F 391 .H185 H64 1976 V.2
Holden, William Curry, 1896-
A ranching saga

P9-CRS-146

GIFT OF

THE EWING HALSELL FOUNDATION

A RANCHING SAGA
The Lives of William Electious Halsell and Ewing Halsell

Volume Two

A RANCHING SAGA
The Lives of William Electious Halsell and Ewing Halsell

BY WILLIAM CURRY HOLDEN

Drawings by JOSÉ CISNEROS

TRINITY UNIVERSITY PRESS • SAN ANTONIO, TEXAS

CITY COLLEGE LIBRARY
1825 MAY ST.
BROWNSVILLE, TEXAS 78520

F
391
.H 185
H 64
v. 2

Copyright © 1976 by Trinity University Press
Library of Congress Catalog Card Number 75-9300
SBN # 911536-59-0
Typesetting by G & S Typesetters, Inc.
Printed by Best Printing Company
Bound by Custom Bookbinders
Printed in the United States of America

Contents

Volume Two

List of Drawings

Volume Two

A RANCHING SAGA
The Lives of William Electious Halsell and Ewing Halsell

Volume Two

Texas Ranch, Spring Lake, Office Staff 17

Ewing Halsell actually operated two separate ranching enterprises: the Halsell Cattle Company and Ewing Halsell's personal ranching business. The Halsell Cattle Company was confined to the Spring Lake ranch. The Ewing Halsell operation included Bird Creek, which he had leased from his sisters, the Osage lease from 1904 to about 1914, the Big Creek (Centralia) ranch which he owned and activated in 1926, the Fall River ranch in Kansas, his Texas leases which he called his "Texas ranch," and, finally, his Farias ranch.

The "Texas ranch" was a lease of 51,000 acres in Bailey County, a strip roughly three miles wide by 28 miles long, east to west. It joined the Spring Lake ranch on the west and extended within two miles of the New Mexico line.[1] The land was a part of the old Muleshoe ranch* and was owned by C. K. Warren and Son.[2] The lease was acquired by Ewing Halsell in 1925 and kept until 1937.

---

*The brand was a muleshoe, and this was the name given the town, Muleshoe, when the Santa Fe built through the pasture in 1912. The town became the county seat and remained the only town worthy of the name in Bailey County.

When he relinquished the Warren land in 1937, Ewing leased the VVN ranch from W. H. Fuqua, Inc. of Amarillo. This tract lay in Bailey County, south of the Warren land.[3] In 1941, it was purchased by the Dora Roberts Land and Investment Company of Big Spring, Texas. G. H. Hayward represented Mrs. Roberts, and Ewing Halsell's dealings were with him. The VVN pasture had only 13,422 acres, and it was necessary to augment it by temporary leases of small tracts anywhere he could find them, such as the Dunn league, the Mallet ranch* in Hockley County, another tract near Bovina and others. These leases were given up later, in 1945, when Ewing Halsell purchased the Farias ranch east of Eagle Pass. At that time the "Texas ranch" books were closed, and the Farias ranch books were started.

From 1916, when the Halsell Cattle Company was formed with Ewing as manager, the home base for it, and all of Ewing's personal operations, was in Vinita. In 1945 he transferred his central office to San Antonio. For several years A. F. Chamberlain was in charge of the Vinita office without assistance. Then Ruby Robbins was brought in and Mr. Chamberlain departed. Next, Miss Nilla B. Hale, a very efficient secretary, was employed in late 1923 and was later in charge of the office until 1936.[4] By this time the business load had increased to the extent that stenographic help was employed.

A rather tragic accident happened to Miss Hale. She washed her hair, rolled it up on celluloid curlers, and lay down on the floor with her head in front of an open gas heater to dry it. She dozed off to sleep, and the celluloid curlers caught fire. Instantly her hair was ablaze. She got a towel and snuffed out the blaze, but not before her hair was completely consumed and her scalp deeply burned. The pain was excruciating for weeks. Ewing Halsell sent her to plastic surgeons for skin and hair transplants. The unfortunate episode affected her personality, and she changed from a happy, outgoing person to a self-conscious recluse.[5]

After the accident, Mrs. Ina Boggs, who worked under Miss Hale, took over the office until her husband, a railroad man, was moved to another division. When it was known she would be leaving, Ewing started inquiring about town for an ef-

---

*Founded by David M. DeVitt, owner of the Mallet Land and Cattle Company, and now (1974) owned by his daughters, Miss Christine DeVitt and Mrs. Helen DeVitt Jones and others.

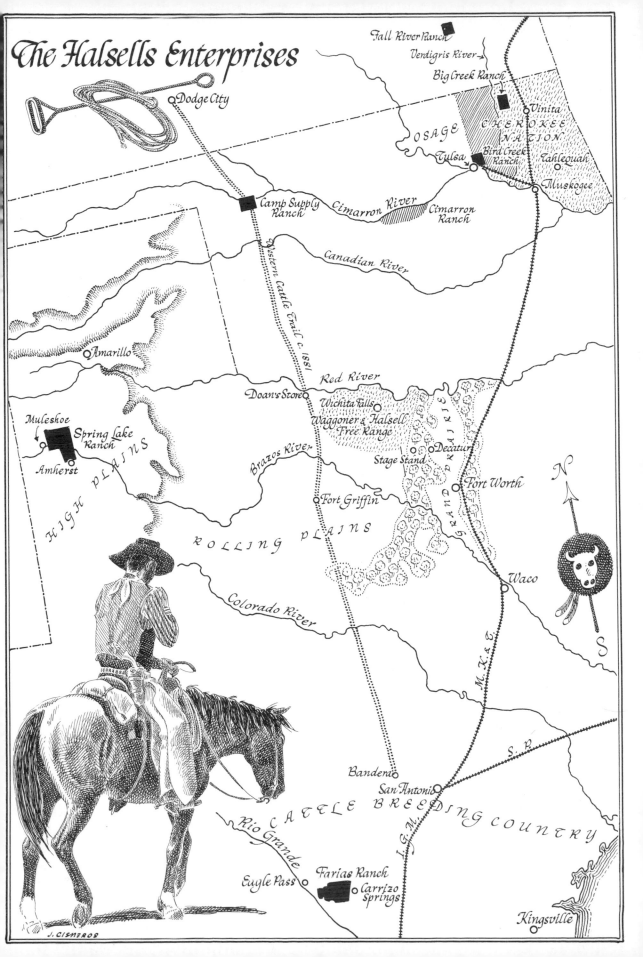

ficient secretary. Someone told him about Helen Campbell who had graduated from Vinita High School and had been working in the First National Bank for a year or more. She was reported to be an extremely efficient and responsible secretary. Ewing employed her and soon found that the reports were remarkably true. This was the beginning of a relationship between Helen Campbell and the Ewing Halsell family which lasted until the deaths of Lucile, Ewing, and Lucile's sister, Mrs. Grace Fortner Rider. Helen looked after and supervised the nursing of the latter, in addition to a heavy schedule involving the estate, for some time after the deaths of Lucile and Ewing. Helen had become "the unadopted daughter" of the family and, after 1944, lived and traveled with the Halsells until their respective demises. She remained on as secretary of the Ewing Halsell Foundation. From 1937 to the present she has been a pivotal factor in the affairs and fortunes of the Ewing Halsell family.

Ewing had a peculiar genius for organizing the working forces on the various ranches. His quiet nature, personal charm, and warm and sincere interest in the lives and affairs of those who worked for him attracted and held responsible, energetic employees who were utterly devoted to him.[6]

For the overall operation of his own ranches in Oklahoma he had George Franklin.* Under George was Hie Spencer, boss of the Big Creek ranch, and Clyte Harlan, boss of the Bird Creek ranch. On the Spring Lake ranch, owned by the Halsell Cattle Company, Ewing placed Ernest Huffman, a tough and temperamental cowhand but an able and dependable foreman.

Huffman's loyalty and devotion to duty was demonstrated during the terrible blizzard of February, 1918.[7] The wind blew with hurricane force, and temperature was below zero, with a chill factor of 50 degrees below zero. Driving snow and sleet covered the land and piled up in great drifts behind any object above ground. Huffman was wise as to how cattle reacted to such conditions. They turned their tails to the wind and started moving south. When they came to a fence, they stopped and bunched up against the fence. With loss of muscular exertion they became stiff

*George Franklin was born in Vinita in 1880. He went to Willie Halsell College, spent some time in an eastern college, and was better educated than most cowmen of his generation. He was an excellent judge of cattle and a superb trainer of horses. He was married and had two children, George Jr. and Beth.

J. CISNEROS

and, after a few hours, would fall over and die. Huffman loaded a chuck wagon with provisions, bedrolls, and wood for fires, and he and his hands followed the cattle. When they came to a fence they cut it and herded the cattle through. The only way to keep them alive was to keep them moving. It was a matter of staying up with the herd and keeping it bunched together. When they came to another fence they cut it, and so on for two days and nights. The cook would stop when he could find a sheltered place, build a fire, make coffee, and cook such items as he could. He kept the cowboys full of hot food and coffee. There was no sleep. The wind was relentless, and the cattle never stopped until they came to a fence. Regardless of the time, day or night, the fence had to be cut.

When the blizzard abated on the third day, the outfit had reached Sulphur Draw in Yoakum County. The cattle and horses were worn out, and they rested. The animals had been without water for three days, and the ice on the lakes, tanks, and troughs was six to eight inches thick. But Huffman had thought of that, and he had placed axes and picks in the wagon so that they could chop holes in the ice. It took about a day to get the herd watered. In the middle of the day the sun melted the snow and sleet in the blowout places where the crust was thin, and the cattle and horses grazed. When cattle and horses had eaten their fill, Huffman began the trek back the way they had come, restoring the fences behind them. In this way, the Mashed O cattle were saved, except for a few that had wandered away from the herd at night when they eluded the dazed cowboys. Eventually these were recovered. Other ranchers who hovered over their stoves in dugouts and shacks lost up to 50 per cent of their herds.[8]

Later a misunderstanding was to develop due to Huffman's temperament and introspective nature, but Ewing Halsell did not let that interfere with repayment of the debt he felt he owed Huffman whose dogged perseverance saved the Halsell cattle. Huffman resigned as foreman, and L. D. Gaither took over the Spring Lake ranch. Gaither had been working as a straw boss under Huffman, but the personalities of the two clashed, and they could not abide one another. Gaither was a head taller than Huffman and was a great, powerful, dominating person, as outspoken as Huffman was noncommunicative. The latter was compact, muscular, and coordinated. In a fight they would have been fairly evenly matched. But it was sometime later before they tangled.

A Ranching Saga

Regarding the organization of the ranches, Ewing's "Texas ranch" had to be administered as a separate unit because it was Ewing's personal undertaking. At least a separate set of books was kept. The actual work was done by the Spring Lake hands, but the time put in on the "Texas ranch" was charged to that account.[9] The Warren pasture had some improvements, and, when needed, a couple of cowboys would stay there and batch. On roundups the whole Spring Lake crew worked the pasture, and the time put in was charged to the "Texas ranch." The cattle bore the Diamond Tail brand. Otherwise the procedure was the same as on the Mashed O, as the Spring Lake ranch was locally called.

About the time the "Texas ranch" was being established a local farm family became entwined with the Spring Lake ranch operation.[10] The Murrells were a large family with about seven boys and a girl or two. Of the boys, no two were alike. They differed in size and temperament so much that a stranger never would have suspected they were kin. In height the boys ranged from about five feet seven to six feet four—the tallest ones were the oldest and the youngest. All of them were short on schooling and long on cowboying. Each one of them learned the business on the Spring Lake ranch. Because of their eagerness and willingness to work, Ewing Halsell developed a fondness for the entire family. Two of the boys later became ranch managers, and another was put in charge of the ranch's farms which started with 3,000 acres and eventually grew to 10,000 acres. H. O., the oldest, after becoming efficient on the Mashed O, went to New Mexico and became manager of the Arnett ranch, which was formerly a part of the old Bell ranch. Johnny, who was about the middle of the Murrell progeny, developed the most skill. He could ride, rope, brand, mark, and castrate with speed and efficiency. He became a good judge of cattle, never shirked, and was always on the job first and stayed the longest. He quickly became what old cattlemen called "a real cowboy." Gaither took a special interest in Johnny and taught him all that he knew about the cow business. The relationship became a father-son affair. Gaither entertained great expectations for Johnny, and the boy did not let him down.

When the Warren lease was relinquished in 1937 and the cattle moved to the VVN pasture, it was necessary, because of the distance involved, to keep a small crew there all the time. Gaither sent Johnny along as straw boss, and Johnny married while he was on the VVN assignment.[11] Eight years later when Ewing Halsell acquired the Farias ranch east of Eagle Pass he sent Gaither there and made Johnny Murrell manager of Spring Lake. At the time Murrell was the youngest manager of a sizable ranch in Texas. He held this position until the Halsell Cattle Company sold the ranch in 1973.[12]

The work on a real cattle ranch was hard, grueling, dusty, and, in warm weather, sweaty and smelly. An element of danger was always present, such as being thrown from a horse, getting tangled in a rope, being dragged by a horse, falling with a horse which had stepped in a hole while running, being charged by an angry cow or bull while on the ground, being run over by a charging animal in the cattle pens or chutes, working on a windmill, and a host of less common accidents.

The working of cattle on horseback was only a small part of the labor on a ranch. Some realistic descriptions of the nitty-gritty chores on the Spring Lake ranch have been described by N. O. (Newt) Robison who started as a cowboy there when Johnny Murrell was just a boy.[13] In physique he was very much like Johnny, small, agile, wiry, dexterous, and a good rider. He could keep his balance on most any pitching horse. More than forty years later he recalls with articulate detail what ranch work was like before the time-honored methods of handling cattle gave way to mechanization.

Branding started right after the Fourth of July.[14] They were still running the chuck wagon all the time Newt was there, and branding was done on the outside, not in corrals. Later they built branding pens in different pastures. It took between 20 and 25 men for a branding crew: a wagon boss, cook, horse wrangler, two ropers, at least eight flankers to throw and hold the calves, two men to run branding irons, one to dehorn, one knife man to mark the ears and castrate, one to vaccinate for blackleg, and one to paint the stumps of the horns and the scrotum cuts, needed to prevent blow flies from infecting the wounds, and several men on horseback to hold the herd. Usually, there were what were called stray men, or reps, from neighboring ranches to pick up their strays.

The wrangler would round up the horses early in the morning, so early he would get off his night horse and kneel down on the ground so he could sky-light the horses. He would round them up and have them at camp by good daylight. By that time the boys had finished breakfast. Several of them would take lariats and make a rope corral around the herd, in all seventy-five to a hundred horses, about four for

A Ranching Saga

each hand. Every horse had a name, usually some distinguishing mark, color, or characteristic, such as Spot, Roan, Speck, Baldy. The wrangler knew the name of each horse. When one of the boys called out a name the wrangler rode slowly through the herd until he spotted the right one, roped, and led him out. When saddled, the boys mounted, and the boss explained briefly where they would begin the roundup, and they set out in that direction in a slow lope (never in a dead run as in the movies). A slow lope for a horse is similar to jogging for a person. A horse could keep at it for an extended period of time without tiring. As the hands went along, the boss would tell one when to drop out until a great line would form and start circling the pasture, driving all cattle found in the area to be covered. About noon the hands, with the cattle collected, would converge at a spot near the camp where the cook had dinner ready (dinner on the ranch was always at noon). Several hands held the herd while others ate, and then they swapped. In the meanwhile the branding iron men had the irons ready. Cow chips were used for cooking and heating the irons. At headquarters they used coal.

Cows were bred so that the calves came in early spring when the dangers of snow and blizzards had passed. By July, the calves were ready for branding. The time required for branding and treating the calves depended on the size of the herd, usually between four and five hundred. After the branding, the herd would be cut for dry cows [cows that did not produce calves]. These were cut out to be sent to market along with the old bulls, strays, and other cattle not to be kept, and they were held in a separate herd to be driven to another pasture. If the roundup had covered the entire pasture, the cook would take the wagon to the next campsite in the afternoon. If the pasture was large, it might take two or three days to work it, doing a different section each day. The bedrolls were on the chuck wagon and supper would be where the wagon was. July was a hot month. If the men were out for ten days or two weeks with one change of clothing, they could hardly stand themselves, much less the other fellows, by the time they got back to headquarters.

Newt Robison recalled that the Spring Lake ranch had 47 windmills in 14 pastures: "Like the horses, each mill had a name.[15] I remember the most of them.*"

*South Hereford pasture: Sage hen, North Mill, Mare Mill, Esther, North Camp, Coursey.

A Ranching Saga

The care and repair of the mills was of utmost importance. With the exception of playa lakes during rainy seasons, the underground water was the only source. The man in charge of the mills was called the windmiller. His pay was $75 a month while the cowboys got $45. The windmiller was the best paid man on the ranch with the exception of the boss. One's rating on the ranch was usually in proportion to his pay. So the windmiller rated along with the cook and straw bosses. The windmiller had his own wagon, fixed up with every kind of tool he might need: big chain wrench, several Stillson wrenches of different sizes, a blowtorch, a vise attached to the wagon bed, hammers, pliers, pipe cutters, threaders, and hacksaws. He had a supply of parts: pitmans, joints of sucker rod, pieces of pipe of different sizes, bolts, nuts, nails, and pieces of lumber for scaffold repair. He also had a small turning plow and a slip scraper used to fill in around the water tubs. The wagon always had an extra cylinder, check valves, and good supply of leathers for the valves.

An ample supply of larger items was kept at headquarters, such as whole sections of wheels, joints of pipe, and sucker rods. If something was needed which was not in stock at the ranch, someone had to go to Muleshoe where E. R. Hart Lumber Company carried everything needed for a Standard Mill.

All of the original XIT mills were Eclipses, with large wooden wheels, some eighteen feet in diameter. They were a direct stroke type; that is, every time the wheel went around once, the sucker rod went up and down once. The mills were

Brown Lee pasture: North Mill, South Mill, East Camp Mill.
North Snyder pasture: North Mill, South Mill, Antelope Mill.
South Snyder pasture: Trap Mill.
West Snyder pasture: North Mill, Road Mill, Osage Mill, South Trap Mill.
Little Sand pasture: Elmer Mill, Homer Bryant Mill, Green Mill.
Spring Lake pasture: Spring Lake Mill, South Soda Mill, Carrols Mill, Feed Lots Mill, Dry Farm Mill, Baldy Mill, Linda Mill.
Bull pasture: Bull Mill, South Bull Mill.
Stray pasture: Stray Mill.
Big Sands pasture: Little Red Mill, Flat Mill, Bull Mill, Shipping Trap Mill, Buck Mill, Jack Law Mill, Oil Well Mill.
Dunn League pasture: Little Six Mill, Charles Malone Mill.
McKnight pasture: two mills (cannot recall names)
Deaf Smith County pasture: two mills (cannot recall names)
Arkansas pasture: two mills (cannot recall names)

powerful and would run on a small amount of wind. However, they had two short-comings. One was that they had babbitt bearings, which was a soft metal. They needed to be greased at least once a week. Even then, in time the bearing would wear out. The only remedy was to take the wheel off, a section at a time, and remove the mill head. To do this, one would have to erect a gin pole which rested on the platform and extended some distance above the top of the wheel. At the top of the pole would be attached the upper block of a block-and-tackle. The removal of a wheel and mill head was a two-man operation. With an eighteen-foot wheel, the section was nine feet from center to outside. The mill head had to be ten feet above the platform. So, to remove the bolts at the center of the wheel, one had to stand on a cleat nailed to the upper part of the tower four feet above the platform and twenty-four to thirty feet above the ground. The sections when detached were let down with the block and tackle. Then came the mill head, which on the big mills weighed between 150 and 200 pounds. It had to be pulled upward until it cleared the base on which it rested. Then it was lowered to the ground. A fire was built under the part containing the bearing, and the remainder of the old bearing was melted and run out. Then the mill head was placed in a sand box and the axle carefully placed in the center of the bearing cavity. Newly melted babbitt was poured around the axle. It solidified quickly. Then the head was pulled to the top, set in place, and the wheel reassembled. This was usually about a two-day job.

In the early 1900's, steel mills began to replace the old wooden mills. The new ones were much smaller and easier to take down when necessary. They were not the direct stroke type but worked with gears so that the wheel would make three or four turns to lift and lower the sucker rod one time. As the old XIT Eclipse Mills completely wore out, they were replaced with steel mills. There were several makes. On the Plains, the favorite brands were the Standard, Star, and Dempster. The Spring Lake ranch used the Standard, not that it was any better but because Hart Lumber and Hardware Company carried a complete line of parts for all models and sizes of Standards.

The windmiller carried a bedroll and cooking outfit and at times might be out for a week. He could do nearly everything needed except pull a mill head. In that case one of the regular hands helped him. Before irrigation wells began lowering the water table, the windmill pipes were set from 30 to 60 feet below surface. To pull

A Ranching Saga

sucker rods, or pipe, was not difficult for one man. But, as the water table fell and the well setting became deeper, the windmiller's job became harder. Red Murrell, Johnny's brother, was the windmiller when Newt Robison was there. Much later, Johnny's youngest brother, Phelps, the tall one, was the windmiller.

The ranch also had a blacksmith shop, and Ernest Huffman was a good blacksmith. On occasion a needed part for a windmill could be fashioned in the shop. However, there were other demands on the blacksmith shop. The steel wagon tires had to be shrunk; horses had to be shod; broken equipment made of iron had to be mended, and it was done quicker on the ranch than by carrying it to town.

When Newt went to the ranch, the Halsell Cattle Company had a Model T flat bed truck, but its use was limited.[16] The road to the trade center, Muleshoe, was a couple of ruts. Much of the land the road traversed was sandy, and it was easy for the truck to bog down and start spinning its rear wheels, which only caused them to dig deeper. Thus, the truck could be used only after a rain and could not be counted on much even then. So the freighting was done with wagons and mules. If the return load was not to be too heavy, a wagon pulled by four mules was sent to town. If a very heavy load was anticipated, six mules would be used. Many times two outfits would be sent in order that there be two drivers to do the loading. The main commodities hauled were cottonseed cake and salt, both purchased by the freight carload. The ranch had a warehouse in town. Freight cars had to be unloaded within two days or pay demurrage. So the freighters would store all the contents of the car in the warehouse except the last two loads. These they took back to the ranch. They also hauled grain. A typical load per wagon was fifty 100-pound sacks, or two and a half tons. Coal was hauled to headquarters. The freighters usually returned with their loads late in the evening after the other hands had eaten supper. In such cases, the other hands unloaded the wagons and cared for the teams while the freighters ate supper.

Fences have always been a problem on a ranch.[17] The outside boundaries of the Spring Lake ranch were well fenced when W. E. purchased the land. Cross fences had to be built; and, as the Halsells put in fields, they had to be fenced. For the pasture cross fences the ranch hands did the work at off-seasons. The farm crews fenced the fields. A cross fence five to ten miles long required a lot of posts, and these would be ordered by the carload and delivered at Amherst, Sudan, or Muleshoe. Most of them were cedar shipped from the Cross Timbers in central Texas. In a mesquite country mesquite was used extensively by ranchers. However, cedar would last much longer than mesquite. The shipping cost of mesquite was about the same as cedar, with little difference in the original cost, so for fencing on the High Plains it was more economical in the long run to use cedar. Bois d'arc made wonderful posts, but the supply was limited and the price higher. Barbed wire and staples were bought in large quantities.

The building of a good fence was an art. Any old cowboy could dig a posthole, put a post in, and tamp it. But it took some expert supervision to get the posts in a perfectly straight line and equally spaced. Posts were spaced from thirty to fifty feet, but the average was forty. The Mashed O outfit took pride in its fences, and the foreman always put a fencing crew under a straw boss who knew how to construct a good fence. Most fences built had four wires.

The secret of building a fence so that the wires would stay taut was in having proper corner posts and gate posts.[18] For a corner post the first pre-requisite was to have an extra large, solid post planted deep in the ground. There were two ways to stabilize it: with a "dead man" or a brace. For the "dead man" a hole three or four feet long and three feet deep would be dug several feet from the corner post on the opposite side and at a 90 degree angle from the direction of the fence line. A short post would be planted horizontally in the bottom of this ditch with a piece of barbed wire wrapped around the middle of the "dead man," and the two ends extending to the top of the corner post. Dirt would be packed tightly on the "dead man," and then the two strands of wire would be stretched with a lever of some sort until the wire was absolutely tight. This kind of post properly installed would withstand a tremendous pull by the wires used in the fence.

Another way of bracing a corner post consisted of planting two other posts within about five feet of the corner post, one in line with one stretch of fence and the other post in line with the other stretch.[19] Another post in each instance would be fitted, notched, and placed from the ground level of the inside post to the top of the corner post. Then a twisted wire brace would be applied from the top of the inside posts to the bottom of the corner post.

For gates the "dead man" type was not feasible because the wire to the "dead man'' would extend out into the gate and would be a hazard. There were two methods of installing gate posts. One was to use extra tall posts, reaching ten to twelve feet above ground, and tie the tops of the two together with a twisted wire pulling brace. This was a good way to keep the gate posts rigid, but limited the heights of loads going through the gate. The other method was the same as the second type mentioned above.

All these details about fence building Newt Robison learned while working on the Mashed O. Many transient cowboys came and went without ever getting in on a fence building job, but all of them had to ride fence. With a pair of fence pliers, which could also be used as a hammer, and a supply of staples in the leather boot top used as a pouch and attached to the saddle, he rode mile after mile of fence to make sure it was in order. If he found something wrong he could usually fix it with his pliers and staples. If a wire were broken, he would report the matter, and a buckboard or wagon with proper equipment would be sent to make the repair. Next to the windmills, the fences were the most important items to be kept up on the ranch.

Gates at the headquarters, corrals, and feeding pens were constructed with wood. Those in the pastures were made of wire which had five or six strands of wire securely held, in equal distance, with wire or wooden stays.[20]

From 1925 to 1945, the period he operated his ''Texas ranch,'' Ewing Halsell had a nagging problem connected with it which did not exist with the other ranches. With them he either owned or controlled the land and could make long-range plans. With the ''Texas ranch'' the leases were for one year at a time. He carried an average of 5,000 cattle on leases, and he could never be sure when his occupancy would be terminated. Any cattleman who, on short notice, might be caught with 5,000 cattle and nowhere to go had something to worry about. Resulting from this kind of uncertainty were typical negotiations between Ewing and the owners of lease lands, first of the Muleshoe ranch and next of the VVN.

The first contract with C. K. Warren was 51,000 acres at 30 cents per acre.[21] Mr. Warren was obligated to maintain the fences and keep the windmills in good repair. The rental amounted to $15,300 a year. The Warrens and Ewing Halsells had become acquainted at a vacation resort in Michigan and had become warm friends. The friendship continued for twelve years until Mr. Warren's death. The families corresponded often, not only the men but the wives. Mr. Warren had a profound respect for Ewing's knowledge and judgment about everything pertaining to cattle and ranching. Their letters always had much to say about cattle, weather, and their families.[22] Mr. Warren often asked Ewing's opinion about trends in the cattle market and sought advice about buying Mexican steers. Warren's health was not good, but he made light of his ailments. The subject became a topic of banter between him and Lucile. She insisted she was keeping a supply of lilies handy just in case of need. A typical retort from Warren was added in a letter to Ewing, September 17, 1926:

With best regards to your good wife, and tell her I have again escaped having lilies sent to me. I remain

Your sincere friend

In a later letter Ewing conveyed Lucile's reply, November 24, 1926:

Lucile joins me in love to your wife and family. She says that the lilies are expensive this time of year, and so she wants you to take care of yourself.

Their business relations were excellent with respect to Warren doing his part about maintenance of the ranch. Fences were kept in good repair, and in 1930 Warren added four new watering places. Ewing wrote thanking him, and adding:

I have felt uneasy about this water situation. While we have not had any trouble, if there should come a long still spell we could be out of water.

Warren replied:

Any time that anything needs fixing, let me know, and I will be glad to follow your instructions, as I want to keep the ranch in first class shape.

So it went. All year until the time came to renew the lease. Then for a short period both men became strictly business. Ewing began by wanting to reduce the lease to

W. E. and Ewing Halsell   307

CITY COLLEGE LIBRARY
1825 MAY ST.
BROWNSVILLE, TEXAS 78520

25 cents per acre. Warren would stand firm. The give-and-take would last by correspondence for two or three weeks. In the end the old terms would be renewed. Then the friendly social relationship would be resumed. In 1931, Ewing held out doggedly for 20 cents an acre. Warren stood his ground, and again Ewing settled for 30 cents. Before another negotiating round, however, Lucile's lilies were needed. Mr. Warren died August 10, 1932.[23] His son wired Ewing and Lucile who were vacationing in Honolulu.

Edward Warren, the son, took over the family affairs. Ewing's attitude towards Edward was warm and paternal, but when time came to renew the lease, Ewing, as was his custom, reverted to strictly business. He wanted the lease reduced to 20 cents an acre and pointed out that was what he was paying the Ellwoods and the Martin Estate.* Edward reminded him that neither the Ellwood nor the Martin Estate was responsible for fences or water. Ewing countered with another offer: he would pay 20 cents an acre and an additional $500 a year for Edward to take care of the fences and water.[24] Times were hard. It was the year the banks were closed by President Roosevelt and at the height of the Great Depression. So Edward agreed, and these terms were observed until 1937 when Edward took back the Muleshoe ranch to operate for the family. The warm personal relationship between the Halsells and Warrens never diminished.

About the time Edward took over management of his father's estate in 1932, Ewing indulged in a running controversy involving Edward, the State Highway Department, and a caliche pit.[25] The correspondence about it is amusing and illustrative of Ewing Halsell's persistence for detail and principle. Highway 84 from Lubbock to Farwell had been fenced and graded diagonally across the Muleshoe ranch, a distance of about six miles. The Highway Department was ready to put a layer of caliche on the grade so as to make it an all-weather road. The engineers found an excellent caliche deposit nearby on the Warren land. The district engineer went to see Edward about arrangements to open a pit. Edward said he would have to confer

*It is to be remembered that Ewing was a trader and a short term operator when need be. He leased every pasture available within a reasonable distance on a one-year basis, and bought steers to stock it with the idea they would be ready to market by the time the lease was up.

with Mr. Ewing Halsell who had the land leased. Edward wrote Ewing a letter, and this is Ewing's reply:

We do not want to stand in the way of your selling anything that will bring money, but our experience with State Highway contractors has always been unsatisfactory. They use your property, tear your fences down and tell you to go to Hell.

If you deal with them, make them put in a cattle guard every place they cross a fence, agree to keep all cross fences up, and stay in a road and not drive all over the pasture. I want you to be responsible for any damages done to my cattle or should they get out into the crops of other people on account of the Highway Department tearing down fences and leaving gates open. I do not want you to give them privileges of getting water at or camping around any windmill. I suggest that you put into the contract your right to cancel it if they become a nuisance.

Edward conferred with his attorney, Mr. Kimbrough of Plainview, with reference to a contract enveloping all of Ewing's provisions. The lawyer advised Edward that he had no legal right to contract for the protection of Ewing's cattle. He suggested instead that Edward agree to give Ewing one-third of the money received for sale of the caliche, and that Ewing contract directly with the Highway Department in regard to damages to grass and cattle.

When he relayed this information to Ewing, Edward added, "I don't believe we will get enough out of this to load a gun. However, the Highway Department is accusing us of holding up construction of a much needed highway."

Ewing then received a letter from Guy R. Johnston,[26] the district highway engineer:

We can assure you that your cattle will be protected from injury and escape from pastures, and that camping around windmills will not be permitted; also there will be no unnecessary damage to the grass by driving over too much territory. This office will cause you just as little inconvenience as possible in hauling caliche across your grass lease.

Ewing replied:

It would be much more agreeable to me if it were not necessary to take caliche from pastures which I use, but if that is the only practical place, I will not stand in the way, but I want a contract from your Department, and one from the contractors who haul the caliche.

The contracts were drawn and signed. Ewing considered the entire matter a nuisance and expressed his annoyance to Edward Warren:

It is not a matter of digging the pits so much as driving back and forth across your pastures. I think it would be a good idea to fence the pit and connect it to the highway with a lane.

Whether or not the pit was fenced and a lane made to the highway is not stated, but two months after the work began, Ewing wrote to Edward:

The road contractors have acted very nice so far, and have done everything they could to protect us, but [he added by way of defending his original theory] you know constant driving of trucks through the pasture *does disturb the cattle* [italics added].

Four months after the pit was opened Ewing received a check from the Highway Department for $587.50 for his one-third of the caliche. After that he did not think quite so badly of the highway people.

The thoroughness with which Ewing Halsell attended to minor operations of his extensive cattle business is indicated in a letter to W. J. Jarboe, October 21, 1932, in regard to wintering and feeding some cattle on land owned by Jarboe:[27]

Am enclosing a contract in duplicate as we agreed yesterday. Will you please sign and return one copy immediately.

In regard to taking care of these cattle, unless it rains, I cannot leave over 500 there, as I feel sure you do not have enough water for more than that number.

If I leave 1,000 cattle there, I will pay you $60 a month to take care of them. If I cut the number down to 500 I will pay you $35 a month.

It will take two men and wagons a half day to feed 1,000 cattle, and one man and wagon a half day to feed 500.

After these cattle are rounded together and fed a few days, I think they can be fed in two bunches.

When you round these cattle I want them rounded very slowly, never make them run nor trot.

Feed the cake on clean ground, and not on the same spot each day.

I will have Mr. [Tom] Huffman or Mr. Franklin come by to help get you started with this

A Ranching Saga

work. While I am sure you can take care of cattle, we all have our own way of doing things, and my own men know better how I want it done.

The main thing now is to get your fences up, and be sure to fence around the stacks of hay Mr. Neville has in the pasture. I want these fenced whether or not I buy the hay. Put good fences around the stacks so the cattle will not break in. I will furnish the wire and posts. When the need is over I can take wire and posts away, or sell it to you if you wish.

I will haul my own cake to your place. Let me know if this is satisfactory.

Ewing's philosophy about having women on the ranches was the antithesis of that of his father.[28] He liked women, and he thought they were a good influence on the men around them. He was convinced that women were better cooks than men. When he could find them he preferred to get a husband and wife team, the woman to cook and the man to grow a garden, milk the cows, and do all manner of domestic chores. He put great emphasis on farms or ranches being as self-sustaining as possible as to food, and was a believer in gardens and orchards for two reasons. First, he loved to see things grow, whether it be flowers, garden plants, or field crops. One of the many facets of his nature was that he was a farmer at heart. Second, it was just good common sense for the people of a rural operation to live off the land. This he managed to do on all of his ranches to an astonishing degree. The amounts meticulously recorded in the records of the different ranches spent for store-bought groceries are unbelievably small. The main items bought, always in quantity at wholesale prices, were flour, coffee, and sugar. Ewing himself loved fried chicken, and he had the chore man get 300 baby chicks at a time, and before they were eaten as fryers, they would have another batch coming on. Each ranch kept from 60 to 80 laying hens. Hogs were raised, killed, and the hams and bacon salt cured. At hog killing, it was his job to season the sausage, which he did painstakingly with his own special formula. The lard was rendered. Nothing was wasted. During the growing season, the cook and husband spent all their extra time canning vegetables, hundreds of jars and cans each year. The same was true when the fruit of the orchards was ripe. Occasionally, the hands got a taste of Mashed O or Diamond Tail beef, but not very often. Ewing was not one for having beef three times a day every day, as was the case on some ranches, especially if it were "stray" beef. He insisted on diversity of menus, with steaks or roast about once a week. In this way it was more economical to buy what was needed at the nearest market. It is amazing how he managed to feed so well on so small an outlay.

The main reason was his ability to establish a rapport with the women cooks, and he wrote them long letters about how to manage and what to cook.[29] It is ironical that a man who was phenomenally successful in directing the cooking could himself cook only one item. Helen Campbell, who lived with the family for twenty-one years, testifies that the only thing he was an expert at was rice pancakes. At that he had no rival, but, according to Helen, he could hardly boil water. However, the following letter to Mr. and Mrs. Tockey (mostly to Mrs. Tockey), at the Big Creek ranch, December 6, 1945, is indicative of his knowledge of what should go on a ranch dining table:

I think at times you have been confused on just what our customs are or what I wanted cooked at the ranch. Mr. Franklin is not very good about helping new people.

The items that we use are, of course, bread and meat, beans, Irish or sweet potatoes, cabbage or turnips, rice and the different kinds of cereals. Occasionally we have canned tomatoes and corn. I would say that once or twice a week is sufficient for these canned goods. I think soup is a wonderful food and should be served at least once or twice a week in the winter time when you have something to make it with. You can serve either creamed tomato soup or vegetable soup if you have any stock to make the vegetable soup from. I would serve hot biscuits for breakfast and supper and have some corn bread or light bread at noon. I think nearly all cowboys and farm hands like hot bread best, but it is nice to have homemade light bread should you have a large crowd, or just for a change. Of course, I do not want all of these items served at one meal.

It has always been our custom to have some kind of dried fruits, but they are very scarce and extremely high, so we will use some dried fruits when we can get it, but will always have some kind of syrup or molasses. When our hens begin to lay, I would have custard pie once or twice a week at noon when you haven't any other dessert. It is all right to have a bread pudding which just requires cream and butter and bread. If we should have raisins, it is all right to put some raisins in the pudding.

I was very well pleased with Mrs. Tockey's cooking and Mr. Tockey's work. I am giving you these suggestions so that you will understand what our customs are and try to vary this diet occasionally. For Christmas, I would like for these men to have a turkey, cranberry sauce, pumpkin pie or some other kind of pie, with the usual potatoes and beans.

Be sure and drain my hot water tank, and put a little salt in these goosenecks and toilets so they will not freeze.

A Ranching Saga

His letter must have done some good. On January 31, 1946, after having made a trip to the ranch, he wrote again, this time to Mrs. Tockey alone:

Am sending you out 25# raisins and 25# prunes. I like to buy groceries in bulk in large quantities. But don't want to serve these every meal until they are all gone. I would have a raisin pie once or twice a week and prunes on the table one or two meals a week.

I think you are getting along with your cooking very nicely. You understand better what our customs are. Am also sending some rice with the other groceries. I think rice is a wonderful food if it is properly cooked, so I would have rice sometimes in place of beans or potatoes. It is better, I think, boiled in a double boiler and plenty of butter, put on it after it is cooked, but you may know more about this than I do.

A few days later, he sent Mrs. Tockey the following instructions:

I am enclosing you herewith an Institutional Daily Record which I wish you would start keeping as of the day you receive it. For the days before that time, we will have to estimate the meals served. Show the total number of people served, including your family, for each meal. I mean, for instance, if you have 4 people for breakfast and 10 for dinner and 8 for supper, your total would be 22 for that day. Of course, the gross revenue dollars does not apply to us. I will talk to you about this again when I am at the ranch.

This must have been Mrs. Tockey's undoing. This much bookkeeping was beyond her, and she and her husband left. Ewing found another husband and wife team, Mr. and Mrs. Emory Moon. On June 5, he wrote Emory:

The screen door on the west porch needs fixing badly. Also the floor. We have a little flooring in the shed that you can use. The flies are bothering, so get this fixed as soon as you can.

Separate your milk as soon as you bring it in. I think that is the reason our milk is getting sour on us. We are not getting it to the ice box soon enough. But it is better to leave it out 15 or 20 minutes after it is separated before you put it in the box so some of the animal heat will go out.

There are quite a few hens setting in the cake house by the mule barn that I wish you would break up.

Gather your fresh vegetables in the morning so your wife can use them at noon.

You are doing a good job with the cooking but there is a right smart to do there, and I would like for you to keep your garden worked, the grass cut in the yard and take care of the cows, chickens and hogs.

On June 29, Ewing Halsell instructed his secretary, Helen Campbell, to write Hie Spencer, foreman at Big Creek:

Mr. Halsell asked me to tell you that he thought it would be a good idea to buy fresh meat about once a week or at any rate every two weeks for your boys. He thought this would give them some variety at the table.

He suggested either a roast or steak. I think you can probably get this at Lenapah. Do not buy the most expensive meat, but get good meat.

Ewing Halsell loved to write letters, but even more he enjoyed getting them. He encouraged everyone to write him: the secretaries in the Vinita office, his foreman, straw bosses, cowboys, and cooks, on all the ranches, and Will Rowland in the Amherst office.[30] This helped him in keeping up with the myriad of details concerning his numerous enterprises. He especially encouraged people to write to him during the three or four months he had to be completely out of the hay fever belt. The belt for him included everything from the Mississippi River to the Rocky Mountains. His chief source of information was from two secretaries in the Vinita office. From late 1923 to 1936 it was Nilla B. Hale, and from 1937 it was Helen Campbell. Both were efficient but entirely different in their work habits.

Nilla B. Hale was strictly an office secretary.[31] She had people come to see her in the office. She used the telephone, wrote letters, and sent telegrams. She seldom, if ever, went out to the ranches or inspected the cattle and properties on the ground. She got the facts secondhand, but she did a marvelous job of keeping up with everything. The information gathered was reported in concise detail to Ewing every week or ten days. Each report required about two pages, legal length, single-spaced, small margins, typewritten. Her style was free, homey, and inclined to be a bit gossipy. Ewing apparently loved to get the gossip though he never passed it on. The office force was composed entirely of women. When away on extended trips he sought to keep up their morale by sending presents. In 1935, he and Lucile were at Santa Monica. Before leaving Vinita, he had managed to get the sizes of the office ladies with the view of sending back clothing. The following is a typical report to Ewing Halsell, September 21, 1935, just after receiving the gifts:

Dear Mr. Halsell:

The income man has finished his examinations. There will be increased taxes on your return of about $50.00. Most of this is brought about by a change in the Farms Company report wherein their taxable income was increased over $900.00. Some payments on horses were left out of the return.

They are paying 60¢ and 75¢ for some extra good corn here from the Churchill place. They are paying 40¢ for corn at Durant and 50¢ at Muskogee. Oats are still 27¢. George said he had 200 bushels offered at 30¢ delivered at Centralia. I think he is going to buy them if he can get them at 27¢.

With reference to the cake. Your letter said you wanted the pea size to go to Lenapah. However, if you want this changed we will have no trouble in doing it. I read your letter as 50 tons for Fall River but have checked back on it and see it was 30 tons. If you want this cut down I am sure we can get it reduced and take this additional cake to one of the other places. Will not do anything about it however until I hear from you.

Think perhaps I can get George to look at the Gravitt land next week.

George [Franklin] said the grass was still green but it is making bad colored hay. He thinks however they will be through haying by the 25th of this month.

He said the boys at Centralia had wanted to come in to the Rodeo. He called last night and told Hie to let Lee, Buck and Neal come in today.

He plans to move the Wallen cattle Sunday.

Our gifts came in this morning. They are all awfully pretty. I am afraid you have forgotten this spread of mine though and I am afraid the skirt is going to be a little tight. I will try it on this evening. The girls will also try on their things tonight.

If these have to be exchanged shall they be returned to you or returned direct to Bullocks. There was no sales ticket with them but the clerk's number is on the ticket pasted to the outside of the package. I told Almeta about hanging up your clothes when they came in. She said she would watch for them.

Next day:

Mrs. Boggs and Ruth's things fit all right but mine is entirely too small. I am awfully sorry

A Ranching Saga

as I think it is very pretty. I wrote you yesterday asking whether I should return it to you or the store. Won't do anything about it until I hear from you.

I know you would enjoy being home if you would be free of hay fever but these people are being hurt too badly by it and I would hate to see you take a chance on it.

[This report went on for another page]

Helen Campbell, quiet, low-key, soft-spoken, and gentle but firm, was logical, articulate, and practical. She was fast, efficient, and thorough in the office, and even more so out-of-doors. She enjoyed going to the ranches and inspecting everything from the bunkhouses to a sick steer out in the pasture. When she wrote a report to Ewing Halsell it was from direct observation and not from second-hand reporting.[32] The following is a typical report which she made to Ewing Halsell while he was a "hay fever exile" in Santa Monica, July 26, 1937:

Dear Mr. Halsell:

Ernest [Powell] and I went to the Bird Creek Ranch and Dairy today. I took the man from the County Agent's office to check the fences at Bird Creek for the range program. There are so many rules and regulations on this program that I am afraid we are not going to get paid for very much of our fence but he was very liberal and has promised to get as much by as possible. He is going to have it figured up in the next few days and will advise us just how much is eligible for this government payment.

George Franklin and George Stall got away early this morning. They spent last night at Bird Creek.

I saw the Mexico cattle or rather the tail end of them that Clyte had on the wheat west of the house. These cattle had just been dehorned and didn't look very good but Clyte said they had improved a lot since they got in and he thought this dehorning had set them back some.

The wheat all looks good. Clyte is getting ready to sow oats.

We went on over to the dairy, got John Stanford to sign the affidavit on the Logsdon land but Mac was in town to see about getting the Mayo Hotel to buy milk so I left the affidavit with Mrs. Taylor for him to sign and mail to us.

They reported that the refrigeration was working all right and had been for the past two weeks, however, Mrs. Taylor said that the people from Tulsa were out and felt sure that the Norge people wanted to put in a three phase motor but she didn't seem to know very much about it so I asked her to have Mac write in what he found out from there.

Mac's wheat looks good. Mrs. Taylor said the production was holding up good.

She said Mac had taken the bull over to Bird Creek and put with the heifers.

I went out to the Big Creek ranch last week, and saw the fed steer that was sick. I believe George wired you about this. He had been cut out to ship and had to be cut back as they were leaving the beef trap. George and I drove down to see him about noon. He was laying down when we got down to see him but got up and started to walk. His left hind leg seemed to give way under him and he fell, however he got up again and walked away, sort of dragging this leg. After he had gone a short distance his leg seemed to limber up and he had better control of it. We watched him for a while and this lameness in the one leg seemed to be all that was wrong with him. His eyes looked all right to me although George thought he looked a little wild. He was in good flesh. George gave you this information in his report but I thought it might give you a better picture after I told you what he looked like to me.

We looked at the cattle in the Hill pasture. This is where George thinks he can cut from next time. They are cleaning up the troughs nicely and are in very good flesh.

I couldn't see a lot of difference in the two year old heifers. The flies are bad everywhere and the cattle are bunching and staying in the tanks. There is lots of water in all the tanks.

Your house is coming along nicely. The plasterers started to work last week and will finish up this week. The bath tub and shower are in. This is running into more money than I thought it would but I believe it is going to be nice.

I went to the bunk house and looked it over. While it was not as clean as it might be it was not as bad as I expected to find it. The closet that Tom talked about has evidently been cleaned out.

I have been writing to Gaither giving him the weights and price on the cattle sold from his place but I have not written to Clyte, however I will do this in the future.

We are all happy to know that Mrs. Halsell's health has improved. Was glad to talk to you [long distance] this morning.

[This report continued for another page]

After she started working for Ewing Halsell, Helen made a practice, often on her own time, of going to every one of the ranches and spending a day with the boss, or straw boss, inspecting the cattle, grass, fences, equipment, everything that pertained to operation. She tried to make the trips every two or three weeks. With her sharp eyes and remarkable memory, she learned quickly. It did not take long

A Ranching Saga

for her to become a good judge of steer meat and horse flesh. Pretty soon she could judge within a few pounds the weight of an animal just by looking at it. Her proficiency in the office was equally as good. The cowboys, who assumed that men's knowledge of "cowography" was naturally greater than that of women, paid her their supreme compliment: "She thinks like a man."

Ewing Halsell soon realized that "he had a jewel of great price" in Helen Campbell.[33] In an interview August 23, 1973, John Mahoney of Vinita related an episode which happened in 1945 when Ewing was planning to move the central office to San Antonio. Someone asked him how he was going to get along without Helen Campbell. He replied, "I have no intention of getting along without her. She is indispensable. She knows more about my business than I do. She can give you from memory a legal description of every piece of property I have, and I could not do that."

World War II, *Shortages, Problems* 18

Ewing Halsell had the gift of remarkable foresight. As early as 1937 the voluminous correspondence he carried on in connection with his many enterprises indicated that he was aware that World War II was in the making and that he had begun making preparations for it. In 1938, his activities in this regard were stepped up. When the German army smashed across the borders of Poland in September 1, 1939, Ewing had his affairs in order as well as was physically possible.[1]

His foresight was explainable by his extraordinary capacity to get information, analyze it, arrive at conclusions, and store it all away in his mind. He had lived through World War I, had kept up with the building of the German military machine, the alliances, the inevitable war itself, and the aftermath. He was 40 when World War I started and 44 when it ended.

In the early 1930's he saw the same manifestations, the military preparations in Germany and Italy under two ruthless dictators, the same alliances, the same unavoidable trend, and he was certain where it would lead. He read the newspapers, and he kept abreast of what was happening in Europe. He correctly concluded that sooner or later the United States would be drawn into war, and there would be shortages, rationing, privations, and sacrifices.[2]

Beginning in 1938, he inaugurated an extensive program of capital outlays, many of which he might have postponed for years had he not foreseen the specter of scarcities on the horizon. On the Spring Lake ranch he installed a number of irrigation wells. He included a surveying program to get the ditches in the right places with the proper gradients. All this would insure more grain and more beef when the need came, as it surely would.

Additional help would be required, and to get it, he would need places for laborers to live. A major building program was begun.[3] Old houses were repaired. Old roofs and floors were replaced with new ones.[4] New rooms were added to existing houses. New houses were built on the farms which were to be irrigated and on new land to be put into cultivation.[5] Bathrooms were installed in some houses.[6]

Ewing took advantage of an opportunity which was offered by the federal government.[7] One aspect of the New Deal program of the Roosevelt administration to counteract the Depression was the Civilian Conservation Corps, which had two objectives. One was to give employment to young men at a time of vast unemployment; second, the jobs the CCC men were to do constituted the first nationally supported efforts at conservation, such as stopping water erosion, wind damage, and natural abuse of forest lands.* One of the panaceas for reducing future wind damage like that sustained during the Dust Bowl era was to plant windrows of trees at intervals across the open plains. The theory was that these hedges would decrease the velocity of the ground wind. Ewing secured authorization to have the CCC set several acres of trees to the west and north of the Spring Lake headquarters, around the Sod House, and at the Spring Lake dams. Also, they fenced the trees and did some work in the blowing sand hills.

Throughout 1939 work went on at a quickening pace. More farmhouses were built, two on the Mitchell farms, one on the Van Ness, and a machine shed on the Forrest Halsell place which Ewing had bought.[8] Telephone lines were put up. Two

---

*The purpose of the CCC program was similar to the Peace Corps of the later Kennedy administration with one basic difference. The CCC men were to do their environmental work in the United States while the Peace Corps members went abroad to teach people how to better use and care for their environment.

large trench silos were dug, one at Dry Farm and one west of the barley field. Mechanized farm machinery was purchased, a four-row tractor, tandem disk, a two-row binder, and an ensilage chopper. A large barn, mostly for baled hay, was erected at the Forrest Halsell place known as the North Farm. A truck with a long trailer "which could be used for hauling feed or cattle" was purchased for the Spring Lake and the VVN ranches.[9]

Four days after the European war started on September 1, 1939, Ewing wrote to Gaither urging him to push all construction, to get salable cattle on feed, to get the silos filled, and equipment repaired. He had ordered 100 tons of cottonseed cake delivered at Littlefield for his "Texas ranch" and 100 tons at Plainview for the Halsell Cattle Company.[10] The tone of the letter reflects the anxiety caused by the state of affairs he had been anticipating for two years. This could be considered phase one of events to come. Phase two would be the interval until the United States would become involved. In World War I, the interval was two years. It might be that long again, he thought. In the meanwhile, with the British Navy in control of the high seas, the United States would again become the allies' arsenal for arms and food. As in World War I, German submarines would take heavy toll by sending food ships to the bottom, ever making food scarcer and more costly.

The eventual entrance of the United States would bring rationing and scarcity of materials and equipment. Ewing feverishly speeded up his preparations. He bought new tractors, quantities of barbed wire, sixteen new windmills which he put in storage, hay mowers, and spare parts for machines. He had all houses painted. The Lamb County R.E.A. had just been installed.[11] All farmhouses were wired for electricity. He bought two new automobiles. His greatest concern was to be able to care for the products of the land. A big barn and hay sheds were constructed at Bird Creek and a huge hay shed built at Big Creek. He wrote his foreman to keep good supplies of sugar, flour, and coffee on hand so that when rationing came they would have a reserve to start with.[12] Repeatedly he urged that farm equipment be kept in good condition, oiled, greased, and under sheds when not in use. The same for cars, pickups, and trucks.[13]

Anticipating rationing, he directed Gaither and Franklin to keep careful records of amounts of gasoline used on the ranches and farms, on the highway, irrigation wells, and other travel relating to ranching and farming.[14] In that way, when rationing did come, they would have a basis for gasoline exemptions for agricultural purposes. Later these records were indeed helpful.

Ewing had foreseen labor shortages.[15] These became manifest in 1940 and increased steadily with the passing months. With the nation's industrial plants going three shifts a day, competing for workers, and wages going higher, more farm and ranch workers drifted to factories. In the summer of 1941, it was hard to get hoe hands, truck drivers, tractor men, or field hands to fill the silos. Thirteen men were needed for filling the silos and the Spring Lake crew consisted of seven.

Hay baling of the native grasses was an important part of ranching in Oklahoma. Until Pearl Harbor, Ewing had contracted the baling. In 1942, the contractor could not find men to run the balers. So Ewing had to enter the baling business and use cowboys to mow and haul. This condition was general throughout the land, especially with ranchers who supplemented their grazing with hay and field crops. It was the beginning of a trend whereby cowboys had to mix farm work with cow work.

Ewing compensated for the labor shortage by mechanization. Tractors replaced horses and mules, and pickups and trucks were used mostly instead of wagons and teams. Due to seasonal differences, Ewing could switch the same crew from the Oklahoma ranches to the Texas ranches, or vice versa. He did have on each ranch a small corps of loyal dedicated hands who were willing to work long and hard. By splicing those together and rotating the crews to the different ranches, he managed to keep essential work going.

However, this arrangement was threatened by the draft. Several times Ewing appealed to draft boards to defer some of his most irreplaceable hands. The following letter, August 26, 1943, to the draft board of Bailey County states his point of view:

I don't think I am acquainted with your Draft Board but I am in hopes that they have some judgment about the needs of ranches and agriculture. It is hardly necessary to explain that all of us are for winning this War and know that there are lots of sacrifices to be made.

In industries that are called ''War Industries'' there are men that simply step into a job without any training, but get into these industries and are exempted. In our Ranch business it takes years to train men to fill the bosses' positions. I believe that the ranch business and

J. CISNEROS

production of beef is just as essential as airplanes or ships, and the ranch industry cannot be carried on without some experience.

When Johnny Murrell's and T. V. Murrell's numbers are called I am going to ask that they be exempted on the ground that they are in essential industries. I am not doing this for any personal reasons. These men are well qualified for the places they are in and are absolutely necessary for the running of these ranches. They can take older men and green men and make them useful help, but if I have inexperienced foremen they have to hire experienced help to run the ranch. I am writing you this in the hope that you know these people. I think you know me well enough to know that I am not basing this on any personal reasons. We are all serious about doing our job. If you can help in this matter I will appreciate it. These draft boards are just our neighbors and are all trying to do their duty, but sometimes their friends can explain a situation better than someone that does not know them so well.

This request must have been effective as both men were deferred. However, both had families and that made it easier for the board to justify its action.

Later Ewing's efforts were not successful in dealing with the army.[16] An old hand, Bassil Pippin, who had only one eye, had been drafted. He wrote Gaither that some men in his company had been released to return to farm and ranch jobs. Ewing wrote the commanding officer and requested Pippin's release, stating, ''I was rather surprised that the army accepted Private Pippin on account of his having only one eye. All good Americans are anxious to win this war and we do not want to do anything that would cause delays. I am giving you the facts concerning this man's work, and if in your judgment, he would be more benefit to his country in his regular work than as a soldier I would be extremely glad to have him.'' The request was denied.

In November, 1942, Ewing wrote to Johnny Murrell, ''We are awfully short of help everywhere, Slaughter is now classified by the draft board as A-1. He may be called any time. We need more help!''[17] So it went. Ewing raised the pay of all hands five dollars a month. They could get a few seventeen-year-old boys, only to have the draft snatch them away before they learned enough to make good hands.

The dairy at Tulsa was constantly having labor problems. The situation there became so critical that Ewing wrote Clyte Harlan that it looked as if they would have to close it and sell the cows for beef even though the town desperately needed milk.[18]

In December 1943, Ewing wrote to Halbert Parsons at Centralia, "I am going to Texas January 2, and am taking a little boy who wants to work. Will be there several weeks and will see if he works out. If not will bring him back. We have just enough men to do the most essential tasks each day . . . there are several sick men at different places. If you get sick get word to the office . . . this flu is not bad, lasts four to five days . . . but take care of yourself until you are over it."

A big flood at Bird Creek did a lot of damage to roads, fences, and fields. Ewing, in desperation, wrote the county agricultural agent pleading for any kind of help—soldiers, prisoners, any sort. The agent replied that none was available.[19]

As Ewing had anticipated, rationing not only limited or completely prevented the obtaining of essential materials but added a heavy load of bookkeeping for the ranches and farms. Records had to be kept for many items in order to get ration stamps or permits to obtain gasoline, tires, parts, machinery, motor vehicles, sugar, flour, planting seed, and on and on. Most materials were unobtainable even if one had the permits. They needed to add a room to East Camp. Les La Grange in the Amherst office wrote that "bath fixtures, sheetrock, and lumber were not available in Lamb County." In Oklahoma Ewing tried to get a power line put from the road into a ranch near Turley. The power company replied that it was out of the question, that the materials required were on the priority list.[20]

Ewing had a way of coping with rationing. In a letter to John Skinner, straw boss on one of the divisions of the Big Creek ranch, January 26, 1942, he gave advice about what to do about sugar:

The government is going to ration sugar and it will be necessary for us to conserve like everyone else. I do not want to discontinue the use of breakfast food, but my idea would be for you to serve prepared foods 2 or 3 times a week and a cooked cereal the balance of the time. I do not think it takes quite as much sugar for cooked cereals. I want to buy syrup to keep on the table at all times. A good syrup will take the place of sugar in most diets. I think in Texas we buy a brand called Sarah Jane or Brer Rabbit which are both good syrups. I want you to buy these by the case, both the prepared breakfast food and the syrup.

We have a little sugar on hand but I do not want to use it until necessary. From the government regulations we are allowed one pound of sugar per week per person, so we will be allowed 12 to 14 pounds of sugar per week.

Let the Ramseys see this letter and you prepare your work together on these grocery bills and follow the government regulations. There is plenty for us to eat, if we will just take care of it. Tell Mrs. Ramsey to have biscuits for breakfast, corn bread at noon and biscuits at night, and any cold breads you have left keep over for dressings and the cold biscuits can be used in bread puddings or toasted for breakfast.

In September 1944, Ewing wrote to Skinner again:

If you find any wild plums while riding around the pastures, gather me a bucket full, and get George to take them to my house in Vinita. Also I would like for the cooks at the ranch to make as much plum preserves as they have sugar. If there are any pears at Carl's place they should be preserved.

With a truly genuine and patriotic desire to help with the war effort Ewing repeatedly stressed the importance of gardening. He had always contended that a farm or ranch should be as self-sustaining as humanly possible, but the exigencies of the war caused him to emphasize necessity more than ever. He wanted a garden on every headquarters, camp, and farm. During the war he wrote hundreds of letters to foremen, straw bosses, cooks, wives of hands, and anybody he thought he could get to do something about raising food at home. He wrote instructions about what to plant and when to plant, and how necessary it was to work the soil and keep the weeds out. He never failed to mention turnips, no matter whether it was spring, summer, or fall.[21] He would say: "It is time to plant some turnips," "I would put in a little patch of turnips," "Do not forget to plant the turnips" and many other variations. The records do not reveal how effective the turnip planting was.

All of his life Ewing had been a believer in raising hogs. He insisted that every one of his ranches and farms raise all the hog meat and lard it could use and then have a surplus to sell. During the war years he was more adamant about this than he had ever been before. Just as he did about gardening, he wrote many letters about hogs. The following to Mr. and Mrs. Elmer Ironsides, September 25, 1942, is typical:

We are in a very bad war, and I am quite sure we all feel that it is our duty to produce and save as much as possible. I am anxious to produce more pork on the different places. So I want you to take good care of the mother sows. See they are bred properly, and that careful attention is given them when they are having their pigs. Make sure they are fed properly at all times.

He urged Clyte Harlan at the same time to increase the hog production at Bird Creek and directed that he buy 5,000 bushels of corn for the purpose.[22] News came to Ewing that at Spring Lake they were feeding corn to hogs with the shucks on. He got off a letter to Gaither without delay instructing him to see that Mr. Palmer, husband of the cook, shuck the corn before feeding it to the hogs. He frequently inquired in his letters to his foremen about how the hogs were doing, how many, how much did they weigh. At one time when the books showed he had 18,000 cattle he was concerned about how a few hogs were doing.

The records show that during the war each operational unit on the ranches had from 20 to 50 hogs to sell each year. The money returns were negligible. In 1940 Big Creek sold 33 hogs with an average weight of 210 pounds at $5.15 a hundred which netted $10.51 each. Two years later prices had gone up. Bird Creek sold 20 hogs with an average weight of 253 pounds at $14.00 per hundred weight, averaging $35.40 each.

Ewing also stepped up the raising of chickens and production of eggs.[23] He installed brooder houses at each place which maintained a cook, especially where there were the husband-wife teams. He insisted that they raise more chickens and eggs than they could use and then sell the surplus. Eggs were most useful in the armed services, and he considered it a patriotic duty to help furnish all he could.

By the same token, Ewing Halsell, untypical of cattlemen of historical fiction, raised sheep, not commercially but for his own use. He loved lamb, but he did not insist that each operational unit raise sheep. He kept a little flock at Big Creek. From time to time he would have a lamb or mutton prepared, to be eaten either at the ranch or at his home in Vinita. He kept the flock small, but he had the sheep sheared, sold the wool, and entered the proceeds in ranch books. He figured the wool, during the war, was needed for uniforms and blankets for the troops.[24]

As the war progressed, feeding problems became more acute. On September 8, 1943, Ewing wrote, almost frantically, that he had been unable to buy a single ton of cake from mills in Arkansas, Tennessee, or Oklahoma. He had previously depended on these sources for his Oklahoma cattle. The problem was not so bad for the Texas ranches but was on a week-to-week basis. The mills only sold for immediate use.[25] There was no chance of getting even a small reserve. There was sufficient roughage (the cattlemen's term for filler, such as grass, hay, and fodder), but protein became more scarce each year.

One of Ewing's grave concerns was keeping the equipment in repair.[26] He had done what he was able to do before the outbreak of the war to assemble reserve equipment. As the war wore on, he was anxious to keep it in repair and usable. Three weeks after Pearl Harbor he wrote to Johnny Murrell:

Take good care of your truck tires. See they are pumped up good and carry lots of pressure. We are not going to be able to get tires. And we must take care of our harness and equipment, as it is going to be extremely hard to replace. We are really in a very serious War, and all of these little things are going to count.

A year later he wrote Johnny again telling him to look over all the pickup and truck tires and if the rubber was worn badly to get them retreaded quickly while they could still get good rubber. The chief source of natural rubber was Southeast Asia, and the Japanese had cut off that supply. If Johnny could find any old tires with the fabrics unbroken, he was to get them and have them retreaded. Then Ewing added a parting admonition, "I would use the pickup as little as possible. When you go to town, try to think of everything you will need, make a list, so that it will not be necessary to make a trip more than once a week, or even less."

The red tape connected with the simplest matter was most vexing and bordered on absurdity. In Oklahoma a tire on the big cattle truck blew out. It was paired with an old tire which did not blow out, indicating the injured tire was faulty. It was guaranteed. The blowout happened almost in front of the tire store which handled that brand. They agreed to replace the tire but could not without a certificate from the chairman of the Rationing Board of Craig County. It took several days to get the certificate and much extra time and many miles on the truck, using up both rubber and gasoline.

The big cattle truck did a lot of hauling from 1943 to 1945.[27] Somehow they managed to keep it shod and running. They moved thousands of cattle with it with a great saving of manpower. Using it, two men could do the work of six or eight men under the old methods of moving cattle. The chief reason that the truck lasted was that Ewing was constantly after the drivers who operated it, telling them to take care of it, to grease and change the oil at regular intervals and "to get the tires tested every day."

Along with the problems occasioned by the war and attending to countless details involved with his personal supervision of several ranches, farms, a dairy, real estate, investments, and an oil company, he had another capacity. He had the time and desire for helping people. A kindly and compassionate man, endowed with understanding and sensibility, he sensed the problems of other people whom he knew and trusted. Unobtrusively, he moved in to help. Many such instances could be mentioned; however, only two will be recounted: one to a neighbor and another to employees. Both had to do with the war.

A personable young man, George Snedden, owned a ranch adjoining one of Ewing's pastures called the Wallen place, which was detached from the Big Creek ranch. George was educated, charming, and had a delightful young family. A very special relationship of a father and son type developed between Ewing and George. In his college career George got into the Naval Reserve as a Junior Lieutenant. Immediately after Pearl Harbor, he was called to active duty. He loved his ranch and was deeply perturbed about what he could do with it when he was leaving for an unknown length of time. Ewing sensed his dilemma and offered a solution. He would buy George's cattle at the market price, lease the land at a dollar an acre per year, keep the place up, and turn it back to George when he eventually got out of the Navy. This was arranged and was a load off George's mind.[28]

The fences were in bad repair. They really needed to be replaced completely with new ones, but wire and labor were almost impossible to obtain. Ewing did not want to make a capital outlay without George's knowledge and consent. He wrote to George, then stationed at a naval air base at Tallamook, Oregon. The correspondence which followed is both poignant and touching:

On June 12, 1943, George wrote to Ewing:

It is awfully good to hear from you. Your nice letter to me would have been answered sooner except I was not here when it arrived. I feel that new fence wire is probably very expensive now and that it would not be wise to refence the ranch. However, I want the fence kept up in good condition, and will very much appreciate it if you would attend to that and deduct the expense from the amount due me next April. It is my understanding that my taxes on the ranch can be deferred until after the War with no penalty. It is my intention to delay payment that long. My naval pay for two years will not pay the taxes for 1942, and this makes my situation a little difficult. It's awfully good of you to offer to loan me the money to pay them. You cannot know how much I appreciate this. However, I can manage.

The work here is very interesting and I like it very much. As you probably know this station is responsible for the patrol with blimps of the northwest seafrontier, which means a lot of territory. I have been in no danger whatever. I have been left in the U.S. for a long time at my commanding officer's request. This cannot last for the duration in my opinion.

Elizabeth and children are well and send their best wishes to you and Mrs. Halsell. We are all homesick, but cannot do anything about it. So we are managing to derive quite a bit of pleasure out of my being stationed here.

Mr. Halsell, I want you to know that my association with you has given me a great deal of pleasure and satisfaction. I am anxiously looking forward to carrying on where we left off when this War is over. Until then kindest regards to you and Mrs. Halsell.

On July 14, 1943, Ewing replied:

I was awfully glad to have your letter. Think you have been rather fortunate in the place you have been in. While I know there are some disagreeable things in these jobs, you still get some pleasure out of it.

Your ranch country is in good shape. We keep the fences so the cattle won't get out. I don't think it is a good plan to undertake any new improvements. We haven't spent any money on them yet but if I could find some posts, I would buy a few just to replace the rotten ones.

Couldn't contract any of my hay jobs so am putting up the hay with my own outfit and it is a lot of trouble. So you boys in the army and navy are not the only ones that have worries. Of course, yours are greater but, believe me, doing business under present circumstances is not a lot of fun. It takes about three weeks to buy a bolt or any kind of repairs for equipment that you have to have on farms and for haying.

Give my love to Elizabeth and the children. Am glad to hear from you now and then. We are all fine.

On May 26, 1944, Ewing Halsell wrote to George:

I just returned home. Have been in California and accompanied Will Rogers' remains here and placed them in the vault at the Will Rogers Memorial at Claremore. Glad to get this accomplished.

On my return home I found your Indian. It is quite unique and really very interesting the way it is made and dressed, and it was certainly nice of you and Elizabeth to remember me.

Your pastures are all in good shape. I have allowed 6 acres to the head for everything that is on this ranch. The only drawback to your ranch is the fences. My men are not doing any too much work in keeping them up and they really need to be replaced with new ones, which I am sure you will want to do when you get home, but under present conditions, we are just going to keep tying these old wires together and putting in a post.

I was through part of the Osage country a couple of days ago. The grass there is fine. I wasn't up in your part of the Osage, however.

I am awfully anxious to see this War over with. I would like to ease up a little bit, and one doesn't feel like doing it while you boys are all in the army, but when you return home, I will be glad to turn this ranch back over to you, and I am sure it will be a pleasure to you to get home again.

Best regards to you and your family.

In 1944 Ewing began negotiations to purchase the Farias ranch in South Texas. To finance the deal he needed to sell the Wallen pasture which adjoined George's place. He knew that George hoped that some day he might obtain the Wallen land, which together with his would make a good workable ranch. Ewing wrote to George giving him the first opportunity to buy it at $25 an acre. The following letter of July 17, 1944, was George's reply:

I very much appreciate your writing me in regard to the Wallen ranch. As you know I have wanted this land ever since I purchased the Centralia ranch. Almost a year ago I was allowed to come home in order to get my affairs in shape before going on foreign duty. My Commanding Officer requested that I be left here for an additional period of six months as the station was still in a formative period. Those six months have passed. I am expecting a promotion to Lieutenant Commander in the very near future which will automatically send me to a bigger job. As badly as I want your land I am afraid to go away leaving the amount of indebtedness the purchase would require.

If the land is not sold I will certainly try to buy it when this damned War is over.

Thank you again for offering the ranch to me first.

W. E. and Ewing Halsell   333

Ewing Halsell's final letter to George, December 27, 1944, was as follows:

I was in hopes you would be back home before now, but looks like you have another year ahead of you. So I am planning to continue using your ranch. It is in very good condition except of course the fences need lots of work, but we are keeping them up fairly well.

I have not been able to sell my Wallen place, although I priced it at $25, and I think it is worth it. I may not be able to sell it before you get home, and if I don't, I will expect you to buy it.

We have had a very pleasant Christmas at home. Had my usual friends in for eggnog. Our old house had a good many flowers which had been sent, and it looked very pretty.

Your present, the cheese, came in very nicely. It has been hard to get here, and besides it takes up a lot of [ration] points. It was a very thoughtful gift.

Another illustration of Ewing Halsell's concern for his employees emerges from his correspondence with Clyte and Mabel Harlan, two loyal, dedicated, hardworking individuals. Clyte was the foreman at Bird Creek and Mabel was the cook.

Beginning in 1940, the ranch was understaffed because of the labor shortage, and the Harlans tried to make up for it by driving themselves harder and longer. Fatigue and frustrations caused them to be irritable and unhappy, to the extent that Clyte even threatened to join the Marines.

Ewing knew of their plight and feared they were headed for physical problems. He realized they were two determined and stubborn people, and, although he knew that something had to be done to get them to slow down, he was also aware that the direct approach might be misunderstood as a reflection on their ability and stamina. So he tried a course of suggestion. In a routine letter to Clyte, July 8, 1940, he casually dropped in the following paragraph:

After your harvest and your hay is up, I want you and Mabel to take a little vacation. You have been there long enough, so you deserve a little time out. I think you would enjoy going to the mountains, and if you would you might plan to drive to Colorado Springs and Denver. The roads are good and it would not take over two days to make the trip. . . .

The Harlans made no response to this suggestion nor to many other similar suggestions which Ewing continued to make in his letters. They kept on with their brutal work schedule through the summer, fall and into the winter of 1940. Then Clyte collapsed and had to be hospitalized. Surgery was required, and Ewing kept close touch with Clyte. As Clyte gradually got better, Ewing began again to urge a vacation on the Harlans. And, as previously, they continued to ignore his pleas and worked at the same pace throughout 1941 and 1942. In August, 1942, Mabel became very ill with pneumonia and had to be rushed to the hospital. Again Ewing showed his concern by writing both Mabel and Clyte, mentioning more rest, a vacation, and the hiring of a cook to ease their load.

The last half of 1942 passed slowly. Clyte was discouraged, for he felt the poor showing at Bird Creek was his fault, although it was really the fault of the adversities of the weather. Ewing tried to boost his spirits by writing a letter full of both consolation and optimism. Throughout 1943 Ewing continued his one-way correspondence, filled with his thoughts for the well-being of the Harlans. He did not neglect the Harlans' children in his concern, affection, and hope for the future. On August 1, 1943, he wrote to Mabel:

Going to send a card to Susanne and Clyte, Jr. Just want to let them know I thought of them. They are both nice children. I am awfully pleased with Clyte Jr.'s work this summer. I know it has been a little hard, but it is good for him and will help to make him a good man. He may not want to be a farmer, or a ranchman, but everything that he can learn will help him in whatever profession or business he goes into.

Many other individuals and families were the recipients of Ewing Halsell's concern and compassion during the war years and afterwards. There was Gaither, Huffman, Tooyah Bean, the Murrell family, and scores of others in the records, and, no doubt, an even greater number of which no records were made.

The war did something to Ewing and those with whom he worked and depended upon. As it progressed the tone of the letters became more mellow and forbearing. Spiritual values, in a worldly sense, transcended material assessments.

Farias   19

In April, 1944, the Ewing Halsells went to San Antonio for their spring vacation. Lucile, her sister Grace, and Helen Campbell were having lunch in the small Sun Room of the St. Anthony Hotel. The room was crowded. Suddenly Ewing, by nature a modest and constrained man, came bustling into the dining room, and excitedly said to Helen, "Young lady, do you think we could get together a million dollars?"

A hush fell over the room. The waiter stopped to listen. The chatter of the diners ceased, and a stillness prevailed. Ewing, conscious of the effect he had produced, paused and glanced about the room. He blushed like a school boy caught in some mischief, then slid into the vacant chair at the table and waited for the talking to resume. Leaning toward the ladies he said in a guarded tone, "I think I have bought a ranch."[1]

This was the beginning of the end of a search which had been going on for years.[2] He had started looking for a sizable ranch in the 1930's for several reasons. The only lands he actually owned himself were the tracts which made up the Big

Creek ranch, the Wallen ranch, the Fall River ranch, and the Jarboe ranch. Bird Creek which he operated was owned by him and his sisters. His "Texas" ranch, which at the time was the Fuqua VVN pasture, was leased on a year-to-year basis. There was little chance of substantially expanding the Big Creek ranch.

Another reason for wanting another ranch had to do with climate.[3] Each passing year he, Lucile, and Mrs. Rider felt more and more the chill of the cold, sleet, and snow of northeastern Oklahoma.* They longed to move south, and San Antonio was their favorite spot. However, one could not go out just any day and find a suitable ranch within a reasonable distance of San Antonio. For several years he had had realtors looking out for a ranch of about 100,000 acres in South Texas, New Mexico, or Old Mexico.[4] He had spent considerable time following up leads, but so far nothing satisfactory had turned up. Several sites qualified as to size, but always with a drawback, such as faulty title, lack of dependable water, too remote, or too arid.[5]

On this visit to San Antonio in April 1944, Ewing, after the family had settled in at the St. Anthony, called a real estate agent he knew, D. K. Martin, and let him know that he was in town. Saturday night Mr. Martin called to say he thought he had found the ranch Ewing was looking for and asked if Ewing would meet him next morning at Martin's office to look at the maps. Ewing went and spent three hours examining the maps and the data. He was familiar with the general area. The ranch contained 97,000 acres and was located near the Mexican border, about halfway between Carrizo Springs and Eagle Pass. The price was reasonable, about $8.65 an acre.[6] Ewing was never one to buy a horse without looking in its mouth; he wanted to inspect the ranch before committing himself. It was arranged that Mr. Hal Mangum, the owner, would show him the ranch on Monday. Like a good trader he concealed his enthusiasm for the prospect until he was out of Mr. Martin's office. On his way to the hotel his excitement mounted. By the time he reached the Sun Room he was fairly carried away.

---

*Mrs. Rider had come to live with the Halsells about 1935. Her husband, Orion, a prominent Vinita attorney, had been drowned while on a fishing trip vacation in 1931. After his death, she continued to live in the home where she and Lucile grew up, then later gave up the home and came to live with Ewing and Lucile. She made her home with them for the rest of their lives.

A Ranching Saga

He and Helen spent the afternoon considering how they could raise $1,000,000 within a reasonable time. Their books and records were in Vinita, but they did not particularly need them. They both knew his liquid and convertible assets. They reached the conclusion that by selling some stocks and several detached tracts of land in Oklahoma they could raise the amount without encumbering any of his major properties.[7]

The entire family decided to make the inspection trip. They were to get an early start, look over part of the ranch before lunch, and eat at the chuck house or the chuck wagon, depending on where the cow work was taking place. Lucile was fascinated with the development and wanted to do something extra nice for the cowboys they would meet next day. She had the chef prepare great quantities of neatly trimmed and wrapped picnic sandwiches and cookies.

Next morning, instead of Mr. Mangum showing up, Mr. William H. George, president of the First National Bank, Eagle Pass, came by to pick them up.[8] Some emergency had prevented Mr. Mangum's coming, and he had sent Mr. George who was acquainted with every part of the ranch, its background, and its present condition. The drive was about three hours from San Antonio, and they arrived at the ranch about 11 A.M. They spent some time looking over one of the pastures and managed to reach the chuck house just before the dinner bell rang. Mrs. Halsell quickly met the cook and arranged to have her dainties placed on a table where the cowboys would file by to fill their plates. One thing Lucile had not anticipated was that the cowboys were all Mexicans, some of whom did not even speak English. The Mexican vaqueros were used to beans, meat, and bread. Most, if not all, of them had never seen party sandwiches, and they went over and filled their plates to the brim with frijoles, meat, and tortillas. Ewing and Mr. George made it up to her by gorging themselves with sandwiches, when they no doubt would have preferred what the vaqueros were eating.[9]

They did not see all the ranch.[10] The roads were inadequate, but Ewing saw enough to satisfy himself. The improvements were practically nil. The only buildings of consequence were the two bosses' houses of three rooms, each without running water. The old main ranch house built by Fleming and Davidson had burned down some years earlier. The cook house was a *ramada*, that is, an arbor thatched with brush on top, an open-air affair, and nearby was a small bunkhouse.

All this did not bother Ewing. In fact, he rather preferred it that way. He would not be hampered by having to save and salvage old structures. He could just move over a little way and start from scratch with his own layout for the headquarters he had in mind.

They returned to San Antonio late in the evening. Lucile and Grace were weary, but Ewing and Helen were so elated they sat up quite late figuring and planning. The next morning Ewing Halsell signed a contract of purchase, and he and Helen started getting the money together.[11]

With the acquisition of the Farias ranch, there was plenty to do. First was the matter of moving the central office of the Ewing Halsell enterprises from Vinita to San Antonio. Second, the moving of the family from the old home in Vinita to a suite of three bedrooms, four baths, and a large living room in the St. Anthony Hotel. Third, the moving of cattle and equipment from the VVN ranch in Bailey County to the Farias. Fourth, the planning and building of an extensive headquarters on the Farias, contracting for additional tanks, wells, windmills, and fences. Ewing was 67 years old, but he went about it all with the buoyancy of a person half that age.

The first two of the items were accomplished with a minimum of exertion on the part of the family.[12] Since their construction about 1910, the Gunter Hotel and the Gunter Office Building had been the headquarters for South Texas cattlemen. Ewing took a suite of offices in the Office Building, which was only a block from the St. Anthony. The only sadness experienced in the transition from Vinita to San Antonio was the moving out of the old homeplace and away from lifelong friends.

In addition to the 97,000 acres in the Farias ranch Ewing leased part of the Chittum ranch adjoining the Farias on the north, bringing his total range to 148,000 acres. This would run from 5,000 to 5,500 cattle units. It was Ewing's intention to have 2,200 mother cows and the remainder of the pasturage devoted to steers. In line with his understanding with Mr. Mangum, he was not to get possession of Farias until December 15, 1944. However, Mr. Mangum shifted his cattle in such a way that Ewing could start bringing his cattle in by November. Ewing had the hunting rights for 1944.[13]

In August, he wrote Johnny Murrell his plan of cleaning out the VVN pasture. The young cattle were to be shipped to Farias and the older cattle to Oklahoma.

340   *A Ranching Saga*

They had 700 yearling heifers which he wanted shipped to Farias in November along with all of the 1944 calf crop. Also he bought 2,323 U Bar steer yearlings from E. K. Warren and Son which he wanted shipped to Farias in November. Two hundred old cows and 700 two-year-old steers were to go to the Big Creek ranch. Later, he would finish stocking the Farias ranch from South Texas sources.[14]

The improving of the ranch was a long, slow process. It was almost like going out on virgin land and starting afresh. There was a fence of sorts around it, and a few earth tanks and windmills. However, the lack of improvements was only a challenge to Ewing Halsell. He lost no time in getting started.[15] The ink was scarcely dry on the deed to the land when Helen opened a set of account books. The first entry was the transfer of $5,000 to the First National Bank in Eagle Pass, June 19, 1944. The first purchase, made June 27, was a new Chevrolet master coach for $1,138.39, but with radio, heater, fender guards, trunk guards, and freight it amounted to $1,537.39. This first item indicates the advent of the motor age in the Halsell ranching operation. The motorized vehicle came before the horses. The second item in the leather bound account book, July 29, was for the salary of John H. Hinnant. He was the first foreman and the highest paid man on the ranch. He left the ranch in October 1945. His salary started at $150 a month and was raised to $175. When he left, he sold his horse to Ewing for $125. The average pay for Mexican vaqueros at the time was about $60 a month. When the first shipment of yearlings arrived from the VVN ranch, Ewing sent Gaither down to help receive them at Farias.

Correspondence as to what actually happened on the Farias the first two years after Ewing Halsell took it over is extremely scarce, but the account book is very revealing. The first purchase, August 9, of equipment or materials was for two tents, 12 by 14 feet of 10 ounce duck, and one 12 x 16 tarpaulin also of 10 ounce duck, all for $159.74. These were used for the first hunting camp, located at Rock Tank. The first hunt was held in December 1944. On August 28, five saddles were acquired from Frank Vela for $515. As yet, there were no horses to put them on. On September 11, five other saddles were shipped from some other place with an express charge of $4.83. These got there just in time. Three days later twelve horses were acquired for $1,200. Each horse cost $3.00 less than the saddles. The horses were secured at Hebbronville and were trucked to Farias at a cost of

$60 or $5 a horse bringing their total cost to $105. So their value on arrival at Farias was a little more than the saddles.*[16]

During October 1944, things began to shape up for a cow camp. Two wagons were repaired at a cost of $86 with no mention of where they came from. Several hundred feet of lariat rope, a horse bell, and a cook pot were purchased from the lumber yard. Then followed nine saddle pads and pot racks and three bridles. On October 23, six more saddle horses were added for $450 or $75 each. On October 31, 2,000 doses of Cutler's Pelmenal were obtained. They were getting ready to receive the young cattle from the VVN, and these vaccines were necessary for the anticipated shipping fever. Seven part-time hands were hired, two Anglos and five Mexicans. On November 18, 1,200 steers arrived by rail at Eagle Pass from Mule-shoe. G. B. McDonald was put on the payroll as hunting camp cook. Ordinary hands were listed as laborers.[17]

In December, 1944, the Farias became a beehive of activity. Brad (G. B.) McDonald, who was on the payroll only during the hunting camp, is listed with $100 salary. Lester La Grange was brought down from Amherst on a temporary basis at a salary of $75 a month. His duties seem to have been to keep up with supplies and run errands. There were nineteen laborers, three Anglos and sixteen Mexicans. Their wages ranged from $45 to $75 a month. No distinction is made between those working at trades and those with cattle. Fabian Lopez was the only one who got $75. All the others received $65 or less, down to $45.[18]

On December 9, the cook department was considerably improved by the acquisition of six dutch ovens at a cost of $23.52. Anyone who has ever cooked at a camp will realize the value of these additions. The grocery bill for December, for twenty-one men, was $129.08 or about $6.75 per person a month, approximately seven cents a meal. However, deer were plentiful, and this was the hunting season. The men had venison with flour gravy and tortillas about three times a day.

In January, the camp really began to go high-class. Four cots, the first mentioned so far, and ten cups and saucers were ordered. The cots cost $23.80, the cups and saucers $1.20, and a tax of $1.20 was added. By the middle of January, goat meat began to supplement venison. Three goats were bought for $4.00 each. The labor force was cut from nineteen to eight, all Mexicans.[19]

*In W. E.'s day the saying was, "He rode a $10 horse with a $40 saddle."

By February, Hal Mangum had turned over the old headquarters and Ewing began renovation of the three-room house. In the expense account book we find hardware, $22.70; lumber and nails, $108.67; paint brushes, $10.80; paint price not given, and Tom Southall, carpenter, $50.00. Abraham Garcia worked on the house the entire month for $75.00. Also lumber was hauled out for a little bridge, probably for a crossing on a small creek between the old headquarters and U.S. Highway 277, two miles to the north of headquarters. During February, Emilio Saucedo sustained a broken leg, and the ranch took care of his hospital bill, thirteen days at $6.00 a day for a total of $78.00. The grocery bill for the month was $129.39. Only one trip was made to town for this purpose.[20]

In March, fifteen laborers were working as carpenters, painters, plumbers, and fence builders. All except one were Mexicans. Abraham Garcia, listed as a mason, was paid $150 for the month. The grocery bill was $87.03. Perhaps the most appreciated addition to the old headquarters during March was one Jersey cow at $110. Now there could be a token amount of milk and butter for each of the hands. The lumber bill for the month "for the boss's house" was $866.86. Screens, electrical wiring, and inside plumbing were being installed. On April 13, $692.90 worth of new furniture was delivered, and also Mrs. Ewing Halsell was reimbursed for $76.71 for shades, blankets, sheets, pillows, and table cloths. The grocery bill for April was $123.36 for fifteen laborers in addition to the salaried men. The Jersey cow was helping out. There was considerable fence repair during March and April.[21]

So it went until December. Up to this time the work at the old headquarters was for the purpose of modernizing it as a major camp. It was near the center of the property and would continue to be a good operational location. For a year and a half Ewing debated whether to build his substantial buildings for himself and his guests here or beside the irrigation canal on the west end of the ranch. If located there, water for household and domestic use would be assured, with plenty for lavish landscaping. He considered putting implement sheds and shops there, a great hay barn, feed lots, and graineries. The site would be ten or twelve miles nearer Eagle Pass. He could have one or two thousand acres of permanent pasture and could look out and see a couple of thousand cattle grazing at one time. What a beautiful sight that would be! In a number of ways it would be similar to the headquarters at Big Creek.[22]

Then he would weigh the disadvantages of having his main headquarters at the west end of the ranch. At Big Creek there were only 17,000 acres between the headquarters and the far side of the pastures. At Farias there would be nearly 100,000 acres to the far side of the ranch. There was a drawback in being too close to town. Maintaining one's privacy would be more difficult, with more opportunity for uninvited visitors to drop in. Being near feed pens, in a rainy year the smell, when the wind was in the wrong direction, could be an awful nuisance. The old headquarters were splendidly isolated. They were completely hidden from the highway. There was only one road and one gate to the highway, and it could be kept locked. As to water, a draw was a mile or two east of the old headquarters, and the first time he saw it, when they came out to inspect the ranch, he had made a mental note that a huge dam could impound an enormous lake. The surface water impounded there would be much better than water from the Rio Grande. On a working ranch there was distinct advantage of being near the center.[23] Ewing considered moving the headquarters nearer the lake he planned to create. Then he would have something comparable to Big Creek, where the headquarters overlooked a sizable man-made lake.

After weighing the pros and cons of the location for a year and a half, he wrote to Les La Grange December 18, 1945:

The more I am on this ranch the more I want to put the headquarters where they are [now]. I am going back again to the idea of adding to the old headquarters. I think my idea of a pipe line from the canal is practical. Regardless of what these engineers say, I think the water can be brought from there.

When John H. Hinnant left the ranch in October 1945, L. D. Gaither had come to live at the ranch and was drawing $75 a month pension. He held an advisory position at Farias. In January 1946, Herbert Meier became boss with a salary of $175 a month. Juan Salinas got $100 a month. Fourteen Mexican workers were on a $75 a month basis, depending on how many days they worked. Gaither's pension was on a par with the vaqueros' pay, yet he was a person of importance on the ranch, someone to be reckoned with.[24]

With Ewing Halsell's decision to expand the old headquarters, he made a plan for a number of new buildings to be used by the family and guests. Lucile was the architect and decorator. She helped draw the plans and selected and purchased all furnishings which were specially made. The layout was something like that at Big Creek, only oriented east and west rather than north and south as in Oklahoma. The employees' quarters at Farias, containing the original houses and those added in 1945-46, did extend north and south. Beginning on the south was the caretakers' house, next was the boss's, then two bunk houses, and the chuck house with large modern kitchen. About a hundred yards to the east of this group was a large, galvanized steel barn. To the north and east of it extended about two acres of corrals and pens with high fences painted red.[25]

Over the years Ewing added four more buildings south of this complex. Today, on the north side of the quadrangle, facing south, is the family kitchen and dining room. The house is T shaped with kitchen, large store room, and servant's room extending to the back. The front with a screened porch has the dining room on the left and two guest rooms with bath on the right. Across an open space the size of a city block, grassed and kept neatly mowed, are three houses, facing north. On the east of this row, Ewing built a spacious, but not ostentatious guest house. A large living room runs across the front. Behind the living room are two exceedingly large bedrooms, each with bath. In the west end of the living room is a large brick fireplace with the mantel which was moved from the old home in Vinita when the house was torn down to make way for the Ewing Halsell High School.

The middle house is long from east to west with a deep screened veranda in front. Being on the shady side of the house, this is where the guests gather in warm weather to drink their toddies and perchance indulge in some hot games of poker. During the hunting season, if the weather is chilly, they move to a large living room inside with an inviting fireplace and comfortable chairs. Also, there are several guest rooms with baths in the rear.[26] The next house to the west is a small house which was designed for Ewing's use. All three of the houses are painted a buttercup yellow, with fenced yards, neatly landscaped.

The compound with the eating quarters across the way was designed primarily for entertaining. There is nothing lavish, but it all is solid, comfortable, and functional. In a remarkable sense it reflects the character and personality of Ewing Halsell himself. He built small houses to increase privacy and to reduce fire hazard. He came to the latter conclusion after having been burned out of a sizable house at Spring Lake when he and Lucile were left homeless.[27]

Ewing Halsell had the misfortune of acquiring the Farias ranch at the end of a series of favorable years. For ten years the rainfall had been average or above. The year he first inspected and bought it was one that was better than average. The year he took over, 1945, was a little below but not enough to cause alarm. The next year, the one of much activity and outlay, was above average. Then a two-year drought began in 1947 and became acute in 1948. Ewing was to learn a method of ranching procedure that was new to him, one called ''pear burning.'' This was a practice entailing burning the stickers off of the prickly pear (*Opuntia*) so that cattle could eat the flat, green, fleshy leaves. The old-timers knew how to resort to pear burning during bad years. They had learned the trick from the Mexicans a hundred years before.[28]

In 1888, Professor James C. Maelin of the University of Kansas traveled through the semiarid area studying the flora. This was towards the end of the drought of 1886–1888, one of the worst of record in Texas. Professor Maelin was amazed at the ingenuity of the Mexican workers who had kept their cattle alive for two years on what was probably less than ten inches of rain during the entire two-year drought. The *Opuntia* grows abundantly in that area, some growing to a height of three to four feet. The plant gets a considerable part of its water content from the air. The region is near enough to the gulf that the southeast winds bring moisture from the gulf even during years of little rainfall. The drought of 1886–1888 had been so severe that much of the mesquite and acacia brush had died. The Mexicans would build a fire of dead brush in an area surrounded by prickly pear. The laborers would cut a bunch of prickly pear, and with a fork hold it over the fire until the stickers were burned off, and then throw the leaves to the cattle who were waiting eagerly and hungrily to consume them.

By the 1890's, Texas ranchers had opened up most of the Southwest Texas area and begun to acquire title to it. They eventually improved on the technique of pear burning. They invented sheet iron tanks which would hold several gallons of kero-

sene or gasoline, equipped with pressure valves and pumps. A burner nozzle was attached to a hose which in turn connected to a spigot at the bottom of the tank. The tank was held by straps on the back of the worker. With his lighted torch he walked about burning the stickers off the standing prickly pear. Cattle followed so close behind the pear burner that they sometimes nuzzled him away before he had finished with a bunch of the pear.

This was the method being used in the Farias country when the drought of 1948 reduced the ranchers to burning pear. Ewing, ever eager to learn new ways to cope with nature, was fascinated by the procedure and lost no time trying it out. His advisor and teacher was Holman Cartwright, who ranched at Dinero just east of the Farias ranch. They spent many rather enjoyable hours figuring up ways to improve the accepted method at the time. Cartwright would go to San Antonio, drop by the Gunter office, and get Ewing. They loved to go to junkyards together and poke around, looking for discarded tanks, pipes, fittings, and all manner of items which they could use to put together a more efficient burner. With the help of a welder they designed a large tank which would hold a hundred gallons or more of butane, mounted on wheels, with a small Maytag type motor which ran a pressure pump. Several long hoses were attached, each with its fire nozzle. In this way four or five men, without burdens on their backs, could burn a swath from fifty to a hundred feet wide through a pear thicket. The new contrivance also reduced the fire hazard for the men. The old type of container, carried on their backs, was prone to drip the volatile fuel on the clothing of workers, causing a constant menace of incineration. Even before the mobile unit was devised, Ewing and Cartwright had provided their pear burners with fire resistant jackets somewhat like firemen use. However, these had limited use due to the fact that jackets deprived the body of its natural evaporative cooling processes. Sweat would accumulate giving the effect of a Turkish bath. The jackets were of little help except in cold weather.[29]

The main value of pear burning was that it kept the cattle alive. They could exist on it for extended periods of time and look pretty good, but the appearance was deceptive. The old-timers knew it all the while, and Ewing had been told what to expect. However, the realization was brought home to him and Helen, who nearly always officiated at the ranch scales when cattle were shipped, when they sent a consignment of steers from Farias to La Pryor, a distance of fifty miles. The steers lost nearly a hundred pounds, and with the shrinkage Ewing lost money. But the occasion was not without its lesson which Ewing heeded. The pear was about 95 per cent water and contained very little protein. A pound of concentrate, like cottonseed cake or even the whole cottonseed, would make a considerable difference in the hardening of the flesh.[30]

The whole matter of burning pear was intriguing and exciting to Ewing Halsell. To make use of what nature had provided in a semiarid country subject to periodic, acute droughts was a challenge, one with which he quickly learned to cope. He developed a profound respect for prickly pear which to the passing stranger was a useless nuisance. With it, a cattleman could weather severe droughts. Without, the land would be burned to a crisp and not even a jackrabbit could survive. The pear was the ranchman's insurance.

A fascinating feature of the Farias country was its unpredictability.[31] With less than seven inches of rain in 1948, the newcomer could not imagine how vegetation could ever return to the dead, barren earth. But the very next year, the rainfall was double its annual average, and the flowers, weeds, grasses, bushes, and trees covered the land with brilliant color and verdant green, giving it a luscious, tropical appearance. Wildlife returned and cattle fattened. The next six years were about average, or slightly below. None necessitated pear burning, and the respite gave the prickly pear a chance to again spread over the land. The pear burning machines were stored in the sheds. But 1956 was a repetition of 1948. The pears were ready and the machines were brought out, reconditioned, and put to work. The drought of 1956, which lasted only a year, was followed by the longest series of average years since weather records have been kept; seventeen years without a general drought. However, even on average years local variations occurred. During the mid-1950's the sheep and goat area of the Edwards Plateau was subnormal for seven years. During locally dry years in the lower Rio Grande country, the rains came usually during the hurricane season of late summer, ending a severe drought with a six- or eight-inch rain all at once. The runoff would be rapid, and the effect on vegetation disappointing. But the flash floods were good tank fillers, provided they did not take the dams out.

Local ranchers, with all their investments in the Farias area, had constant financial problems, their ups and downs and their booms and busts. After a few good years they could get the bank paid off and maybe a little ahead, and then the cycle would start again. Ewing Halsell was in a position to cope with adversities of weather. When conditions were awful in South Texas, he could start the pear burners for the cows and ship the steers to the ranches in Oklahoma and Kansas.

Over the years improvements were built. More tanks were made by damming draws with watersheds covering several sections of land. The Comanche Lake created by the big dam southeast of the headquarters never went dry. A pipeline had been laid from it to the headquarters, and Red Caldwell, a jack-of-all-trades with an engaging personality, contrived an ingenious filtering system to cleanse the water of silt and humus matter. He utilized abandoned oil field equipment, steel tanks, pipe, and valves. With a blowtorch and know-how he produced a filtering plant, at small cost, capable of serving all the buildings and grounds at headquarters. Red rigged up a circuit so that the filtering tanks could be backflushed and cleaned of accumulated silt simply by closing and opening some valves. The construction of this plant was a matter of compelling interest to Ewing, who spent considerable time watching and even acting as Red's assistant. Two aspects of the project appealed to him. One was Red's ability to recycle materials rusting and going to waste into something that was usable and economical.[32] The other item was the convivial and captivating personality of Red himself. Although Red was an entrepreneur, who finagled around with many projects such as slot machines, liquor store, and bottling works, he was a master craftsman with his hands and a schemer with his brain. He had a big heart, was honest, and never imposed. A close friendship and camaraderie developed between Ewing and Red which lasted as long as Ewing lived.[33]

Ewing Halsell spent much time and money developing irrigation lands at the west end of the ranch. An irrigation ditch, belonging to the Maverick County Water Control and Improvement District, Number One, extended from northwest to southeast across the extreme west end of the ranch. It serviced irrigated fields between the south boundary of the ranch and the Rio Grande. The former owner of the Farias ranch had not joined the Water District but had granted the District permission to place the ditch across the ranch. It did provide water for cattle in that section.[34]

Ewing, as previously indicated, loved to farm and see useful plants grow. He studied the flow of water in the ditch and was convinced that considerably more water passed through his property than could be used by the farmers below. He studied the lay of his land along the ditch and estimated that he could get water to about 2,000 acres. He arranged a meeting with the Water Board of the District to discuss his securing the necessary water. The Board was quite willing provided he would be committed to pay his pro rata share of the bonds and maintenance to the District. This, Ewing did not intend to do. He wanted to be able to discontinue irrigation any time he found it unprofitable without putting a permanent water tax on his land. He proposed that he contract to buy the water he used from the District. After considerable wrangling, with Ewing remaining adamant, the Board, realizing it had nothing to lose and something to gain, agreed to a time limited contract subject to renewal. The agreement was reached in March, 1946.[35] The cost of the water was $3.50 per acre for each six month.*

Ewing lost no time getting the project underway. He employed a surveyor and an engineer to lay out the first 1,000 acres, of which 641 acres were put into a farm the first year. A contract was made with Vernon Standifer to prepare the land. The first job was to clear the brush, a growth of mesquite, catclaw, white brush, and other semiarid plants. There was very little prickly pear in this area. The brush was bulldozed off with a D6 Caterpillar tractor owned by Vernon Standifer and a D7 belonging to Ewing Halsell. The same tractors were used to do root plowing and raking. Root plowing was accomplished by pulling an underground blade behind the heavy, giant tractors, about 24 inches below the surface, cutting the roots of all trees and bushes. A heavy rake would then be used to pull the roots to the surface. Then the roots and brush would be pushed into piles. The brush and roots would be allowed to dry, and then it was burned. Next came the leveling of the surface of the land. A heavy grader on a long frame, called a Land Plane, filled the holes and gullies and levelled the surface. The land was then ready for breaking to a depth of 12 to 18 inches two ways with a heavy breaking plow. Lastly, the clods were broken and the surface smoothed with a large harrow. An engineer was then employed to run levels for the ditches which would convey water by gravity flow.[36]

Ewing purchased a ditching machine to make the ditches. He organized his own

*The cost of the water gradually went up. By 1970, it was $12 per acre per year.

crew with a boss. The land was ready to sow to oats, but the ground was so dry that it had to be watered before the seed could be planted. Mr. Standifer instructed the crew as to how to handle the water. It was taken from the ditches with siphons, which at first were made of rubber and later of plastic. After the land was watered the oats were sowed with a Wheatland drill in early September. The field was ready for pasturage in the fall by the time calf weaning was completed.

With the first unit in production, other plots of land were prepared. By 1965, 2,000 acres were under irrigation. After a few seasons of irrigating by gravity flow, Ewing Halsell put in a sprinkler system, purchased from the Oaks Irrigation Company of Pharr, Texas, at a cost of slightly more than $9,000 installed. It consisted of a General Motors Diesel 3-71 Motor, a suction hose, a huge valve and pump mounted on a four wheel trailer, 2,714 feet of sprinkler pipe, 66 sprinklers, and all necessary connections.[37]

After two years, Ewing began to feel that sprinkling was more expensive than the gravity method. He had his bookkeeper, Emil Weilbacher, who worked for Ewing Halsell from 1946 to 1965, prepare a comparative cost statement. This confirmed Ewing's conviction, and he reverted to the gravity system.*

While Ewing Halsell was undertaking the purchase of the irrigation water at Farias, he was also negotiating to sell water rights on the Spring Lake ranch. One of the interesting aspects of the farms surrounding the Spring Lake ranch was that the water table in the irrigation wells in that area was far more stable than the water level in most of the South Plains area. Extensive pumping did not seem to have nearly as much effect on lowering the water as it did in most other areas. In the late 1940's some alert engineers and geologists came to the conclusion that the underground water in this area flowed from the Northwest to the Southeast, and that along the Southeast line of the Halsell properties was an underground ridge of a somewhat impermeable limestone which slowed down this flow. This ridge sup-

*Later Clyte Harlan, on a hunting trip to Farias, noticed the abandoned sprinkler system and asked if he could take it to Bird Creek to irrigate the bottom farms from the creek which ran through the ranch. He had some difficulty getting permission from the state and federal water authorities to take water from the creek. This was finally arranged, and the sprinkler system was trucked to Bird Creek. However, Clyte was never able to make it work economically. Red Murrell then hauled the system to the Spring Lake ranch, where he used it on a personal pure seed project in the Big Sand Pasture.

posedly acted like an underground dam, backing up the flow of the underground water, so that a virtual lake of water was maintained in this vicinity so long as there was any flow of water through the underground reservoirs. This theory gained considerable acceptance and it probably led to the numerous offers to purchase water rights which the Halsells began to receive.

Ewing was very concerned about the tax consequences of any such sale and also about the possible resulting diminution in value of the land with the water rights sold.

Negotiations with various possible buyers went on for years, and finally in 1950 the first sale, to Southwestern Public Service, was made, subject to the Halsells obtaining a favorable ruling that the proceeds of the sale would be treated as capital gains rather than as ordinary income at higher rates. This sale to Southwestern Public Service retained the right to all water which might be useful for watering livestock, domestic uses, or for drilling wells but not for irrigation or industrial uses other than oil exploration. The buyer was prohibited in all sales to remove the water for irrigation or navigation purposes. This sale covered more than 44,000 acres of land and, in the center of this tract near the middle of the ranch, was sold a few hundred acres of land as a site for an electric power plant.

This sale was followed by other sales to the City of Littlefield, the City of Lubbock, and further sales to Southwestern Public Service, the last sale having been closed in November 1957. No water rights were ever sold under land which was subject to cultivation, but only under the sandy pasture lands which had largely been excluded from the XIT ranch as unsuitable for agriculture. This land had been acquired from County School boards after the Sod House and Spring Lake pastures had been purchased out of the XIT ranch.

The prices received for these water rights ranged from $15 to $35 per acre. One of the neighbors, the late John S. McMurtry of Muleshoe, Texas, sold the water rights under his sandy land at the same time Ewing was selling to one of his buyers. John was out of the state when this matter came up, and he gave his power of attorney to the Halsells' lawyer, Gilbert M. Denman, Jr., authorizing him to make any trade with regard to the McMurtry water rights provided it was identical to the trade Ewing Halsell made for himself and his sisters. On that deal the top price of $35 an acre was obtained.[38]

A Ranching Saga

Back at Farias, the improvements became considerable. They consisted of the boss's house, two bunk houses, a chuck house, a bath house, a cold storage plant, a cow barn, a huge machinery shed, extensive feed lots, which included a storage barn, a feed grinding mill and equipment, and two sets of scales. Farias was more than a ranch with irrigated fields to Ewing Halsell, his family, and his friends. It was a home, a place of retreat, something to be shared with the extended family, friends, and faithful employees. One of the charms of the ranch was that it was devoid of ostentation. Allan Shephard, an occasional guest, described it "as a working ranch, not a show place. The furniture was plain, but comfortable, and the food was excellent."[39]

The most important occasion of the year was the hunting season, which came in the late fall when the weather was cool and bracing and the deer were fat. A wonderful deer country, the ranch carried about half the number of deer as it did cattle, and Ewing was as concerned with their welfare as he was with that of his cattle. He never leased hunting rights for money and guarded against poaching. With the help of the regional game warden he kept a fairly accurate estimate of the number of deer and maintained it on an even keel. If the number became excessive during a series of good years, they permitted the killing of a few does. On bad years the does were zealously protected.[40]

The hunting season was looked forward to from one year to the next. Plans were made long in advance. Careful attention was given to scheduling. The visitors were classified and grouped according to compatability and interest. For instance, old friends from Vinita and Tulsa would be invited as a group. Then there were the friends from San Antonio, those who enjoyed playing poker or gin rummy together. A time was reserved for the neighbors and friends in Eagle Pass. Another interval was devoted to the foremen and top hands of all Ewing's ranches.

Ewing enjoyed all the groups, but especially the latter. He had a twofold reason for giving them extra attention.[41] First, they were men whom he had practically raised and with whom he had shared many experiences. They were dedicated to the cause which was his supreme interest, working with cattle. Bringing them together for a social and sporting occasion was a unique and effective method of building morale. Second, after the day's hunt was over, the employees, mellowed with Bourbon and Scotch and filled with prime beef, settled down to talk shop. Ewing drew from them details and problems of each of the ranches. He was one who could listen as well as talk. He elicited their ideas and sought their advice about many aspects of the business, such as what pastures were overgrazed, which cattle were ready for market, what repairs should be made. Everyone knew he would make the decisions, but all felt that he valued their advice and judgments. Of his poker-playing friends from Oklahoma or San Antonio, he knew the nature, temperament, tastes, and peculiarities. Ewing himself was the bartender, and, like a professional bartender, he never drank but knew what each guest preferred and how strong or how mild he liked his toddy. It was understood by all guests that Ewing wanted everyone to feel the mellowing and relaxing influence of liquor, but that he disapproved of excesses. One neighbor who attended the hunting parties for years reported that only one time had he ever observed a guest, a newcomer, "get out of line" and that he was never invited back.

Among the card players were conversation, banter, poker, and pitch. Ewing had the rare quality of keeping the party lively, with wit, stories, anecdotes, buffoonery, repartee, and a remarkable ability to recall some incident about a guest of which the victim would not like to be reminded. For instance, when the ranchhands were the guests, Johnny Murrell went out early one morning with one of the other hands. Johnny spotted a deer lying under a bush and shot him. When they returned the partner had a fantastic tale to tell about how Johnny shot the deer at a distance of 400 yards while running through brush. Ewing was not fooled. He got the partner off and got the truth, that the deer was asleep when Johnny shot him. Ewing then named the draw where it happened, Sleepy Hollow. Thereafter, as long as Ewing lived, when Johnny was in a crowd Ewing never failed to recount some incident or other that happened in Sleepy Hollow. His story would not allude to a deer, but everybody knew what was meant and had a wisecrack to make about Johnny.[42]

Another incident was told by Emerson Price of Vinita. The Vinita group was at the ranch. Everyone who had been there before knew about Cha Cha, a pet deer which had been raised from a baby bottle stage at headquarters. He was as gentle as a lapdog and was a favorite of everyone on the ranch. Cha Cha ranged near the house, and during hunting season he wore a leather collar with a bell attached, so that no one would mistake him for a wild deer. Kelly Hartley, Mike Snedden, and

Emerson had been out since before daylight in a car and had had no luck. Going back to headquarters with Mike driving and Emerson on the back seat, Emerson saw a deer behind a bush some fifty yards from the road. He touched Mike on the shoulder and he stopped. Emerson got out, observed the deer lift his head, and shot him. Mike ran out to make sure he was dead. He yelled back, "You have killed Cha Cha. He has a leather collar and a bell." They examined the bell and the clapper was missing. The two loaded poor old Cha Cha on the fender of the car and drove on to headquarters, feeling like thugs caught beating a baby. When they arrived Ewing was serving highballs in the guest house just before supper. Emerson sidled in like a penitent sinner approaching the confessional, holding Cha Cha's collar behind him. He held it out, and sorrowfully he said, "I've done it! I'll pack my bag and get going."[43]

Ewing recognized the collar, looked at the bell, saw the clapper was gone, and said with not a trace of rancor, "Don't give it a thought. Poor old Cha Cha was getting old, and it was better for him to come to his end with one clean shot than to have eventually died of a smooth mouth and old age." Ewing had a marvelous way of relieving an immediate anguish, but, in the future, after the hurt was gone and the right people were present, he would say something like, "Emerson, when you go out tomorrow, remember I have a pet three-legged javelina up Sleepy Hollow, look out for him." or "we have a Jersey cow with a bell on in the horse trap. Just at daylight one might mistake her for a deer. Be careful."

Of all forms of indoor entertainment, Ewing liked poker the best. Whether the stakes were low or high, he had a facility for keeping them in the range of those playing in any particular game. He did not like to lose. He would play just as hard for a two-bit pot as for one of a thousand dollars. It was said of him that he had a good poker face, but he had a sort of Achilles heel. When young he had thrown a thumb out of place in a roping accident. Ever since that time, when tense and concentrating, that thumb would twist. Most all his old poker-playing friends knew this, and in a game they never watched his face but his thumb. He was conscious of this and devised all sorts of ways to casually conceal his thumb. If he put it under the table, that was a dead giveaway. So he resorted to various little strategies to cover his thumb. One evening after a dinner of expensive Kansas City cuts of steaks, a poker game was in progress, and a banker friend was in the game. The banker was not a great poker enthusiast. When he lost his two dollars' worth of chips, he said he thought he should go to bed. Ewing said to him, "Sit down, you have not lost enough yet to pay for your meal!" The good banker took the dry grins and asked for another two dollars' worth of chips.[44]

Dining was a ritual whether it was breakfast, lunch, or dinner, only on the ranch they called it breakfast, dinner, and supper. Whatever meal it was, the procedure was the same. The dining room was plainly furnished with a long table which accommodated fourteen to sixteen persons. It had benches along the sides, a host chair at the end nearest the kitchen, and a regular dining chair at the foot of the table. Ewing took his place at the head of the table and designated where the others were to sit. According to Jay Taylor of Carrizo Springs, who started going there as a young man, one could tell how he rated his guests by the order in which he seated them. His most important guest would be at his right, the next most important at his left, and so on down each side and the least important at the other end. Jay said that he, as a young man, was always at the opposite end.[45]

The knives, forks, spoons, glasses, and napkins would be at the places. All the plates were stacked at the head of the table in easy reaching distance of Ewing along with carving knives, forks, and serving spoons. The main dish which might be a large standing roast or a platter of huge sirloin steaks would be brought in and placed directly in front of Ewing. He would glance down the table and size up about how much he thought each could eat. Beginning at the far end he would skillfully slice the meat, add from the side dishes, and pass the plate down. Then he would take the measure of the next person and serve him accordingly, and so on up to the head of the table, and himself last. Jay Taylor observed that, regardless of Emily Post, Ewing had one habit which he envied. Always in the bottom of the enormous meat platter was the natural brown gravy of the roast or steaks. Ewing would during the meal reach over and dip his bread in the gravy. While carrying on an engaging chatter, he kept an eye on the plate of each guest and offered refills. Especially at the table he was the perfect host.[46]

Ewing had some rules which were understood and respected by guests and employees while hunting on the ranch. No drinking of liquor was permitted before or while hunting. Hot coffee in a thermos was recommended. Each guest was permitted only one deer per season and when the deer was shot, the guest became the

J. CISNEROS

driver or caddy for those who had not yet gotten their deer. No shooting with deer rifles was to be done within a mile of headquarters. This was for the protection of the help and children connected with the ranch. Guns were to be unloaded before returning to headquarters, and no liquor to be served until guns were put away. Probably as a result of these requirements, no accidents occurred during the twenty-two years that Ewing Halsell enjoyed the cherished hunting seasons on the Farias.

Another pleasure Ewing indulged in was driving over the ranch and showing it to new acquaintances. He often had one of the hands do the driving. Then he could concentrate on explaining about the various grasses, shrubs, trees, flowers when in season, wild life, and, of course, the cattle. He would have the driver go several hundred yards out of the way just to inspect a horse, cow, or bull. He would have the car stopped on some eminence, and he would expound on the vistas in various directions. He would delight in watching a fleeing deer, a covey of quail, or a road-runner. A sensitive guest was soon aware of Ewing's kinship with the land and with the life which it sustained. For the average person, one or two trips like this would suffice, but not for Ewing Halsell. He could have done it every day for a year, and each day would have been a new adventure.[47]

Heel Flies, Screwworms, Bedbugs

20

Cattlemen in South Texas during the 1930's engaged in considerable controversy regarding the merits of spaying heifers intended for the beef market rather than for breeding. In a measure the question was academic for the cattle raiser. Nature determined how many heifers were born each year, an average of 50 per cent of the total. Unless the rancher was expanding his operation, he needed to save about 20 to 30 per cent of each year's heifer crop to replace old cows beyond calf-bearing age. The other 70 to 80 per cent of each year's heifer crop he would have to carry until they were ready for the beef market. Whether or not they were as profitable as steers was something over which he had no control. He could spay the heifers and they would put on more weight and bring more money. But spaying was an internal operation requiring a veterinarian's services and considerably more time than for castrating the male calves. Also, the spaying was much more risky because of the chance of infection. The shock was greater and recovery slower than was the case with steers. When these factors were taken into account, cattlemen differed as to whether spaying was economically worthwhile.

One aspect of dealing with spayed heifers had not been resolved. For a cattleman who wished to buy three-year-old cattle in South Texas and take them to the bluestem grass areas of Oklahoma and Kansas, graze them for the summer and ship to market in the fall, which would be the more profitable per hundred weight—spayed heifers or steers? South Texas ranchers had their ideas about this, pro and con, but no one had actually experimented with it on a large scale and under controlled conditions.

In 1938, Ewing Halsell, always one to try out new methods, conducted an interesting experiment.[1] He made the following arrangement with Tom East, whose wife was the granddaughter of W. E.'s old friend, Captain King; the East ranch was near Hebbronville:

Mr. Tom East
% King Ranch
Kingsville, Texas

Dear Tom:

In regard to the steers that we traded on while I was at your ranch last week. I am to take between six and seven hundred of your three and four year old steers out of about eight hundred.

These cattle are to be delivered to me between the 10th and 20th of April on board the cars at Hebbronville. The cattle to be delivered from your pasture about four miles, stood in the lot about an hour and weighed with a three (3) percent shrink and not to be watered or grazed the morning they are weighed.

I am to pay you 5½¢ a pound for these cattle at the time of delivery.

After cattle are sold you are to have a one-half interest in any profits they make above the purchase price, the freight and sales cost and $7.00 a head pasture bill.

I am to handle these cattle according to my own judgment and to give you reports at the end of the year, showing account sales and to pay you any moneys that are due you on profits.

If this is satisfactory to you and covers your understanding of the trade you can just write, ''Accepted,'' on the copy of letter enclosed herewith, and return.

This was accepted by Tom East.

A Ranching Saga

At the same time Ewing negotiated for 394 spayed heifers from the King Ranch[2] as follows:

The King Ranch
Kingsville, Texas

Gentlemen:

I am writing, setting out my understanding of the trade on the spayed heifers. I have received three hundred ninety-four (394) spayed heifers and paid $14,835.32 for them which was at the rate of 5½¢ per pound.

I am to pay the freight on these cattle from the loading point to my Oklahoma Ranch and pasture them at $7.00 a head, market these cattle this summer or fall according to my best judgment and after deducting the cost, freight, yardage, commission and $7.00 a head pasture bill from the sales price we are to divide equally the profits or loss. It being understood that there is no interest to be charged on the money paid by me for the cattle. But should there be a loss instead of a profit you are to remit to me the difference.

If this is plain to you and according to your understanding, please sign accepted and return the letter to me keeping the enclosed copy.

This was approved by Robert J. Kleberg, Jr.

Both the steers and spayed heifers were shipped by rail to one of Ewing's Oklahoma ranches and run in the same pasture so that all the conditions would be identical. They were separated for shipping, weighing, and sales. Careful records were kept throughout every step in the procedure from the beginning to the end. The average sale price per hundred weight for the steers was $6.17, for the heifers, $6.16. The average clear profit per steer after purchase price, freight, feed, and grazing was $6.70. For the heifers it was $3.08. This experiment, as far as the participants were concerned, demonstrated that for the buyer wanting three-year-old cattle for summer grazing and fall marketing that steers were more profitable than spayed heifers.[3]

During the late 1800's and early 1900's cattlemen could be consistently divided into two categories, breeders and grass feeders. Texas ranchers were mostly breeders. Each stocked their ranch with cattle units, that is a cow and a calf, according to the carrying capacity of his land.[4] On the coastal plains of Texas it might be one unit to six acres. In some parts of the Trans-Pecos region it could be one unit for a hundred acres. On the average ranch the cattlemen handled only what he raised. Each year he sold his steers and heifers after selecting just enough of the latter for breeding to replace the old cows. He kept and rotated just enough bulls to service his cows. Only on exceptionally wet years, which happened about once every eleven years, did he consider buying extra steers on a single season basis to use the surplus grass.

The other category, the feeders, operated like W. E. Halsell when he went to the Cherokee Nation in 1881.[5] They did not breed cattle and thereby keep a large capital outlay tied up in cows. They followed the pattern of bringing from the South Texas breeders two- and three-year-old steers and heifers in the early spring, fattening them on the summer grasses of the Northern Plains or the limestone or flint hills of Oklahoma and Kansas and shipping them to market in the fall. Later, with the advent of the feed lots, first in the Corn Belt and then everywhere grain sorghums could be produced, the old operation pattern changed. In the feed lot business, Ewing Halsell pioneered.

The undertaking, in a measure, had two origins: the one man, or a family unit, which originated in the Corn Belt of the mid-west during the 19th century, and the large scale commercial operations which began in the ranching areas of West Texas, Oklahoma, and Western Kansas during the 1920's and 1930's. It was with this latter movement that Ewing Halsell was primarily involved.

The Corn Belt type of feeding was based on corn as the basic protein in the fattening process. In the western feeding enterprises, sorghum grains, principally milo maize, provided the fattening ingredient. For a half-century or more the raisers and users of beef were convinced that milo maize produced an inferior quality of meat as compared with corn. As long as this prejudice prevailed, cattle destined for feed lot finishing were shipped to the Corn Belt for fattening.

Corn, without irrigation, was not a dependable crop in the semi-arid Southwest, while milo maize was much more dependable. After the 1920's several agricultural experiment stations, along with a few adventurous individual ranchmen, set about to demonstrate that milo maize-fed beef was just as palatable as corn-fed meat. Ewing Halsell was among a relatively small group who pioneered in this movement.

The first feed lots in the Southwest were started in connection with the cotton-seed oil mills. At the outset the oil mills utilized cottonseed for obtaining the kernel of the seed which was made into cottonseed meal and cottonseed cake, both of which were accepted as a valuable protein concentrate. An oil was squeezed from the kernels, and this was soon utilized to make a substitute cooking shortening for hog lard. The first to be merchandized was called Cottelene. This staple was later further refined and sold under such trade names as Crisco.

At the outset of the cottonseed milling enterprises, the bulk of the seed, the hulls, were not merchandizable. So great piles or sizable hills of hulls grew around the mills. Cattle would eat them, but they were only a filler. It was discovered that by mixing cottonseed meal or cake with the hulls cattle did well and fattened. Partly to get rid of the hulls, and partly to have a market for the meal and cake, most cottonseed oil mills built pens nearby and started fattening cattle for market. These were the first feed pens in West Texas where both cotton and cattle were raised.

Ewing Halsell installed feed lots at Bird Creek, Big Creek, and Farias ranches, and had a quarter interest in one at Spring Lake, with the Halsell Cattle Company as the other partner. The Bird Creek, Big Creek, and Spring Lake lots were built and put into use in the early 1930's. The one at Farias started in 1947.

He was among the first to build feeding pens on the ranch where the cattle were and to experiment with finishing cattle with the ingredients close at hand, milo maize, cottonseed meal or cake for concentrate, and whatever roughage, or filler, was at hand. This might be sorghum cane, alfalfa, prairie hay, or cotton hulls. The latter could be had for two dollars a ton at the mills. The determining factor for hulls was the transportation.

At the outset of the feed pen era the lots were small, accommodating from 200 to 300 cattle. The grain was ground on motorized hand-fed feed grinders, scooped into a wagon, mixed with the concentrate, hauled to the pens, and shoveled into troughs, all by hand. The roughage was delivered the same way. As time went on, the processing was gradually mechanized. The lots were made larger and the number of cattle fattened increased accordingly. In the 1930's one man could feed about 200 cattle in a day. By 1960 two men could take care of 3,000 cattle so far as the actual feeding was concerned.

It was not until the late 1950's and 1960's that feed pen operation became a truly big business on the High Plains of Texas, New Mexico, and in western Oklahoma. By this time the meat consumers had become convinced that there was no difference in corn-fed and milo maize-fed meat. Cattle were shipped from all the southern states to where the milo was raised and packing houses moved to where the fat cattle were. By 1973 the feed lots on the High Plains were fattening five million head a year.

Before the operational pattern changed with the advent of feed lots, Ewing Halsell was operating in both camps—breeders and feeders.[6] He was a trader as well as a cattle raiser. He did not confine his efforts to one category or the other but mixed them with appreciable results. If he had some spare grass on any of his ranches, he would buy 300 or 700 or whatever number of cattle he could take care of for the foreseeable future and send them to a place where the extra grass abounded. This one operation might net several thousand dollars which otherwise might not have materialized. He was not content in taking up the slack on his own land but was on a constant lookout for opportunities to take advantage of surplus grass of others. He had a wide and intimate relationship with many ranchers and owners

A Ranching Saga

of ranches in Texas, Oklahoma, and Kansas. If he heard, for instance, that his friend, Horace Barnard, who had a ranch in the Osage country in Oklahoma, had a vacant pasture with grass, Ewing would lease it for a limited period, buy the number of marketable cattle the pasture would conservatively accommodate, and ship them there.[7] This he did with 591 mixed cattle in October 1953, with a resulting profit of $5,490. He carried out numerous short-term operations of this nature, but always within a reasonable distance of one of his four owned ranches where the cattle involved could be looked after by one of his foremen. A typical dealing is described in a letter to George Franklin[8] from Helen Campbell while vacationing with the Halsells in Santa Monica, September 9, 1940:

Go and look at the Deshazo yearlings and write Mr. Halsell what they are like. Look at any other cattle you hear of for sale and which are the kind he is interested in. Did you ever go see the Todd yearlings? Write Mr. Halsell about these matters at once.

A few days later Ewing wrote:

Keep looking at any cattle that are offered for sale and make me a report. As I have said before I do not want to buy young cattle that are not good. They cost just as much to winter and do not make the gain.

The following indicates the extent to which Ewing utilized temporary leases for herds he purchased for short term processing. George Franklin mentioned four instances in his weekly report, July 1, 1940.[9] The Callaghan herd and Kone cattle were doing well on the Jack Montgomery ranch, and the Brunson cattle and Mexico shipment were making good progress at the Wallen ranch.

The fact that he had four ranches widely separated geographically and staffed with dependable crews afforded him an opportunity which the man with one ranch seldom had. As previously pointed out, drought never struck all of his ranches at the same time. On average years, the rainfall on one ranch and its adjoining area might be extensive, creating a condition favorable for an extra short-term profit. That Ewing Halsell kept up with such matters in addition to the thousands of other details established him as a man of extraordinary ability and decision.[10]

The entire year's work was scheduled at the first of the year and was coordinated with all four ranches, always subject to variations of weather and markets. The practice of rotating the cowboys, which began as a necessity during World War II, was continued in a modified form. Latitudinal differences in the location of the ranches made possible the rotation of the labor force. Branding, dehorning, marking, and castrating began at the Farias in late February or early March. Next, most of the crew moved to Bird Creek, Big Creek, and Fall River; finally, the branding routine ended at Spring Lake. With this finished, the circulating cowboys went back to their respective home stations.[11]

In the late summer or early fall the process was repeated. In this way the crew caught unbranded calves, whether they were missed in the spring work or had been born afterwards. However, the main purpose of the fall work was to separate and regroup the herds according to what was to happen to them. The cows with calves were driven to the nearest pens. Here the calves, then seven to eight months old, would be separated from their mothers and kept in the pens for the weaning ordeal. The mothers would be kept outside or driven to another pasture. For several days the calves moped and bawled continuously, day and night. The sound of their bawling could be heard for a mile or two on a still night. The mothers, if within hearing distance, would bawl back, each one seemingly recognizing the cry of her own calf. Feed and water were available for the calves in the pens. As time passed, the bawling decreased and eating increased. After five or six days, the calves were thoroughly weaned. If the mothers were allowed to return to the locality of the weaning, each cow would go to the spot where she last saw her calf. By this time her milk had dried up.

Some of the cattle would go to market as grass-fattened stock, some to feed lots, old cows and bulls to the slaughter houses for hamburger and canned meat, some heifer yearlings to replace the old cows in the breeding herds, the remainder of the heifer yearlings and steers to pastures to grow another year.[12]

A considerable amount of shipping from ranch to ranch took place, originally by rail, later by truck and rail. Rail transportation of cattle did not entirely cease until the 1950's. The movement of cattle was usually from south to north. Normally, by July the weather patterns had been established and the overall conditions determined. Ewing, with the assistance of Helen Campbell, would make a precise schedule of shipping.[13] So many cattle cars of a certain size would be or-

dered to a particular shipping point on a given day at Eagle Pass, Muleshoe, Bovina, or at stations between Tulsa and Nowata in Oklahoma. Cattle cars came in two lengths, 36 and 40 feet. Ewing usually preferred the 40-foot cars. On occasions he ordered 40-foot cars and 36-footers arrived. This really messed up that particular operation. If he had ordered ten forty-foot cars and ten thirty-six-foot cars arrived, he would have about twenty cattle left over after loading all the cars. This made a problem which the traffic department of the railroad would hear about in language it could understand.

The fall shipping schedules were made while Ewing Halsell, his family, and Helen Campbell were at the Miramar Hotel in Santa Monica. This was the temporary central office during the "Hay Fever" season. Even without the ranch books, files, records and maps, the detailed operations were carried on in a marvelous manner. Farias had sixteen pastures,* each designated by a name, earthen tanks, each known by a name, and five windmills, known by the pastures in which they were located. Spring Lake ranch had twenty-two pastures,† thirty-three windmills, two natural lakes, and two man-made lakes on Black Water Draw, which seldom held water.

Bird Creek ranch was not so large as the Big Sand pasture in the Spring Lake ranch but was originally consolidated from many allotments varying from 20 to 80 acres. The same was true of Big Creek ranch, which had later been grouped into eight or ten pastures.[14]

*The pastures included: Little Sauz, 8,000 acres; Big Sauz, 16,000 acres; Fresnito, 11,000 acres; Cantina, 4,000 acres; Armadillo, 5,000 acres; Walker, 4,400 acres; Rock Tank, 5,300 acres; Big Beef, 7,000 acres; Little Beef, 4,400 acres; Loma Dinero, 6,700 acres; Latigo, 6,000 acres; Coyote, 2,300 acres; Nopalosa, 1,200 acres; West Llano, 4,000 acres; and East Llano, 4,500 acres. In addition there were numerous smaller paddocks, referred to as traps, each with its special name, and other areas leased from neighbors at different times.

†In 1950 the names of the pastures, and the acres they contained were as follows: Dunn, 5,000; McKnight, 5,000; South Sand, 8,800; North Sand, 5,200; Spring Lake, 1,000; South Spring Lake, 1,300; Soda Lake Trap, 160; Horse, 300; Stray, 814; South Bull, 1,100; Little Sand, 6,320; West Snyder, 6,505; Snyder Trap, 600; North Snyder, 4,966; South Snyder, 3,536; Sudan, 1,204; Nix Trap, 320; North Meadow, 350; Sod House, 890; Arkansas, 1,680; Brownlee, 4,932; Hereford, 11,312; in addition there were a dozen or more farms. Total acres in pastures, 71,289.

Ewing Halsell and Helen Campbell knew the names, exact locations, and carrying capacity in terms of animal units of all pastures on all ranches. At any one time they knew from memory fairly well how many cattle and what kind were in each pasture. While in California, Ewing had newspapers from the vicinities of the four ranches sent to him. The papers would be two or three days late when he got them, but in a general way, with Helen's help, he kept up with the weather conditions in the locality of each ranch. These sources also kept him informed of the local cattle markets. Rains were such good and rare news that every foreman had orders to telephone or telegraph him when and how much rain was received. Added to this information were the detailed reports from the secretaries in the Vinita, Amherst, and San Antonio offices. While in Santa Monica he kept up with what was going on at all the ranches, and at the same time he was not ignoring the stock markets. In the forenoon, he dictated letters to a stenographer, giving minute directions to his foremen and other employees in Texas and Oklahoma concerning small as well as important matters. He had the capacity to get the information, assimilate it, and give directions quickly without frustration and agonizing. In two or three hours in the morning, he could accomplish as much as it would take the average person all day to do. When finished with his business, he could devote his full attention in the afternoons and evenings to his family and friends, playing gin rummy or going to shows or on excursions. This schedule helped him to endure the enforced sojourns in California. In San Antonio, his business hours were longer and his recreation was usually poker and gin rummy with his cronies.[15]

In an exchange of correspondence incident to Ewing Halsell's finding some available outside grass in Oklahoma, and being able to acquire 592 head of mixed cattle to put on the temporary grass lease, one discovers that some cattlemen possess a sensitivity that would do credit to a temperamental virtuoso. Historical fiction has endowed the typical rancher, who has created his holdings by his own efforts, with an image of toughness, and it is easy to confuse toughness with roughness. In many instances this was true, but not always. One of the best friends Ewing Halsell had was Jack Barfield,[16] who ranched in Oklahoma. The relationship between the two friends was such that they could make a $50,000 deal on the telephone. The misunderstanding hereafter referred to had nothing to do with money, but it was about an imagined implication concerning two little heifer yearlings which did not exist.

The oral agreement was that Ewing would ship 593 cattle from Muleshoe, Texas, to Barfield's Oklahoma ranch, and he thought that number was shipped. Later, after Mr. Barfield had had his feelings hurt, the railroad records revealed that only 591 had actually been shipped. With this in mind, the following will show how sensitive and human some cattlemen really were.

On October 20, 1953, Ewing wrote to Jack:

Dear Jack:

Helen sent you a check for the pasture bill and you will note in her letter we are short in the total number of cattle. Am sure you had two or three death loss, as I remember 1 yearling and some cows. In checking our records we are short in the heifers and I would like for you to check your records as to the number of heifers that you put in this pasture with your own and the number you took out.

I am very much ashamed of sending unbranded cattle but I know you do not want anything but what is yours whether it was branded or not. Check your records and see what you think this shortage might be.

Talked to the ranch here this morning. Roy said it was trying hard to rain but apparently we didn't get any as he hasn't called back.

Best regards.

October 24, 1953, Jack replied:

Dear Ewing:

I am in receipt of your letter of the 20th, with the enclosed statement for the cattle shipped to us, and am enclosing herewith a statement showing the number of cattle we received, the number of cattle shipped out, and the number of dead ones.

In connection with the heifers we had in the pasture with your cattle, when we cleaned the pasture we were one heifer short.

Ewing, I am surprised and shocked at the attitude of your letter, and it has hurt me more than you can ever know.

We have two pastures more to clean, adjoining the pastures your cattle were in, and we will certainly work them hard and be sure that we have none of your cattle with them. It is also possible that they could be in our neighbors pastures, or a slim chance that they might have died.

Hoping that this report is what you were asking for, I am.

Yours very truly,

Two days later Ewing wrote to Jack:

Dear Jack:

I hurry to answer your letter. It makes me feel very badly to know that I hurt you. It was certainly not my intention to cast any reflections on you, or your men. I work a pretty good sized outfit myself, and I have men who are careless but absolutely honest, but they are careless in their counts and reports to my office, and I have trouble in accounting for my own cattle. I felt it might be possible that your men in gathering your heifers gathered anything that did not have my brand on it which I am pretty sure my own outfit would have done unless I called their attention to just the number that was in there.

I do not think I am any cattle short but you did not tell me about all the death loss until this report.

There was no intention of any reflection on you, and I want you to forgive me if my letter showed any reflection. I am very proud of my friendship with you and I want it to remain as close as it has been, so please write me that you will accept my apology as meaning no reflection on you, and if I had had your report it would not have been necessary to write at all. It hurts me to think that I have hurt you.

Jack, it has rained all around our country down here but has not rained on me except .15. It is possible I may hear of some rain today as the Black ranch just reported about an inch last night.

We do not have Jack's reply, but we know he continued to be one of Ewing's dearest friends until his death.

Ewing Halsell's computer-like memory, his capacity to visualize about a hundred different pastures from distant Santa Monica as distinctly as if he were hovering over them in a helicopter, his ability to know how many cattle were in each pasture, their classification, ages, and conditions—all this is exemplified in small part by the letter to George Franklin, July 30, 1937, and this is typical of one or more he wrote every day while on his hay fever exile:

The cattle sold about as well as I expected them to yesterday according to the market, but they are not making much money. We made a mistake in not shipping more of these cattle when the market was good, regardless of whether or not they were fat.

I want to ship next week three loads of fed cattle, and hope you can get these cattle out of the Coker and Hill pastures, without working the Middle Pasture, or if the Middle Pasture cattle are the fattest take the three loads from there instead of from the other two pastures.

When you write me tell me how you are getting along with the haying; whether your rains made any water or not; whether the grass has greened up, and whether the flies are bad.

I think it would be a good time to ship a carload of dry cows, either this week or the week following. What did you do about building your new shipping pasture?

I understand that the new tractor has not been delivered. Try not to tear this old one up before we can make delivery.

Write me carefully what you think of the yearlings at Montgomery's. The monthly weight on the little bunch of cattle has not been reported to me. I suppose Vivian sent this in to the office. This is the little bunch of cattle that is in the small pasture just North of the house, that he had been weighing each month.

My plans are to ship six to ten loads of cattle a week from now on, if these cattle are fat enough. Do you think you can get four loads of good cattle out of the Jarboe country; and are there any fat cattle left in the South Pasture?

When you answer this letter try to have it before you so that you can answer all the questions I have asked.

Is anyone stacking hay, and did this last rain help the meadows any?[17]

The number of cattle Ewing Halsell shipped to market from his Oklahoma ranches each year fluctuated between 2,500 and 3,000, with an average of about 2,800. They were sent to Kansas City, Saint Louis, and Chicago by rail. In the correspondence, the shipping unit is often referred to as a "load," which meant a railroad cattle car. On a typical year he would send between 140 and 150 carloads.

In 1950 from his Oklahoma ranches he marketed 2,871 cattle of all classes with a total weight of 3,316,400 pounds. The average weight per animal was 1,175 pounds and the average price was $25 per hundred weight making a total gross income of $859,468.64.* Of these cattle 273 were grass-fed, that is, they were kept

*This amount does not include the Halsell Cattle Company, of which Ewing Halsell owned one-fourth interest, or Ewing's Texas ranches. In all he marketed between 5,500 to

A Ranching Saga

in the pasture and had a supplement of cottonseed cake fed to them on the ground for a period of 30 to 60 days. The straight grass-fed, with no supplement, numbered 2,071. These were shipped to market in July, August, and September. The number of 379 head were feed lot steers shipped in December and January. It is to be noted that, as late as 1950, approximately two-thirds of the cattle shipped to market by Ewing Halsell were grass fattened.[18]

August was the most important month for shipping grass-fed cattle. The following letter written from Ewing's hay fever retreat to George Franklin[19] shows how he kept up with every detail including the shipping schedule for a week:

Was disappointed in the sales of all the cattle last week, especially the South Texas cattle. I think the Kennedy cattle sold about where they should with the 25¢ to 50¢ break in the market. Am writing Helen for you to ship the following cattle, unless I wire different instructions.

One or two cars of spayed heifers to John Clay, Kansas City;

Three cars of Alberty pasture cattle, Montgomery ranch, to Cassidy, St. Louis;

Two cars of Kone steers, Jarboe, to John Clay, Kansas City.

Will be glad to know how you found the Kansas Cattle. I feel quite sure it would pay us to feed these Kansas two year old cattle, but do not know just how good a job Gene does. Do you think he is giving these cattle plenty of water? I am sorry that it is necessary to pump as I thought our windmill would take care of all these cattle very easily, and it would if we had sufficient storage. How did you find the grass? Has it burned up very badly, or has the rain helped it? Tell me what you think of the VVN steers and the pasture they are in.

I wish it was so we could sell some of these cattle at home. If we could do it, we would net a lot more money. I wish you would look at the Lowery cattle and see how much fatter they are than ours. They are selling well on the market.

If the Jarboe cattle are not fat, let them alone, but I feel quite sure you can get two loads of good cattle out of them. Cut these cattle so that they will be something alike, not a big tall rough steer and a smooth steer together. These cattle we have on feed I want to feed long enough to make them good, not just fairly fat. I think in another two weeks they should be carrying lots of flesh and I believe it would be a good idea to add another pound of cake

---

6,000 cattle each year. All of the records of the Halsell Cattle Company are not in the Ewing Halsell Collection. However, a summary of sales of the Halsell Cattle Company for 1954, a typical year, is available. It shows that 362 cows were sold for $29,350.97; 216 bulls for $32,363.22; 669 steers for $129,715.82; 892 heifers for $124,259.07; 472 calves for $47,091.80, all for a total of $362,780.88.

to this feed and give them five pounds of feed instead of four, especially to the cattle in the Hill Pasture and the North Sheep. The cattle at the Montgomery ranch we will feed just as we are. I may decide to feed the two year old cattle at the Montgomery ranch. I believe we may have a worse market next year, so it is probably a good time to get rid of these cattle. I am writing the Indiana man, and hope we get some results from it.

Did Tom Walker's cistern hold after he fixed it? Did you get enough rain to fill your wells and help the tanks any?

How are the hay fever sufferers getting along? Do you ever see Pitt Carroll? It is just about the time of year they begin to have trouble, and it is just about the time of year that I begin to get anxious to come home.

Cattlemen had a multitude of problems which were annoying and could be costly. Among those on the Halsell ranches were flies and bedbugs.[20] There were three kinds of flies: the house type, cattle flies, and heel flies. The house variety could be coped with by the use of screens. There was no defense against cattle flies. They were seasonal and disappeared with frost; so there was a respite. They appeared again with warm weather in late spring and increased in numbers and ferocity until a benevolent nature wiped them out again in October or November. They were worse when the hair of the cattle was short and at a time when the grass-fed animals were at the peak of their corpulence and ready for market. During the still, dog days of late summer, they literally covered the backs, necks, and flanks of the animals. Each fly was equipped with a little drill-like proboscis which it inserted into the skin of the victim and drew out the substance on which it lived. Several thousand flies could extract the weight gain the animal had made for the day. The constant irritation caused the bovine to continually switch with its tail, twist its neck, go under limbs and brush to swipe the flies off. In addition to weight being lost through the snouts of the flies, the animal was fighting flies when it should have been grazing and putting on more weight. Repeatedly, during shipments of cattle to market in August and September, if the sale did not reach expectations, the failure was attributed to the flies.[21]

Another species of fly, commonly called the "heel fly," appeared occasionally and dealt cattle and horses considerable anguish. They were larger and not nearly so numerous as the cattle flies which fairly covered the animal. One heel fly could get more action out of a victim than a thousand of the species previously described. The heel fly had a long, sharp snout which he dug into a tender spot just above the hooves of the animals. It was something like a dull hypodermic needle hitting a nerve. The animal would stamp, and, if loose in a pasture, it would run from the place in an effort to elude the tormentor. If there were a tank, creek, or mud hole, the animal would go and stand in it. The sensitive place above the hoof seemed to be the only spot the heel fly bothered. The season for this annoying pest was of short duration, but while he was around, he caused both cattle and horses to expend more needless energy than the common cattle fly.

Every bunkhouse the Halsells had in Oklahoma and at Spring Lake in Texas was periodically infested with bedbugs.[22] This was practically true of all bunkhouses at the time. Unlike cattle flies which were seasonal, the bedbug was perennial and perpetual. They had been spread during the period of the professional, migratory cowboys, the chuck line riders, who traveled from ranch to ranch with their skimpy bedrolls and with their old clothes which were rolled up, put in a flour sack, and tied on behind their saddles. It was not necessary to carry the bugs themselves but just their eggs which were plentiful. The bedbug is a very shy creature and is endowed with great speed. They seek out their human victims and extract blood only in the dark. How they find their way between the covers is a mystery. In a room infested with bugs the victim can ease out of bed, turn on a light and throw back the cover, assuming the bed has white sheets, and there may be dozens of bugs. In a twinkle of an eye every bug disappears so quickly one cannot see where they go. In the daytime they are not to be found anywhere. They hide in cracks in the floor, walls, and ceiling, and under the slats and in the grooves of the bedstead. It is almost impossible to get rid of them in a bunkhouse which has been thoroughly infested.[23] The only sure way is to burn the house down.

Time after time Ewing wrote his foremen to get rid of the bedbugs in the bunkhouses. He would tell them how to do it: clean up the place, take everything out and sun it, rub bedding with rags saturated with kerosene, pour kerosene in the cracks, make the boys send their clothes to be washed in boiling water, wash the woodwork with lye water, clean out the closet and bathroom, scrub everything. He always ended each admonition: "I hate bedbugs!" The clean-up helped temporarily, but results were never permanent.

Bad things happened to the cattle. Occasionally an animal developed blackleg, a fatal disease. It was controlled by vaccination, usually at branding time. Sometimes a calf would escape the dosage and later might contract the malady. The carcass was burned to prevent it from contaminating other animals which might not have had the vaccine.[24]

An ailment called "sore foot" bothered the Oklahoma cattle occasionally.[25] It was not fatal and apparently was curable. In one of his reports to Ewing, George Franklin explained his treatment. He made a vat several feet long, placed it in one of the chutes, and poured three or four inches of creosote in the vat. The animal would be made to stand in the solution for a short time and then put into a segregated pasture. Apparently the treatment worked.

Another bovine sickness, hemorrhagic septicemia, was not regarded as a plague.[26]

A scourge much more dreaded was screwworms. They developed from eggs deposited by a blow fly in an open wound. The flies were especially bad after a rain when the horn paint had rubbed off and the brand scab had begun to peel, leaving fresh exposed tissue. Newt Robison described the symptoms and treatment,

You would prowl the pastures, or go to a windmill where the calves watered. It was easy to spot a calf with worms if you knew what you were looking for. The calf would be sort of sick looking with blood oozing out of the brand, or the top of the head if the animal had been dehorned. You would cut it out and rope it, just like in the rodeo, and tie it down. You had a bottle which you carried in an old boot top attached to your saddle. The bottle contained a mixture of creosote and chloroform. You poured a little of the liquid into the wound, and the screwworms, little white creatures, would come backing out in a hurry and were dead in seconds. The creosote usually kept the blow flies away until the wound healed. If it was real bad it might get reinfected and have to be treated again. Johnny Murrell told me that they had eliminated the blow flies and did not have screwworms any more. Something else modern.

A serious cattle disease in Oklahoma was called at the time *splenic*, or Texas Fever.[27] It was transmitted by ticks similar to the dog ticks in the piney woods of East Texas and Louisiana. South Texas cattle had developed an immunity to the malady, but carried the ticks up the trail to Oklahoma and Kansas, where they were transferred to native cattle not immune. Kansas passed, and rather rigidly enforced, a law prohibiting cattle from tick-infested areas in Texas and other southern states from being brought into the state. Oklahoma, which did not become a state until 1907, was dilatory in regulating the fever tick problem. The first efforts were voluntary on the part of the Texas cattlemen operating in Indian Territory. The Halsells were among the first to do something about it. The following article from the *Owasso Ledger*, September 15, 1904, gives an account of the method used:

On the Halsell ranch, two miles west of Owasso, 450 steers were "dipped" Tuesday to kill the fever tick,—the remedy now being employed as a preventative against Texas fever.

The process is a bigger thing with the cowboy than branding or dehorning. A huge vat, some six feet deep, wide as a branding chute, 20 to 30 feet in length, is constructed, dug into the ground and cased with lumber, and arranged with an incline for the steer's assent.

The tank, or vat, is nearly filled with water, then a couple of barrels of crude oil is poured in. The oil rides on top of the water. Into this mixture the steer is jumped. He reaches the bottom completely submerging, and emerges on the cleated incline with ears, nose, eyes and mouth filled with oil, which is also clinging to every hair on his body. He comes out of the chute snorting, and cutting such capers and antics as the sizzling branding iron never provokes. It is said to be a great benefit, if the remedy proves effectual, as is now claimed for it.

The Halsells used other dipping vats. There was one at Vinita and another at a shipping switch south of Tulsa where cattle from Louisiana, East Texas, and New Mexico were unloaded for the range in the Creek Nation. Improvements were made in the dip mixtures when effective chemicals not nearly so hard on the cattle as the crude oil were discovered.[28]

As time went on, veterinarians, when at a loss to account for some new and different cattle ailment, were prone to recommend dipping. By the 1940's, the Department of Agriculture, well financed by the Federal government, resorted to many experimental programs. On the advice of veterinarians, the Department of Agriculture offered to furnish materials to build a dipping vat in every county. The program was administered by the county commissioner's court. Judge Haynes of Craig County wished to place one on the Snedden ranch which Ewing Halsell had leased. By this time Ewing had lost faith in dipping. His reply to the Judge was rather curt, "I do not want a vat on any of my property or land leased by me."

Coyotes gave some trouble. They subsisted for the most part on small game, such as rabbits, ground squirrels, and other rodents, but when hungry enough, they would gang up on a newborn calf if they could find one whose mother was away. Also, they were especially fond of lambs or even a grown sheep. In a report September 25, 1940, George Franklin mentioned that coyotes had gotten about a dozen of the sheep. This brought a quick response from Ewing, who really relished lamb chops and mutton:

It is cheaper to kill these wolves than to hire a sheep herder. I want you to put out poison for them. It may be you can set traps and catch them. But, let's do something!

Occasionally, there would be an outbreak of distemper among the horses. This always disturbed Ewing. The foremen had standing orders to get a veterinarian at the first symptoms of the disease. The ailment did respond to treatment, but if left to run its course, it could ruin some good horses.

Ewing Halsell's fondness for horses was almost equivalent to that which he had for some people. George Franklin wrote to him that a horse named Teddy was going blind. Ewing replied immediately from California:

This Teddy horse is a good horse, and I wish you would put him in a truck and take him to a good Vet and see if there is anything he can do for his eyes. I doubt it, but there might be something that could be done.

Sleeping sickness was another occasional, dreaded horse ailment.[29] In his weekly report, September 25, 1940, George Franklin mentioned a case:

The good Mashed O bay horse Lee used to ride has sleeping sickness pretty bad. We had a Vet with him last Monday night. I got home about midnight after taking the Vet back to Welch. Saw the horse again yesterday, and he was about the same. Have not heard from him today. The Vet has a reputation for curing about all the cases he has treated, but I doubt very much that this one gets well. This is not good news, but I think you always want to know about everything. Sorry these things have to happen, but it looks like we can't help it.

Ewing was a believer in raising sorghum cane on the farms connected with the ranches. When mature, the cane had a high content of sugar and made good roughage both in bundles or in ensilage. However, at a certain stage in its growth it con-

A Ranching Saga

tained an acid which, if eaten, would cause cattle and horses to bloat and was dead-ly. Ewing would direct his foremen to see that the fences around the cane fields were in good repair and to have riders inspect them daily to make sure no cattle or horses were able to get to the growing cane.

Aside from the bedbug problem, Ewing got reports, almost always from a wo-man, concerning the terrible condition of the bunkhouses. Then he would get off a letter to each of his foremen.[30] The following to Hie Spencer, April 28, 1939, at Big Creek is characteristic of the round of instructions he would send out about once a year:

Want you to have a special cleaning of your bunk house. Take all of your bedding out and mattresses and bed springs and sun them. Wipe off all of your beds with a cloth with coal oil on it, mop your floors with water with lye soap in it.

Clean out the bathroom and toilet by scrubbing.

I think it would be a good idea to clean out the storage room that adjoins the bathroom, take everything out and clean it out good.

The Price's will help you do this work when you get ready, but I would have my men take out their bedding and sweep the floors out. Get the Prices to do most of the other work, as Mrs. Price will know how to do it better than anyone else. In fact if you will show her this letter she can pretty near tell you what to do.

Then he added a postscript to Mrs. Price, the cook.

Mrs. Price: —I am sure you are taking care of my own room up at the ranch house but I wish you would have this bedding sunned for me sometime.

Another seasonable problem on the Oklahoma and Kansas ranches was prairie fires.[31] There were two types of fires: one unintentional and the other on purpose. The unwanted fires usually occurred in the late summer and fall, after the grass had matured and begun to dry up and turn brown. With an annual rainfall of about 40 inches, all vegetation was lush during the growing season and fires were no prob-lem. By September, the tall grass became dry and brittle. A month or two of dry weather would cause the short grass below to become ignitable. Then there was a serious chance of having a winter's source of roughage wiped out. During September, a system of fire guards was made. Ewing had a method for making fire guards for all the ranches. It was a controlled plan of back-firing.[32] The outfit would take a wagon with two or three barrels of water, buckets, gunny sacks to be used as wet mops, spades, and a plow and go to the side of the pasture that the wind was blowing towards. If there was a road along the fence, the party would back up twenty or thirty feet into the wind, then, keeping the wagon alongside, set fire to the grass and the wind would take it towards the road. If there was not a road they would plow two or four furrows, depending on the velocity of the wind. With wet sacks they made sure the fire did not work back into the wind. When the first section was safely burning towards the fence the crew moved on and started another section, while keeping careful watch on the first section. If there was a road or highway to stop the fire they had little to worry about. If it were only the furrows, one man with a wet sack followed along to make sure the flames did not leap the furrows and that no posts caught fire. With proper wind conditions a crew could make about two miles in half a day or night. Sometimes the most ideal conditions were at night.[33] For the opposite side of the pasture the crew would wait until the wind was blowing in that direction. The same was true of the two ends of the pasture. If the pasture was large, one or two cross guards would be burned. In these instances the plow would be used for the stop. In this way a fairly safe system of guards provided protection against chance prairie fires until the next spring.

The Spring Lake ranch was in the short grass country, and a grass fire at any time was a catastrophe. The Mashed O had its own fire wagon ready at all times. It was a regular wagon with a barrel or two of water, a plow, gunny sacks, spades, rakes, and fence equipment. Newt Robison tells what happened when a fire was spotted:

When a fire would break out in a reasonable distance, we would hitch four mules to the fire wagon and head for the fire. All the cowboys would go on horseback in the middle of the night or any other time. When we got near the fire we stopped the wagon, hitched the mules to the plow and three or four cowboys would hitch their lariats to the plow and get out ahead of the mules, so we would have four mules and three horses pulling. We would plow three or four furrows around the wagon to protect it, if the fire got that far. Then we would plow a furrow at a right angle to the path of the fire. When we reached a point beyond what would be the edge of the fire, if we had time we would turn back and double the width of the furrow. If we did not have time we would move farther away and make another furrow parallel to the first one. In the meanwhile the other men would be coming along the first furrow with brooms and wet sacks swatting out blazes which had jumped the furrow. This method worked if the wind was not too high. If it was, nothing could stop the fire. It would race along until it came to a highway, fields or some place where there was nothing else to burn.

The intentional prairie fires in Oklahoma were called pasture burning. There were two schools of thought about this practice. The difference of opinions persists to this day between Burners and Anti-Burners. When used, the burning took place in March when the short grass was just beginning to "put out," as the ranchers called it. With a fair wind, ten to fifteen miles per hour, the old grass would be ignited on the side the wind was blowing from, and the fire would move across the entire pasture consuming the old dry grass and weeds. The ideal time to burn was about three days after a rain. The growth for two or three inches above the ground would be too wet to burn, and the growth of the new grass would not be impaired. Within two or three weeks the whole pasture would be like a well-kept lawn and ready for grazing. The Burners contended that the ash from the burning would compensate in chemical value for the humus material consumed by the flames. The Anti-Burners took the opposite view, that the humus loss far outweighed the residue remaining in the ashes. Ewing Halsell was a militant Burner, and so are Clyte Harlan and Helen Campbell who today own, separately, parts of the old Big Creek ranch.[34]

During the burning period, the cattle had to be switched to the hay stacks left over from winter. Ewing's letters of instruction contained admonitions about the burning. The following one from San Antonio to George Franklin indicates his concern:

Be careful with your pasture burning, and try not to burn up many fence posts. Take along a wagon with water and put out any that catch. Do this while you are burning. Wish we could get a good rain before we start to burn. The grass will not burn so short. After we burn these pastures off the cattle will have to eat hay, and I want them to have all they want.

Three Bosses

21

Ewing Halsell had a unique quality of inspiring loyalty and devotion of employees. In this respect he differed from his father, who, by his presence and dignified reserve, demanded and received respect from his hired hands. Ewing acquired support and affection by his understanding, thoughtfulness, gentleness, and capabilities. With some of his helpers, this personal relationship was marked by lifelong loyalty. These were people who would go with him not only the second mile but for many miles. Unlike his father who was accompanied by Frank Billingslea during the last years he lived in the Cherokee Nation,[1] Ewing had few, if any, enemies. It might be said that he had no known enemies.

Hundreds of people worked for him during his long and active career. Many of these were persons of passage, with no interest other than the pay checks. These people wandered on, leaving only their names on the ranch records. Those who were industrious, dependable, and trustworthy stayed. In some instances they were boosted by Ewing Halsell into higher positions in other fields worthy of their talents. Others, dedicated to cattle raising, he placed in positions of responsibility in

387

his own extended enterprises. A number of these employees could be considered as characters. It would be difficult and unfair to rate these unusual personalities, so they will be taken at random.

Leslie Davenport Gaither was born in Milam County, Texas, May 20, 1882, and shortly after that his family moved to Buffalo Gap in Taylor County.[2] He must not have liked his given names for no one knew what they were until he died, and then they had to write his sister, Mrs. Rex E. Dillard of Tuscola, Texas, to find out.[3] He signed his name L. D. Gaither, and to all he worked with during his long and rather eventful life he was simply Gaither.[4] He grew up in Taylor County while that area was changing from a free range country to one of big, enclosed ranches, offering opportunities for cowboys, and that became his career. In his early twenties he married and started working for Jim Cage, father of Bob Cage of Eagle Pass.[5] Mr. Cage was a cattle and hog dealer and did considerable business shipping cattle and hogs to Mexico City. Cage also bought steers in Mexico and brought them into Texas to sell to cattle ranchers in Oklahoma. Gaither was most useful to the Cages in this two-way cattle traffic. It was, no doubt, in this connection that Ewing Halsell came to know Gaither, and this accounted for his starting to work for the Halsell Cattle Company's Spring Lake ranch January 1, 1923.[6]

Gaither was married but the union did not last long; his wife divorced him and remarried. He never mentioned her after joining the Halsells, on whose payroll he remained until he died twenty-nine years later.[7] This did not mean that he had no interest in women. He did, indeed. It could be generally said of him that, with a few exceptions, men hated him and women loved him. For the few men he liked, which included Ewing Halsell, Johnny Murrell, and Red Caldwell, he would have done anything on earth.[8]

Bob Cage, much younger than Gaither, remembered him well as being six-foot two, weighing about 230 pounds, of sandy complexion, tough as a boot, and mean as hell.[9] He was a top hand, an excellent judge of cattle, hardworking, honest, and utterly dependable. In the early days, he always wore a white shirt with a vest which he never buttoned. He seemed impervious to weather.* All day he would ride into

*Helen Campbell is of the opinion that Gaither's disregard for adverse weather may have been responsible for severe pulmonary trouble towards the end of his life. Helen was not among Gaither's female admirers. Although she respected his skill as a cowboy and his

a freezing wind in his shirt sleeves and with his vest open. He always wore a Borsalino hat, when a larger Stetson would have been more becoming and given more protection from sun and rain. After a few months on the Spring Lake ranch, Ewing Halsell, recognizing his ability and dependability, sent him to run the Surratt ranch which was detached from the Spring Lake ranch.[10] He held this job for several years until the Surratt was traded for a business building in Kansas City.[11] At that time Ewing Halsell made Gaither manager of the Spring Lake ranch, a position he held until he retired some twenty years later.[12] During this period, a friendship which transcended the relationship of a loyal and faithful employee and a grateful and appreciative employer developed between Gaither and Ewing Halsell. This friendship, both touching and admirable, was revealed in the voluminous correspondence between them. Always a courteous formality prevailed. Gaither always said ''Mr. Halsell,'' and Ewing addressed him as ''Gaither.''[13] At the same time Ewing was carrying on an equal number of exchanges with George Franklin, in charge of the Oklahoma ranches. There is a vast difference in the tone of the letters Ewing wrote to and received from the two men. With Gaither it was friendly, and warm, man to man, making suggestions, asking advice, and concerned with Gaither's health and welfare. With Franklin it was business, impersonal, giving instructions, and demanding reports.[14]

In the Ewing Halsell collection is a folio containing some 300 letters between him and Gaither.[15] Both, with limited literary education, had a unique ability to write logical, interesting, informative letters with a compelling style. When these letters are arranged chronologically the result is a commentary of a myriad of details associated with operating a ranch. A few extracts will suffice to show the personal relationship between the men. On June 29, 1933, Ewing wrote to Gaither from Vinita:

. . . I think little Billy McCluskey [Ewing's nephew] will come out to Spring Lake right after July 4. He can either use my house or a room at the cottage. He can use my saddle and outfit. Would want him to have a regular mount of horses. Put him on the payroll at $25 a month, and have him do something every day. Any time you are riding through the pas-

---

judgment of cattle, she has said, ''Of all the men I have ever known he could make me angry quicker and with less effort than any other.''

tures, or driving, you can make it his job to go with you. You can explain things. He could not learn from a better source than you.

Have you had any rain? . . .

Billy McCluskey came to the ranch several summers after that and apparently fitted in very well.

Ewing was concerned about Gaither, who at 55 was doing the hard, rough work of any two men on the ranch, and thought that he needed a vacation and a chance to get rested for a spell. In the spring of 1935, he extracted a promise from Gaither that he would see about it when the summer cow work was over about August 10.

On July 27, 1935, Ewing wrote to him, reminding him of the conditional promise:

. . . The 10th of August will be here soon, so I hope you can make your plans to come West. Let me know before you leave so I can get your apartment here. If you can come, I would leave the ranch in charge of Tipps. I am sure he will make you the best man. Let him use your car and see after the entire ranch [including the VVN].

I was invited to fly with Will Rogers and Wiley Post to New Mexico, but declined the invitation on account of hay fever in the mountains.*

Ewing wrote Gaither, July 31, 1935:

Would like to hear from you just how bad the screwworms are; whether it is necessary to doctor these cattle more than once or not. If it does not rain, I am quite sure they will let up very soon, but if it continues to shower, we may have considerable trouble.

If you decide you can make the trip here, and drive, I would try to come here in the day time; there is too much traffic here for even a good driver at night. If you will let me know about the time you leave, or expect to be here, I will have you some rooms, or an apartment. I am sure that you will enjoy the trip here, and the ladies will be delighted with it. If you decide to come on the train, let me know, and we will meet you at the station and bring you out; we can rent a car here very easily any time that our car is in use.

Gaither replied August 3, 1935:

*This was only a few days before the fatal airplane crash in Alaska.

The way it looks I doubt very much if I can make the trip, but I appreciate your invitation very much. I have practically all the wormy calves gathered, and all doctored once, something like 300 of them. I will work them again tomorrow and I will write you then how many I had to doctor a second time . . .

We had some good showers on different parts of the ranch last night . . . .

The next day Gaither wrote again:

I worked the 300 cattle I gathered today and put them through the chute and caught them with my dehorning gang. About five out of every hundred that we had doctored show worms again today. I put tar and grease all over them and do not think will have much more trouble. I feel much better about it.

Jimmie Rogers [Will Rogers' son] and Jimmie Blake [Mrs. Will Rogers' nephew] are planning on leaving in the morning for Oklahoma City.

If we don't develop a lot more new cases of worms and my haying outfit gets along good, I may try to leave here Monday week and spend a few days in California with you.

We are still having cloudy weather and local showers.

I think Billy Mc is getting along nice, and is liking the ranch.

We have had a few calves the worms have hurt very bad.

Gaither did leave on August 12 and took two lady friends with him, Mrs. McFall [who operated the Amherst Hotel for the Halsells] and Miss Ruby Mashburn. Ewing knew they were coming because he had apartments arranged for them.[16] They had scarcely settled in when the tragic deaths of Will Rogers and Wiley Post were flashed around the world. It was useless for Ewing to go to Alaska to accompany the bodies back to California. The arrangements would be attended to before he could get there. So it was a matter of waiting for the sad rites in Beverly Hills. All the Halsell family along with Gaither and Mrs. McFall had known all the Rogers family, especially Will and his boys who had been on the Spring Lake ranch many times.

On August 19, Ewing wrote Mrs. Palmer, the cook at the Spring Lake ranch:

I know you have been reading of the death of Mr. Rogers. I think Jimmie was in New York when he heard of the death of his father. Bill, his oldest brother was just fixing to sail as a seaman to the Philippines but they got him the morning before he left. He flew to New York and is going back with his mother and the rest of the family, and will be here tomorrow. It is one of the greatest shocks we have ever had. I know you feel it also as you knew Jimmie and Mr. Rogers.

Gaither, Miss Ruby and Mrs. McFall are here, and I think they are having a wonderful time. They have gone to Catalina Island today, and that way have a little ocean trip, and some very pretty sights to see on the island.

Mr. Rowland wired me of the rain and I hope that your garden got some of this as well as the dry farm.

Wish you would write me how you are getting along. I think it is about time to plant anything that you want for fall now.

Give Mr. Palmer my regards, and have him tell you how his hogs are getting along so that you can write me.

Five days later Ewing wrote R. A. [Boots] Tipps whom Gaither had left in charge of the ranch:

Glad to have your letter of the 15th.

Have you been over in the Muleshoe country, and how do you think this boy is getting along there? I think he is a good man, but he might need some help, especially if the screwworms are bothering any, so be sure to cover all your country, either in a car or horseback.

I have been a little uneasy about the wind not blowing, and be sure to keep someone riding these water places, and if the water is low anywhere, and wind not blowing, start your gasoline engines.

I think Gaither is having a pretty good time, but doubt if he is enjoying it as much as the ladies are; think they are planning on starting home about Tuesday of next week, which would be the 27th, and if they do, they will arrive at the ranch about the 29th or 30th.

I shall be glad to have a letter from you, telling me where you had rain and how your cattle are. Did this rain help your crops a lot at dry farm?

By August 31, Gaither and his lady friends had returned, and Gaither wrote a long letter to Ewing reporting on how he had found conditions on the ranch. He ended with two short, terse paragraphs:

It still stays cloudy and looks like we might get more rain.

Want to thank you again for the very nice time you, Mrs. Halsell and Mrs. Rider showed to the girls and myself.

The day he received Gaither's letter Ewing replied.[17]

Was glad to get your report on the ranch.

Tipps has been there for a long time, and I think that it would be a good plan for you to let him have about ten days or two weeks off, and this is about the best time for his vacation as we will be busy after October 1 . . .

Glad you had a nice trip here, and we all were delighted to show you around.

I have had all the vacation I want, and am anxious to get home.

The last reference to Gaither's 1935 vacation was made in a letter from Ewing to Gaither, November 20:

Wish you would let me know how you are getting along; just how you are feeding the calves, and whether they are eating or not.

We are having wonderful weather here. Franklin is getting his trail wagon out and getting ready to go to moving cattle, so I expect it to snow or rain soon.

The beef market is worse than it has ever been, and am still undecided what I will do with about 800 two year old cattle. They are fat enough to ship, but I can't hardly stand the market.

I saw Miss Ruby in Amarillo. Just had a nice little visit with her. Think she was disappointed that you were not along, but I did the best I could to make up for your absence. She would probably consider it a poor effort.

Hope Father is getting along all right.

On June 10, 1938, after inquiring about rain, invariably the first line of the first paragraph of a letter, Ewing wrote about the pumps on Dry Farm (why 3,000 acres with good irrigation wells should be called Dry Farm has never been explained), that George Franklin was going to Texas from Big Creek to help with the branding on the VVN, and about counting the old cows to be shipped that year. Ewing added rather wistfully:

I would like to be there and help with this work, just for the pleasure. I know you will get along all right, and will take care of everything just as well as I could.

I think Mrs. Wood and her daughter, Lucile, plan on coming by the ranch in September on Lucile's way to school in the East.

I hope Mrs. Holmes and Jean will come by the ranch in June. They are to be here in California on July 7, and they may stop at the ranch.

Ewing made a short visit to the ranch in mid-June. He had learned from his sister, Mrs. Holmes, that Gaither was not feeling well. Gaither was having some pulmonary trouble, but he would not admit it and would not slow down. Ewing went to check on him. He did not stay long, because the hay fever started as soon as he reached the Plains. However, he did persuade Gaither to go to Lubbock and see the doctors. When he returned, on July 22, 1938, he wrote:

I had a very nice trip here. The hay fever lasted until the second morning, but it is practically over now. . . .

I had a good time with you at the ranch and wish it was so that I could come back a little more often, but am afraid to try it before fall.

Write me what the doctors told you. If they found anything wrong, I think you should have the diagnosis checked by some other clinic. I am sure that there is nothing wrong except your throat trouble and that may be in part due to cigarette smoking. . . .

Three days later Ewing wrote again. This time he put Gaither's health ahead of the rain:

I have been anxious to hear from you, especially about what the doctors thought, and how much rain you have had over the ranch . . .

On July 26, Ewing got a letter from Gaither and replied:

This letter was very slow getting here. . . .

You did not tell me anything about yourself. I am quite sure there is nothing wrong, but am anxious to know if I am right. . . .

Two days later he got another letter from Gaither. He went on for nearly a page telling about details of the work and no rain, and at the end, added:

I went to see the Doctor. Think they did everything to me except operate. They said they found nothing the matter except my heart is a little weak which causes me to have these short breaths. He gave me some medicine for that, and I think it is helping me.

I branded steers all morning . . . [which meant he had not slowed up any].

On August 1, Ewing wrote a long letter and did not mention rain until the last sentence:

Glad to know what the doctors thought of your condition. It is not necessary for you to do all the heavy work, and I want you to let some of the other boys brand the steers instead of doing it yourself. . . .

I hope you will get enough help so it will not be necessary for you to do all the work. You just sit still and point out the old cow you want cut and let the other boys do it. . . .

On August 5, Ewing tried a new tactic to get Gaither to slow up:

Was awfully glad I caught you at the office this morning and had a little talk with you . . . you sounded like you are feeling all right . . . and I hope you will have another rain.

I just wrote Mrs. McFall [the lady who operated the Amherst Hotel for the Halsells] and told her that I wished you and she could get a vacation. She is having hay fever so badly that I hate for her to stay there. If you could get one of her sisters or someone to go along, you and Mrs. McFall could take my car and drive to Colorado, New Mexico, or come out to California. If you should come to California it would be better for all of you to come on the train . . . [He went on to tell about 20 day excursion rates.]

Five days later he heard from Gaither who had the lingering habit of telling about the cattle, the crops, and the rain, and saving the part Ewing was most anxious about for the very last.

I went to my doctor Saturday and he says I am getting along good.

I think it is mighty nice of you to offer me a vacation, but we have a lot more work to do, and if it continues dry our early feed will be ready to fill our silo. We are building our concrete water tubs.

Ewing replied:

Wish you would write me what the doctors actually found out the last examination. If I keep asking you about it I am afraid you will think there is something seriously wrong, but am sure there is nothing that care will not clear up. . . .

Gaither was a spendthrift so far as his own money was concerned, but when it was Halsell money he was a tightwad.[18] He would haggle with the merchants for a discount, but if it were something for himself, he would do without. For instance, the Halsell Cattle Company had an old Model A Ford roadster which Gaither used to run about the ranch and farms. Somehow the windshield got broken out. Instead of going to Muleshoe and getting it replaced, he rigged a piece of screen wire in its place to keep the bugs from hitting him in the face and drove the old car winter and summer as long as he could make it run.[19]

As an example of Gaither's meanness, he was old-fashioned in his ideas of running a ranch. He thought cowboys should be up and have breakfast eaten before daylight so they could start to work at the first break of day, and work all day until it was too dark to see at night, then have supper. It did not matter whether it was winter or summer, the hours were from ''can to can't.''[20] Then what one did between supper and breakfast was his own business. For that short period there was no curfew and no rules. One summer, Will Rogers' son, Jim, and his cousin, Jim Blake, were cowboying on the Mashed O.[21] The outfit was working at a camp with the chuck wagon. One of the boys had a car. One night after supper the two Jims took off for a night on the town. They went by Amherst where they picked up some girls and drove them to Clovis where there was a ''night club'' with a juke box and plenty of ''moonshine.'' They had a gay old night, just managing to get the girls home before daylight, but it was nearly sunup when they got back to camp. Gaither had sent the other hands off sometime before, and was waiting, scowling, and grinding his teeth. The coffee pot was still on the coals. Gaither did not say a word, he just stared at the boys, who, after an alcoholic night, needed coffee badly. They grabbed tin cups and started for the pot; Gaither beat them to it and kicked it about twenty feet. The next best soberizer was water. So the boys started to the water keg. Gaither beat them to it and kicked it over. Then he spoke for the first time and told them to get their horses saddled. He marched behind them to the remuda pen and pointed out two of the wildest, most outlaw horses. Knowing the boys were not good with a rope, he did unbend enough to rope one horse and with his 230 pounds of bone and muscle, eared the horse down while the boys got a saddle on him, and one of them mounted. The horse did a good job of pitching but the boys were good riders. Gaither roped the other horse, eared him down and got the other boy mounted. Then he told them where to go, what to do, and not to come back until dark. All day the boys were famished for water. They went by windmills with clear cool water running into the stock water tanks, but they knew that if they got off their broncos they would not be able to remount. So they could only watch their horses drink. All day they went without water or food. When they returned to camp that night Gaither had relented sufficiently to let them drink all they wanted. Then with considerable irony he suggested that the boys might like another night on the town. It was little incidents like this which "endeared" Gaither to his hands. This was a side of Gaither which Ewing never saw. He knew him only as a foreman who got the job done with no foolishness.

Gaither was honest—rigidly, provokingly honest. He might permit himself to be fleeced a little bit, but when it came to Halsell business he was as firm as the proverbial Rock of Gibraltar. Bill Eden, son-in-law of Clyte Harlan, was at Spring Lake one time while Ewing was rotating his hands for cow work. Gaither sent Bill in to get something at Gus Parrish's Hardware Store at Earth. Bill, who was quite a joker, asked Gus how he managed to get the Mashed O business if he did not manage a little kickback to Gaither. Gus was dumbfounded, "Hell no! I had rather try to bribe Ewing Halsell than old Gaither!"[22]

Ewing Halsell's confidence in Gaither's honesty and judgment was complete. He was in full charge of hiring and firing the help for the Halsell Cattle Company and for Ewing Halsell's "Texas ranch." He kept no books, except a checkbook. He wrote checks and kept the data on the stubs. These he mailed to Helen Campbell in the Vinita office. She kept the accounts in order the best she could. Sometimes they were confusing, but when finally unraveled, Gaither never came up short.[23]

As he grew older and his pulmonary and heart ailments increased, his disposition became more cantankerous and irritable, making it increasingly difficult to keep hands on the ranch. The two people he idolized most and treated with faultless respect and consideration were Ewing Halsell and Johnny Murrell. Although there was only five years difference in their ages, Ewing, for him, was a father image. Johnny Murrell, on the other hand, was like a beloved son.[24]

Ewing was aware of the Gaither situation on the ranch and pondered how it could be handled. The acquisition of the Farias ranch offered the solution. He convinced Gaither that for the sake of his health he had to give up the mental and physical strain of being responsible for the operation of a ranch, that he could best serve Ewing by going to Farias to act as a consultant with no assigned responsibility, that the South Texas climate would be beneficial for his health, and that Ewing would put him on a $75 a month pension and keep.[25] Gaither was reluctant, but when the first trainload of cattle was shipped to Farias, Gaither was quite willing to go along and receive the cattle at Eagle Pass. This transitional episode made Gaither feel needed and marked the beginning of the transfer.

For the next few years Gaither was a privileged character at Farias.[26] As such he soon began creating new problems.[27] He felt himself the emissary of the owner and, as such, would countermand instructions of the foreman. The foreman, never sure of just how much Gaither represented Ewing Halsell, was confused and puzzled. The result was a constant turnover of foremen. About 80 per cent of the hands on the ranch were Mexicans, for the most part good, reliable men who understood the treatment of cattle and horses in a warm, semiarid environment. Gaither had a "gringo" attitude towards Mexican Americans. This he did not bother to conceal, which made for trouble with the working force.[28]

Ewing Halsell had no trouble adjusting to the Mexican American population.[29] He loved Mexico; his dealings with Mexican cattlemen had been not only satisfactory, but rather delightful. He had once wanted to own a ranch in Mexico, and the reason he had restrained himself was not because he did not like the people but was because the Mexican government had no firm policy concerning investments by foreign cattlemen.

Eventually Ewing was forced, in spite of his affection for Gaither, to get him off the ranch.[30] He did this with the cooperation of Red Caldwell, to whom Gaither was also devoted.[31] It was arranged that Gaither would move into Eagle Pass and live in Red's guest house. Red and Gaither had a great deal in common. They hunted and fished together. Red had, in addition to a number of small business enterprises, the supervision of some residential rental property. There was always something to be fixed, repaired, or painted. So Gaither could fiddle with the chores and keep from being bored.

Then something happened which made it necessary to send Gaither to the La Retama Motel, which was under the management of a woman.[32] Now it had happened that many years before, Ewing, realizing Gaither's proclivity of squandering his own money on his few friends, had started withholding a part of Gaither's salary each month and placing it on time deposits in the First National Bank in Vinita.[33] He convinced Gaither that he must live on his $75 pension and not withdraw any of his savings. Over the years the amount exceeded $8,000. About once a year the bank would send Gaither statements of the accounts.[34] The motel manager had become very attentive to Gaither, who was ailing and lonely, was suffering considerable pain and discomfort, had taken to drinking heavily and had resorted to pain-killing drugs.[35]

The condition of Gaither's health became acute. Ewing Halsell heard about it and had him transferred in an ambulance to the Nix Hospital in San Antonio.[36] The motel manager went in the ambulance with him, and, as Helen was at the Farias ranch, Ewing insisted that she stay in Helen's room in the Halsell apartment in the St. Anthony Hotel.[37] Gaither died in about two weeks.[38] Ewing took care of all the expenses, more than $2,000, drawing on Gaither's savings. Then the motel manager told Ewing that Gaither had a will in his billfold.[39] Ewing realized that he had a legal problem and turned the matter over to the family attorney, Gilbert Denman, Jr. Observing all legal procedures, the wallet was opened and, sure enough, there was a note in it in Gaither's handwriting which stated that whatever he had in the First National Bank in Vinita and the Frost National Bank in San Antonio was to be given to the motel manager.[40]

The Halsell family was appalled. No mention was made of Gaither's brother and sister or of the Caldwells who had taken care of him for several years. Under Texas law the note probably constituted a holographic will. Ewing Halsell felt that Gaither had been unduly influenced while in an unstable condition and employed Denman to contest the will on behalf of the legal heirs.[41] The first legal action was to establish jurisdiction in Lamb County where Gaither had retained his legal residence, rather than in Maverick County where he was alleged to be only a visitor, and where the woman would have a better chance to win her case. She had many

A Ranching Saga

relatives there who were on the voters' list. The principal witness for Gaither's family was Ewing Halsell who testified that Gaither was in Maverick County only on his orders, and that he had never transferred his legal residence. The star witness for the woman was her daughter who testified that she had taken Gaither to the polls to vote in Eagle Pass. Her testimony was shaken when she voluntarily said Gaither told her he had voted for Taft. This was in 1952 when Taft was not a candidate. Also Gaither's name was not on the voters' list. The judge took the case under consideration for more than a year. In the meanwhile he kept urging the parties to compromise. Finally, this was done with one-third of the estate going to the motel manager and two-thirds to Gaither's family.[42] So ended the hectic, colorful career of Leslie Davenport Gaither, devoted friend and employee of Ewing Halsell.

Entwined with the Gaither story is that of Ernest Huffman. He was several years older than Gaither, and he began working with the Halsells on the Spring Lake ranch about ten years before Gaither showed up. The two men were opposites in every respect, physically, in personality, and temperament. They did have three traits in common: honesty, dependability, and utmost devotion to Ewing Halsell. It was inevitable and regrettable that a feud eventually developed between them.

Huffman came from the vicinity of Snyder, Texas, and started working on the Spring Lake ranch when Will McCluskey was manager.[43] Huffman was little, dark, sour, and silent. He would go for hours without uttering a word, then he might open up and be rather pleasant for a period. But when he was silent everyone kept still because he had a bad temper. He was five feet six and weighed about 130 pounds. He gave the impression of a bantam rooster on the peck and looking for trouble. When he blew up, he was like a tornado. In a crew of hands, all much larger than he, everyone treated him with utmost respect.[44]

He had no concern about his physical appearance. He would wear a pair of pants until holes came in them. Instead of getting them patched, he would buy a new pair and put them on over the worn pair. When spring would come, he would be wearing three or four pairs of trousers. It was several years after he started working on the ranch before he had a suit of clothes. It was given him by Will McCluskey, but it did not occur to McCluskey to supply a belt or suspenders. The trousers were a little large at the waist. Huffman used a rope for a belt. It is doubtful if he ever wore the suit out because he never put it on more than once or twice a year.[45]

Huffman was a valuable man on the ranch. His sinews were like fine-tempered coiled steel. He never tired and never stopped while doing the most arduous labor. He was the first to take hold and the last to let go. After Will McCluskey left about 1917, Huffman acted as foreman until the Halsells disposed of the Surratt ranch. Then Gaither was brought to Spring Lake as foreman of it and Ewing's "Texas ranch."[46] Huffman lacked Gaither's personality and dominating appearance. A stranger, just looking at him, would never have taken him to be boss of what was then regarded as a big outfit. However, his diminutive size and vagabond dress were deceptive. In a fight he was figuratively a wild cat tangling with a big clumsy dog in close quarters.

He was especially rough on hunters and trespassers.[47] The lake, from which the name of the ranch was derived, and Soda Lake, nearby, were perpetual watering places, and countless flocks of wild ducks and geese wintered there. Also there were playa lakes which often held water during the duck season. The Halsells kept the pastures posted for several reasons: hunters were prone to leave gates open, in their thoughtless exuberance they might shoot a horse or a cow, they disturbed the cattle, and they injured the grass. Huffman had orders to keep the hunters out. This he did with gleeful diligence. He would shoot at them across the lakes with a Winchester, which he always carried in a leather scabbard attached to his saddle. He would curse them, fight them, and line them up with his gun on them and march them to the edge of the ranch, usually on the opposite side from which they had left their car. Then he would keep an eye on them to make sure they walked outside the ranch to get back to their car. On occasions when he would find the car or cars and not the hunters, he would shoot holes in all four tires. This left the owners, when they returned, to walk to Amherst, Sudan, or Muleshoe for assistance, distances which varied from twelve to fifteen miles. Huffman was certainly not the most beloved ranch foreman in the land. On the other hand, for people he liked and trusted he would go to any length to accommodate them. He was entirely dedicated to the interests of the Halsells, father and son.[48]

When the Surratt ranch was traded off and Ewing Halsell started his "Texas ranch" adjoining the Spring Lake ranch, he wanted to administer the two operations with one crew. Knowing the temperaments of the two men, he was positive that he could not do it with two bosses. So he had to decide between Huffman and Gaither. Both men were equally good in seeing that the work was done. Neither ever shirked, both controlled their hands by example, by taking the lead in what was to be done, and making it uncomfortable for the lazy and the laggards. Gaither's personality and business judgment turned the scales in his favor. Huffman, deeply hurt and uncommunicative, let it be known indirectly that he would not live at headquarters with Gaither. He preferred a distant line camp. Also he acquired a little house in the new town of Earth. For a year or two he helped on the ranch as a common hand, but from time to time he would hear of remarks that Gaither was making about him.[49]

Gaither, a big talker, ill-advisedly told people that Huffman was getting too old to "cowboy," that he was not well, and that he ought to get a little farm and raise sheep. Huffman's seething hatred of Gaither grew until finally he resolved that he was going to whip Gaither. Huffman decided to go to headquarters and have it out with Gaither there. He did not want anybody else around, so he waited until Saturday evening when the hands would be in town. He had heard that Gaither had been somewhere and was expected home on Saturday. Huffman went to the headquarters and no one was there. So he sat on Gaither's porch and waited. It was almost dark when Gaither drove up in his old car. Huffman walked out to the yard gate to meet him. Gaither was within a few feet of Huffman before he saw him, and it must have flashed over him that Huffman was there for no good purpose. So he started talking, attempting to divert Huffman from whatever he had in mind. Huffman said not a word, but kept coming, like a cat approaching an unsuspecting rat. When within about three feet, with one lightning stroke with his pistol, he whammed Gaither across the temple. The blow floored Gaither flat on the ground. Huffman threw his pistol aside, jumped astride Gaither and pounded him unmercifully with his fists. He beat and cursed until his fury was spent. Then he picked up his pistol, walked away, mounted his horse, and rode back to Earth, feeling infinitely better.[50]

The next day when Ewing Halsell arrived at Spring Lake, Gaither was a sight to behold. One eye was black, swollen, and completely closed. Gaither was reluctant to talk about what had happened, considering there was a hundred pounds difference in his and Huffman's weights. Little by little with the assistance of some of the other hands who had come in the night before shortly after the fight, Ewing got the full story.[51]

Ewing had long known that a feud existed between Gaither and Huffman and feared the encounter might be the beginning of a more violent stage, and he agonized most of the day about it. He felt deeply indebted to both men. He could not forget how Huffman had followed the cattle for days, cutting fences, keeping them together, and bringing them back with little loss during the great blizzard of February 1918.[52] Nor could he overlook Huffman's complete and untiring devotion to duty and to the welfare of the ranch since 1913 when he came there. Huffman's honesty and dependability were beyond question. On the other hand, Gaither was the foreman. Ewing was very fond of him, his management was without fault, and his business judgment was invaluable. In the end, Ewing concluded his only recourse was to back his foreman.

Regretfully and sorrowfully he wrote to Huffman, July 27, 1935:

Dear Ernest:

I was at the ranch the morning after you had been there the night before. I am very sorry the attitude you have taken, and as long as Mr. Gaither is working on this ranch I do not want you to ever come on it. We have been friends a long time, but I could not permit you to have the privilege of this ranch as long as you feel as you do toward Mr. Gaither.

That same day, in a routine letter to Gaither, Ewing ended with a one sentence warning: "I want you to be very careful when you go to Earth or Amherst."

In a few days, in an envelope with the post office stamp on it dated August 9, 1935, Ewing received a handwritten letter from Huffman. The reproduced typed copy below is an exact arrangement of the original. It is a deeply moving expression, in blank verse, of the wounded feelings of an honest, illiterate man:

Mr. Ewing Halsell

      Dear Sir

I did not go to the ranch
to dowhat I did do

I went to Earth to get
Gro Mr. Deoverfort
tole me he thought you at the
ranch.
I went there to see you
I was mad at Gaither
about some of his talk
I tried to talk to him
lost my head
I have not been to the
for a long time only you
were there never will
go there there a gain
I will never give you ore
folk any trouble
you paid me well for eve
day work I ever did
help me a lot beside
Gaither has been puting it
that I am crazy for
the last two year and
look like from what I
did do I proved he
was wright
so I am appoligiz to
you for going there

            Your friend

        ERNEST HUFFMAN

This was the beginning of a long standoff between Ewing and Huffman.[53] In fact, the rift never healed completely, yet a deep, unspoken affection, one for the other, remained as long as they lived. Although there is no record of their meeting and personally resuming their old relationship, they did manifest their mutual regards in exceptional ways.

George Kuykendall went to Muleshoe the same year Huffman started working for the Halsells and came to know Huffman's peculiarities, his honesty, his industry, and his devotion to his work. Not long after the Gaither fight, George was passing through Muleshoe and saw Huffman standing in front of the post office, gazing at a long envelope he was holding. George stopped his car and went back to visit with his old, respected friend. Huffman, silent as usual, handed him the opened envelope. George pulled out the contents. It was a deed for 320 acres of rich, level land with abundant irrigation water beneath it, signed by Ewing Halsell. The consideration mentioned "for one dollar and for long and faithful service." Huffman was so deeply touched that he could not talk; he just continued to gaze at the deed with misty eyes. George, knowing all that was behind it, put an arm around Huffman's shoulders and gave a squeeze, conveying silently his understanding, and walked away. He, too, was deeply moved.[54]

A few years later, George was involved in another episode dealing with the two men who would not speak to each other. Ewing went to Lubbock for the sole purpose of asking a favor of George Kuykendall. He said Huffman was in a hospital in Lubbock, and apparently was recovering from a serious operation. Ewing wanted George to confidentially take care of all hospital, medical, and doctors' fees, and Ewing would reimburse George. There was one condition: Huffman was never to know that Ewing was involved in any way in the matter.

George went to see Huffman, had a nice visit, and when he started to leave Huffman called him back and said he wanted George to promise that George would not let Ewing Halsell know he was in the hospital. George almost told Huffman that was the very reason he was there, but refrained, passing the matter off lightly to the effect that he probably would not be seeing Ewing for a long time. Huffman, being a man of few words, never pushed George to learn who his benefactor was, but no doubt he knew.

George thought up many little schemes to bring the two together with the thought that the rift would be cured, once they were face to face. But both men were proud and stubborn, and he never brought it off.[55]

Later, Ewing made a direct attempt to renew relations with Huffman.[56] He wrote to him from Vinita:

Was at the Texas ranch the other day, and wanted to come by and see you. But it was hot and did not want to take time to stop.

Haven't heard anything of you in so long, was anxious to know how you are getting along; and would like for you to write me sometime.

Any time you hear I am at the ranch, wish you would come and see me. Will always be glad to see you.

Huffman had vowed he would never again step on Halsell land, and he did not go. But he continued to help the Halsells indirectly. Back in 1913, just before he started working for them, about 400 dry cows were stolen from the Sod House pasture. Their disappearance remained an unsolved mystery. Huffman had quietly spent thirty-seven years trying to uncover the theft. In the late 1930's he leased his farm near Earth and went to Arizona to oversee a ranch owned by a Mr. Warren. In November 1940, he wrote to Bill Rowland and wanted Bill to tell Mr. Halsell that he had found out who had stolen the cows in 1913 and how they did it.[57] He got the information from an old drunk cowboy. The two who stole the cattle spent the night at the Sod House camp and learned that all the Halsell crew would be working in a pasture to the north. Next day the rustlers rounded up about 400 dry cows in the Sod House pasture and after dark started with them to the New Mexico line. They reached it without detection. A timely rain had obliterated their tracks. Then they started driving during the night down the state line on the New Mexico side to the Pecos River, then southwest to Columbus, New Mexico, which was just a few miles from the Mexico line. Here, in case of suspicion, they could quickly drive the herd into Mexico. They started a ranch with the O brand. It was "mashed" ever so slightly. In 1940, the original thieves were dead, but the O ranch they started was being operated by presumably innocent people. So Huffman had never given up trying to do something for Ewing Halsell.

A short time after writing Bill Rowland, Huffman returned to Earth to see about his farm. Bill learned he was there and went to see him. When he returned to Amherst he wrote to Ewing:

Had dinner with Ernest in Earth today. He is looking good and is in good spirits. He is here to see about his farm and will go back to his job. He makes $45 a month, but no expenses, not much to do, a comfortable place to stay and good eats. Says he has a cancer behind his ear, and he is saving his money to have it treated.[58]

The cancer turned out to be a cattle tick which had dug in.

Six years following this there was actually an exchange of letters between Ewing and Huffman. Ewing learned by the cattlemen's grapevine that Huffman was in the Sisters Hospital in El Paso with a broken hip. He at once wrote to him:

Dear Ernest:

Just learned that you have had an accident and got your hip broken. They do some wonderful things with these hips now and I expect with a nail and little baling wire they will have you fixed up in good shape. Will McCluskey's son-in-law is one of the best men on hips there are in the country, but I am sure you have some good men at El Paso.

I just came up to Oklahoma about a week ago and am going to spend the balance of May here, and go on to Spring Lake Ranch and start our branding the last of this month. We have had good rains here and the country is very beautiful. Also Spring Lake has had rains. It has been very dry in South Texas but have had some rains since I left there.

Take care of yourself and I would be glad to hear from you how you are getting along.

Huffman replied May 24, 1947. He evidently dictated the letter to an understanding nurse, because the spelling is most un-Huffman-like:

Dear Sir:

I had a letter from Bill Rowland. He thinks he sold my farm to a boy who is making a good crop, and Bill believes he will make the payments.

It has been quite a bit of punishment staying in this Hospital, but I am getting better slowly. I was working for Mr. Warren who was awfully nice to me. He got the best bone specialist in El Paso. My thigh bone broke just below the hip. We put a silver plate on the break and bolted it up. So far as the broken leg is concerned it is well. I think I will get O.K. now. The Doctor ordered me a pair of crutches so I can learn to walk again.

> Yours truly,
> Ernest Huffman

Huffman signed his name himself. It is scarcely legible, but it is genuine.

So far as the records show this was the end of a third of a century of turbulent, stormy waters above, while down underneath there existed a strong undercurrent of friendship and mutual respect which was always there. Nothing could alter it.

Huffman was the boss at Spring Lake when Johnny Murrell joined the crew. Johnny was fifteen years old when he started working for the Mashed O.[59] He thought Ewing Halsell was something out of the story books.[60] Johnny, thin, of small stature, admired the foreman, who was about the same height but more mature. He especially respected the older man for his horsemanship and the way he took the lead in whatever was to be done.[61] However, there was one basic difference between the two. Whereas Huffman was morose and silent, Johnny was outgoing and could get along with everybody.

Johnny's first job was to assist the wagon cook and help wrangle the horses. Soon something happened to the cook, and Huffman told Johnny to take over. He burned the biscuits, made the coffee too weak, and undercooked the beans. He received a lot of nonconstructive criticism, but he got better with practice. When the branding season was over, he was put to doctoring screwworms.[62]

Being with the wagon when he started work turned out to be a break for Johnny. When Ewing was at the ranch during the branding, he sometimes stayed at the wagon when no one else was around. He would give suggestions for improving the cooking, would mend the fire, and be real friendly. In this way Johnny came to Ewing's attention early in his career. A relationship began which was to be a decisive factor in Johnny's life.

Ewing taught him a lot of tricks with the rope and told him to practice and practice. After a few years, Johnny, although still young, became the top roper; that is, when Ewing was not around. After he became the main roper, he and Ewing would team up together at the roundup and compete. Johnny was never quite as good as Ewing, but one day Johnny beat Ewing by one or two calves. Ewing, who never liked to be beaten at anything, whether poker or roping, said, "Dammit Johnny, you've been practicing over the hill!"[63]

Another important break for Johnny was that Gaither liked him.[64] In 1931 Gaither made him a straw boss in charge of a wagon. A wagon crew would be made up from eight to fifteen men, many of them older and more experienced than Johnny. Yet, there was no complaint. In 1940, Johnny was put in charge of the VVN which was Ewing's "Texas ranch." It was under the overall supervision of Gaither, and the general cow work in spring and late summer was by the Mashed O crew. The remainder of the year Johnny was in charge. When Gaither retired and moved to the Farias ranch in 1945, Ewing made Johnny foreman of the Spring Lake ranch, a position which he held until 1973.[65]

Johnny was with the ranch for more than forty years and saw many hands come and go. In the early days before paved roads and when cowboys and field hands could not afford cars, life was pretty dull when they were not working. On the Spring Lake ranch boredom was diminished by periodic sessions of kangaroo court. The boys in the bunk house had a set of rules. For instance, it was a triable offense to stand on the porch and urinate. If one did and got caught he would be tried and whipped. Newt Robison was the official whipper. To quote Johnny: ''He would jerk the chaps off the offender and fairly tear the seat out of his britches. When he got through with you, you knew you had been whipped, but it was all in fun.''

Johnny told a story about a session of the kangaroo court when Newt Robison was the victim. It was conceived by Jack Woods who was a genius at thinking up pranks. Nine new hands had been added sometime before, and each of them had been tried, convicted, and whipped by Newt, who had really laid it on. They conspired to try Newt and beat him up ''until he hollered calf rope.'' Jack spread the word around that Newt was a little crazy and when he got mad he was dangerous. After supper Jack tipped Newt off and told him to conceal a butcher knife under his shirt and what to do when the trial was over. They had the trial, convicted him, and appointed a big fellow to lay on the strap. Newt whipped out the knife, began cussing a blue streak, backed into a corner, waving and slashing about with the knife, and told them to come on, he would fight them all at once. Not a one made a move. After a stand off, the ''judge'' asked him to put the knife down and fight the big fellow fair with fists. Newt said he did not want to fight one but all of them at the same time. He was doing a good job acting like a crazy man. The new men backed off, stayed clear of him, and went to bed. Newt took the knife to bed with him. Next morning when they got up Newt pitched the knife to one side and said, ''Boy, I have decided to take it. Come on and lay it on.'' But the act Newt had put on the night before had been too realistic. Not a one made a move. It took days for the new hands to decide that Newt really was not crazy.[66]

Another rule was against lying. When there was nothing else to hold court about, someone would make up a lie, not a nasty, insidious little lie, but a whopper about another one of the hands. This might be good for an hour or two of evidence, arguments, and deliberation. Johnny took a big hand in these pranks until he got to be foreman, and then he had to be neutral.

Ewing Halsell had complete confidence in Johnny Murrell and his judgment. In 1942, Ewing wrote to the Draft Board of Bailey County: "This boy has worked for me since he was fifteen years old, and is in charge of the VVN and Jennings ranches (Ewing's "Texas ranch"), which consists of 90,000 acres. He is very capable and has a dependent wife, and in my opinion he should be deferred."[67]

On November 11, 1944, Ewing wrote to Johnny:

You have plenty of judgment, so any time that you feel that my plans will not work out best, it is all right to change them. You know what there is to do, so you can just go ahead and work it out, and if you have some bad weather you will just have to lose a day.

There are few instances, if any, in all the Halsell records of where Ewing Halsell gave so much leeway to a foreman, except Clyte Harlan, the trusted foreman at Bird Creek.

John K. Skinner 22

John K. Skinner belongs in a category all to himself. He was boss of Big Creek ranch for six months, and Ewing Halsell found he could not supervise other men.[1] In his later life he was featured in regional newspapers on the front pages as the Floating Cowboy,[2] but he was by no means an ordinary cowhand. John was one of a kind. No other was ever like him. The motive for treating him in a special manner in this narrative is to interplay and contrast him with Ewing Halsell.

Both were one-eighth Cherokee.[3] About the same time, their fathers married women who were members of the Cherokee tribe. John was the son of Nat Skinner. Nat, like W. E., used his wife's Cherokee status and privileges to make a big fortune off of Cherokee grass. The two men were closely associated geographically, though they were not partners. Between them they controlled most of the Cherokee grasslands from Tulsa to the Kansas border on the north, and from the Verdigris River to the Osage Nation on the West. The families of both men lived in Vinita.[4] Nat Skinner was more prominent in politics and public affairs than was W. E. His name appeared often in the Vinita newspapers as a man participating in many political movements and causes, mostly concerning cattle and politicking for the interest of the non-Cherokee adopted citizens and their use of the Cherokee grasslands.

John was born in Vinita in 1880, making him three years younger than Ewing, but he had been in Vinita a year when Ewing arrived there at the age of four.[5] John attended Worcester Academy and later Willie Halsell College. There is no information as to whether he graduated from the College, or whether his family sent him elsewhere, as was the case with Ewing. His letters in later life indicate he was much better educated than the average cowhand. In short, his early social status and family background were comparable to that of Ewing Halsell.

About the time John was grown, his father had financial reversals and went broke, never to recover.[6] Up to this point, the careers of Ewing and John had been very similar. Both had learned the cattle business, were good hands, and were skillful with the rope. W. E. did not go broke and was able and willing to back his son. John Skinner had only his horse, his saddle, and his rope. So the parallel careers of the two boys diverged, one to become a successful cattleman and the other to spend his life as a cowboy. However, their early association had created a bond between them which lasted, although severely stretched at times, throughout their lives.

John did not start working for Ewing Halsell until he was sixty-two years old,[7] a rather advanced age for a professional cowboy who made his living on horseback from early morn until late at night. We have no record of where he went and for whom he worked prior to 1942 when he asked his old boyhood friend, Ewing Halsell, for a job. In the meanwhile he had married and had two daughters and a son who became an Army Captain in the Korean War.[8] Never in the correspondence in the Halsell Collection, dating from 1942 to 1955, does he ever mention his wife. They were separated.[9]

John had many admirable qualities. Although he had been a little wild in his youth, he was an able, competent, dependable cowman who was not lazy and never shirked.[10] No one ever accused him of not carrying his end of the log. His shortcomings were few but flagrant. He was unpredictable and he could not get along with people, especially the cooks.[11] He was known for his cussedness. Physically, at sixty-two he could outride and outwork most young punchers in their twenties. Nearly every limb and every rib had been broken at least once, one leg three times.[12] It was stiff, and he had a hard time getting it limbered up every morning. Otherwise he ignored it.[13]

John had not been at Big Creek long when Ewing made him foreman.[14] Then trouble began. The variance between the contained, patient, and understanding Ewing and the proud, independent, touchy John can best be set forth in their own words, extracts from the numerous letters which they exchanged. It is to be borne in mind that John had a finicky stomach, which in a measure explained his difficulties with the cooks. It is also of note that of the hundreds, perhaps thousands of people who corresponded with Ewing Halsell, John was the only one who called him "Ewing." His sisters began their letters with "Dear Brother." With every one else, it was "Mr. Halsell."

February 19, 1942

Dear John:

Beginning the first of March I am going to increase your salary to $65. I think you are getting along with your work better and the only thing that has bothered me with you is the question of getting along with your men and your neighbors. You are still inclined to be too fussy. There is a way of telling men things about work without making them mad. So be careful with yourself and don't just criticize all the time. It is a good plan once in awhile when a boy does a good job to tell him about it.

I think these Ramseys are going to work out their job all right. Maybe they will not be the best of cooks, but will be better than some. Of course, you can't tell as to their wastefulness. That is the thing that I can't allow. Have always tried to be saving with food. But I think with a little help they will be all right. . . .

Very truly yours,
Ewing

Nearly every day reports came from the ranch complaining of John's disposition. Three days later Ewing wrote again:

February 22, 1942

Dear John:

You know your work; you know where your cattle are and how they are getting along, and those are the main points, but I have had more trouble with help since you have been there than with any man before. It isn't because that you want to be mean to someone, and I have tried to work out the causes, and I am going to tell you frankly that the biggest part of it is that you talk too much. You are just not going to be able to handle this job unless you can get you some men or get along with what men you have. . . . John, try to hold yourself down and get along with your help a little better. You are doing your work all right, but it is very disturbing to have everybody complaining and am quite sure if you will just make yourself quit talking to your men about each other, you will get along lots better. These cooks are trying to please you. They may talk too much, but I think they will do the work if you will just give them an opportunity. I think they even want to cook what you want for yourself. And you should try to eat some substantial food. However, I am sure you are looking lots better than you did a month or two back.

Yours very truly,
Ewing

Two months went by and Ewing made another effort:

April 27, 1942

Dear John:

Will have you some new cooks there the first of May and maybe a day or two sooner, that I think understand this work from what you have all told me about them. I want you to try to get along with these people. You have got a very gruff way and if people don't know you, they think that you are awful, and I don't want you to be proud of that. There are ways to tell people what to do without making them mad. And it would be very easy to get this woman to cook what you need for yourself. I think it is better for you to keep eating eggs and milk with a piece of beef broiled once or twice a week. If I don't send it to you, I would just buy it for myself when you are in town some time. I hope you get your diet and the cook question settled. I don't mind hiring new men, but I certainly hate to be taking on different cooks so often.

Yours very truly,
Ewing

The problems with the cooks continued:

August 7, 1942

Dear John:

I think Helen has found you some very good cooks and I want you to try very hard to get along with them. I know that you are trying to run this place as it should be, but when you criticize your men you do it in a very gruff way and not in a helpful way, and it is easy for them to find another job so they just quit. It helps a cook every once in a while, when they are doing good work, to tell them that they are getting along well, and this applies to any other workmen. We have a very good organization there now, with Tom Miller riding the line, and the cooks we have, with Carl and the feeder we can do almost anything.

Very truly yours,
Ewing

In the fall Ewing received a letter from John:

November 23, 1942

Dear Ewing:

In regard to the cooks, they are getting along fine. They seem to think that I am a good man to get along with. Vaccinated Hogs the 16th, they are doing fine. Hoping this letter will find yourself and family feeling good and enjoying yourself. I am as ever

Yours truly,
John K. Skinner

P. S. Feeling all right myself.

Obviously, John considered bedlam as a normal state of affairs, and when he wrote the above letter he was unaware that not only the cooks, but all the hands at Big Creek were on the verge of leaving. Ewing pondered what to do. He had to move John, if possible, without hurting his feelings. He knew John would not fit in at Bird Creek or at Spring Lake. He and Gaither would not get along. Finally, Ewing had an idea. Johnny Murrell was the straw boss on the VVN ranch. He and his wife Mickey were living at a camp west of Muleshoe. Johnny was young, but he was easy to get along with and had extraordinary facility for working with hands much older than himself without incurring their resentment. So Ewing went to Big Creek and visited with John and explained how his greatest need at the moment was to have a good, experienced, dependable man to go to Texas and help Johnny Murrell feed some cattle during the winter. He made a big point that John would not be worried with administrative responsibilities down there, something that made his stomach worse, and that Mickey was a good cook. John agreed to go. It was his understanding that it was a temporary assignment, so he took a few things in a valise and left his trunk at Big Creek. It is of interest to note here that it was four or five years before this trunk would catch up with him.[15] He apparently got along with Johnny fairly well. Ewing did not hear from him for quite a while and wrote him a letter:

November 28, 1942

Dear John:

You were becoming so badly worried and bothered that I thought your health was going to give out and while you have lots of work there, where you are, you haven't all the responsibilities. You know how to do that work and I want you to help Johnny Murrell every way you can, I am sure you will. If you get yourself in good condition, and I need you here, I will send for you. Take care of your stomach. Drink all the milk you can.

If you haven't plenty of warm clothes, you had better send for them, as I don't think [I] will want you to come here for a month or so.

Will be out to see you about the 7th or 8th of December.

When spring came and the steers were shipped, John wanted to go back to Oklahoma. Ewing worked out another arrangement whereby he could keep John on a separate job where he would not be involved with other people. He would put him in charge of a pasture which had a camp house and was not very far from the headquarters at Big Creek. John went to Big Creek and Ewing wrote to him:

June 12, 1943

Dear John:

George is going to help you move right away. I want you to fix yourself up comfortable and take care of yourself. I know you will take care of the fences and cattle. I don't want you to keep any liquor at this camp.

Ride your fences. Get into headquarters at whatever time they are going to have their noon meal. Take your time and eat a good meal. Drink lots of milk. You can take light bread, butter, eggs and milk from the ranch. You may be able to keep some butter and milk by keeping it in a bucket of water.

Don't keep any money hanging up in your clothes at the Camp. This place is too near the road and they may steal some of your things. I think it is better to leave most of your good things at the headquarters. Keep George posted on how your cattle are.

A Ranching Saga

John stayed at the camp, rode the pasture, fixed the fence, and fretted. He had a growing feeling he was just being passed around and farmed out. On August 22, 1945, he expressed his unhappy state of mind in a short, terse letter to Ewing, then in California:

Dear Ewing:

Will be surprised to hear from me. But as I feel this way about myself in regard to how I am working for you, I am going to give you three ways to go. Fire me. Raise my wages. Cut my wages. I have worked like hell to make a good hand for you. What you do in regard to this matter with me, *I will take it*. So let your conscious be your guide to this matter. I am as ever

Yours truly
John K. Skinner

Ewing immediately and soothingly replied:

Dear John:

Am glad to have your letter but am sorry if you feel that I haven't been paying you enough wages. You do lots of work, but I started you in at very good wages.

I do not want to raise wages at this time, but to show you that I appreciate your work I am going to pay you for an extra month besides your Christmas bonus. I am glad to do that just to show my appreciation because you have been a good worker and very loyal. I hope this is satisfactory to you.

Am having a pretty good time here but would also have a good time working with you.

Would be glad to hear from you now and then how you are getting along. Take care of yourself.

In the meanwhile an office had been opened in San Antonio, where the Ewing Halsells moved in 1945. Gaither had been retired from Spring Lake and sent to Farias, and Johnny Murrell had been made boss of Spring Lake which included the VVN operation. Ewing realized that with all the people on all the ranches, John could get along with Johnny better than anyone else. So he sent John to Spring Lake to help Johnny.[16]

As with his other select hands, Ewing made an effort to help John save part of his monthly earnings.

December 14, 1945

Dear John:

Am enclosing you copy of letter to the bank at home which is self-explanatory, that is, I am buying you a bond to put in the safe and depositing your bonus check and you will receive duplicate deposit ticket from the bank.

Yours truly,
Ewing

John replied:

December 20, 1945

Dear Ewing:

Received your letter of 14 December was glad to hear from you. . . . I am feeling all right, working hard too. I am feeding 600 cattle. I am feeding two hundred and twenty-nine weaned calves every day. And better than four hundred cows and calves every other day. . . . Seems as though I am the only Oklahoma boy that can take it down here. They cannot get too tough for me here. They can work one like hell but I am what can take it.

I am yours truly,
John K. Skinner

P.S. I certainly appreciate you taking care of my money, also buying bonds for me. I need to have my money where I cannot spend it. Nothing here to spend it for.

John wrote to Helen inquiring whether or not Ewing was going to keep him at Spring Lake through the winter.

From Ewing to John:

December 1945

Dear John:

You will probably be in the Panhandle all winter. Quite sure they are going to get an extra man to help with feeding or will take Floyd Templar to help do the feeding. I know you will do your work alright but I want you to be careful and not get yourself hurt or do too much work. The Palmers will take good care of you and I am sure you will be nice to them.

Yours truly,
Ewing

In the spring John wrote to Helen Campbell at San Antonio about his trunk.[17] Helen had had a little confrontation with John a year or two before.[18] John was subject to spells of melancholia. When he was in the dumps, he was impossible. Helen went by his camp to check with him on some matter. John was in a temper about something he had heard, or imagined, regarding Ewing's attitude toward him. Helen later said, "He was the only man who ever cussed me out. He really let me have it. However, the next time I saw him, he had apparently forgotten all about it and was very pleasant." It did not matter that he was cussing the big boss' first lieutenant. He spoke his piece. Had Ewing been there he no doubt would have let Ewing have it. In his letter in April, he wanted Helen to locate his trunk, which he thought was at the Big Creek ranch, and have it sent to the Spring Lake ranch.

From Ewing at San Antonio to John:

February 1946

Dear John:

Was just thinking about you and thought I would write you a little note. Very beautiful day here and warm but not hot.

Just spent three days on the ranch [Farias] here and we are still burning lots of pear but any time we can get just a little shower we would have some weeds and grass. Cattle are not poor but have lost a lot of flesh.

Hope you are getting along alright, keep well and enjoy your work. Am sure you have some help now so you will not have to lift quite so many sacks of cake.

From Ewing to John:

March 20, 1946

Dear John:

Haven't heard from you in some time, and was just wondering how you are getting along.

Did you get your saddle that Clyte shipped and how did you like it?

Would like for you to write me how your cattle are doing and are you getting many calves?

Just fixing to commence shipping cattle from here the 11th. I think Sam Cobb, Elmer Hall and York are coming down [to Farias] to help me drive these cattle to town, and load. That will give me a good Mexican outfit to gather these cattle and put in the trap. Wish you could be down here with me, but I think they need you there.

This is the dryest country I ever saw but the weather is nice, otherwise. We are all getting along fine and would be glad to hear from you. Tell Mrs. Palmer hello.

Give the Palmers my best regards.

> Yours very truly,
> Ewing

On April 26, 1946, John wrote Ewing a six-page letter, a record for John. It was in beautiful longhand. After discussing the weather, condition of the cattle and grass, he had some comments about the modern cowhands:

I figure that these boys that come to work and draw as much money as I do and who have never seen a cow outfit before, know more than I do. I used to think I was a cowboy, but now I just figure I am here and that is all. Of course they can drive a car or a truck, and I cannot. It looks now that to hold a job with a cow outfit you have to be a car driver and a truck driver. I feel myself slipping, and it won't be long till I will be out of the picture. I hate to say it, but I guess I won't last long. I was born thirty years too soon. I had a man tell me that yesterday, and I had to admit he was right. . . . Gaither told me, "John, you have worked like hell here this winter, and I think Mr. Halsell knows it." Johnny Murrell said he would like for me to stay here. He knows dam well he can't find another boy to do what I have done, one that takes an interest in his work. He knows that I know this ranch from A to Z. That don't make any difference. It don't get you anywhere with the outfit. Have not heard from any of my children for some time. That don't make any difference with me. They know I am getting old, and why worry about me.

Am feeling alright. Helped Johnny McMurtry brand his calves yesterday, about 200. . . .

> I am, as ever, your truly
> John K. Skinner

About the same time John wrote to Helen Campbell:[19]

I don't know what Ewing is going to do with me this summer. I wish you would have my trunk sent to Texas. Seems like I have been farmed out so much I don't know where I am at. I was talking to Johnny Murrell today, and he wants me to stay here with him in Texas. He said he had talked to Mr. Halsell and he said that was alright with him.

Ewing to John:

July 3, 1946

I don't feel like I am paying you such bad wages while I know there are some men who get as much as you do that do not do as much work, but I am just paying them too much. But just in order to keep you happy I will raise your wages and you can write me what they should be. If I can't pay you what you think you are worth I don't want you to work for me.

You are doing good work and I depend on you a lot. You would last longer and be in better condition if you would take a vacation. If Johnny Murrell can get some one to take your place for awhile it would be good for you to rest awhile. I know if you stay there you will do your work alright.

John to Ewing:

July 7, 1946

I am leaving next Sunday, the 14th on that truck that goes to the South Texas Ranch [Farias] from here. Will stay a day or two there and then go to San Antonio. . . . I want to see a doctor there. If you are not there, I wish you would leave word about a good doctor to see . . . hope to see you in San Antonio.

Ewing and family, including Helen, had left for California before John got to San Antonio. He did see the doctor whom Ewing had arranged for him. He returned to Spring Lake on one of the Halsell cattle trucks.

Ewing to John:

October 4, 1946

Dear John:

Am sorry I had hay fever so bad in your country that I could not stay but I did stay long enough to see that this country is in fine condition and you were all getting along alright.

Was going to talk with you about your salary. Am going to put it up to $90.00 per month and I will start it as of Aug. 1st, 1946. You do lots of work and I appreciate it. I think this is in line with what I am paying the rest of my men.

Was out with Tom Fields yesterday trying to buy a bunch of cattle he has but haven't been able to trade yet. The doctor he sent you to is the same man I use and is a good man and he can probably help you if you will stay on your diet. If your stomach doesn't get better I would suggest you lay off for awhile and go stay with one of your daughters until you get your stomach in better condition. Am not suggesting this to get rid of you but because I think you are a good enough man that I want to take care of you.

John did not take off to see his daughter, but was feeling better, and seems to have mellowed a bit when he wrote Ewing:[20]

Got a good place to stay here, in the bunk house, all by myself. Don't bother any body and no body bothers me.

The Palmers treat me fine. They are good people to be around.

It is ironical that about the time John had settled in at Spring Lake and had begun to like the place and the Palmers, he received an anonymous letter from someone whom John had probably told off. Although the information contained in the letter was not true, John assumed that it was and wrote to Ewing:

October, 1946

Dear Ewing:

It will be a surprise to you. Am leaving the Mashed O Cattle Co. Oct. 6. That is tomorrow morning. Have tried to make you a good cowboy, but cannot get the job done. If you had told me when you were here that you wanted to get rid of me I would have left then. But that is alright, Ewing. I think just as much of you as I ever did. There is not nothing I would not do for you yet. Am enclosing a letter that was written to me. Don't know who wrote it. Probably will never know. Read it and see what he said about what you said about me, and also you told Gaither what to do with me.

I certainly appreciate what favors you have done to me. I hope some day I can repay you for them. I have another job to go to. But why bring that up now.

I am ever yours truly,

John K. Skinner
Address unknown at present

P.S. (next page)

In this letter it also stated that you did not want me in Oklahoma either. The letter I am enclosing is hard to read, but I think you can figure it out alright.

Upon the receipt of John's letter, Ewing wrote immediately to John's daughter, Mrs. Nan Houston, Boise, Idaho:

October 14, 1946

Dear Mrs. Houston:

Am enclosing you copy of a letter I just received from your Father. I have no idea what brought this on except that he sent me an anonymous letter that he had received. This letter stated that I did not want him which is not true, but quite frequently he gets some hallucinations and becomes disturbed.

I just wrote him what I thought was a nice letter and raised his wages and had suggested that if his stomach did not get better that he go and stay with you awhile so that he could be on the proper diet. He was examined here in San Antonio by a very good physician and his doctor was quite sure that he had ulcers.

Mr. Gaither, my foreman there, thinks that John is going into New Mexico to work for a man that used to work for me but he hasn't his address. I feel quite sure some of the men will hear from him soon and I will keep you posted.

Other than his stomach trouble and his worries that he takes on sometimes he has been quite well and has always worked too hard.

I wanted you to have this information.

Yours very truly,
Ewing Halsell

More than two years went by before Ewing heard from John again. He had been, and still was, working for Hal Bogle who had a ranch east of Roswell, New Mexico. John had evidently been to San Antonio to see the doctor again.

March 10, 1949

Dear Ewing:

Left San Antonio. Did not get to see you before I left. Feeling lots better. The Doc helped my nose alright. Am asking you in regard to a man I met here. His name is Merle Teeter from Eureka, Kansas. He had a ranch on the head of Fall River. Said he has pastured cattle for you there. He offered me a job up there. Would like to know if he would be [a good] man to take a job from.

Have a good job here, but [there are] too many Mexicans to suit me.

Mr. Bogle is a good man alright. Handles lots of cattle. Am at feed lot now, but will leave about the 20th of April to go back [to] the old Turkey Track ranch he owns. Will be in a side camp alone this summer, same as I was last year.

Would like to hear from you in regard to this [Kansas] man.

I am yours truly,
John K. Skinner

Ewing to John:

March 10, 1949

Dear John:

Was glad to have your letter of March 10th. Was sorry I missed you when you were here but I was not in the office very much at that time.

Have had good rains down [San Antonio] here and this ranch is in good shape. These cattle are going out of here nearly half fat. Oklahoma has had a hard winter, and it is still freezing there at night. Am trying to get this big tall grass burned off but talked with George the other night and he has had a case of the flu but thinks he will be about able to work soon.

You inquired about Merle Teeter. I know him fairly well. He has a very good ranch in Greenwood County Kansas just west of Eureka. Think you would like the work in the summer but don't think he handles many cattle in the winter. Am afraid you would run into a part time job. I think he is a good man.

Awfully glad to know your nose is in good shape but watch it and don't let it get bad again.

Best regards.

Yours very truly,
Ewing Halsell

A year and a half went by, and John wrote to Ewing from Milan, Tennessee.

October 1, 1950

Dear Friend:

Be surprised to hear from me. But as I am in Tenn. trying to be a cowboy among these Hillbillys and Pumpkin Rollers, thought I might let you know where I am at. I was sent here by Mr. Hal Bogle, the cowman I was working for in New Mexico. He leased a lot of grass on one of these Ammunition Plant [reservations] owned by the U. S. government. They have about 40,000 acres fenced, and he has a lot of cattle on it. He shipped them from New Mexico [by rail].

I wrote George Franklin since I came here. I told him to have you to send me the *Cattleman* [published] by the cattle association out of Fort Worth. He probably forgot about it. I want it for a year. It is just like being in the army here. They have guards all around the place and keep locks on the gates. There are about 2,000 men working here in the plant, all civilians. Only ten army officers, and they are the boss of it.

Am feeling fine. Tennessee is a good country alright but Texas and New Mexico look better to me than this part of the world. I have been here two months and it has rained most all the time.

George [Franklin] was telling me about Tommy Fields passing away since I was in San Antonio. That is one debt we all have got to pay, and some of us may be next. But why bring that up.

My boy is in Korea. Have not heard from him in three months. I never see a newspaper or hear any news. All I know is what someone tells me. That's the reason I want the *Cattleman*.

I trucked three saddle horses here with me. It was 1,600 miles. Came through Lubbock and called Charley Middleton the night I stayed there. He sure was surprised to hear I was going to Tennessee with saddle horses in a truck to be a cowboy. I told him about Mr. Bogle. He knew him.

How is Mrs. Halsell? Hope all are in good health. Tell Helen Campbell I am still going strong.

> As ever, yours truly,
> John K. Skinner

Ewing to John:

> October 7, 1950

Was glad to hear from you. I had heard before that you were in Tennessee but I did not know what kind of work or cattle you had to handle.

We were very dry at Spring Lake this year. Did not get any rain until July 4th but I think it has rained three times a week since then. The South Texas Ranch is good and so is Oklahoma.

Am writing the *Cattleman* to send you their magazine for one year. If you leave you should notify them to change your address.

Best regards.

Yours very truly,
Ewing Halsell

John to Ewing:

September 27, 1950

Dear Ewing:

Received your letter today. Sure do get lonesome here in this part of the country. Am getting very good wages, $1,800. a year. Am saving my money too. Got a letter from George Franklin's daughter. She lives in Memphis which is 100 miles from where I am located. George was not feeling well, not able to do anything at all.

Am glad I can work and handle these wild Brahma cattle here in this brushy country. It is quite a job but am getting it done alright. When I get up to $2,000. a year I am going to try to hold my job for awhile. Am sending you a paper that is printed here. My pictures is in it. Had been working some cattle and it had been raining all day on me, but you can tell it was me. Thanks a lot for the *Cattleman*.

Hope to see you sometime in 1951. Glad to hear from you any time.

Yours very truly,
John K. Skinner

Taking care of several thousand cattle in a brushy country was a pretty good record for a 70-year-old cowboy.

Helen Campbell to John:

October 14, 1950

Dear John:

Mr. Halsell and I just came in from the ranch and found your letter of Sept. 27th. We are glad to hear from you and to know you are still able to be a cowboy—think you and Mr. Halsell will out last all of us.

We were in Vinita a couple of weeks ago. George Franklin is in very bad shape—has had a series of light strokes and is almost helpless. He lives in Vinita and I am sure would be glad to hear from you. Nannie Collins has been in the hospital—had a light stroke but I think is better now and will go home as soon as they can get some help. Mr. Collins has been awfully worried about her and not doing too good.

All the ranches have finally had rain and we are in fairly good shape. Have had to move almost 2,000 cows off the Mashed O, but were lucky to find a country down by Sundown, Texas. Has been lightly stocked past year and had pretty good rains. Did not sell the calves this year as they are just too light.

Mr. Halsell is feeling fine and going as strong as ever. Rest of family are well too.

We are always glad to hear from you.

Four years went by before John got around to answering Helen's letter. He was back in New Mexico, with Roswell as his post office:

September 27, 1954

Dear Helen:

Be prepared to hear from me. Got your most welcome letter sometime ago [four years]. Should have answered it before now.

I had my eyes operated on. Gave me quite a bit of trouble, but seem to be alright now. . . .

Helen, I am getting along alright after being sick and in the Hospital four times in the last eight years. Cost me lots of money, but I now feel fine. Getting a little grey hair and not as fast on my feet any more. But why bring that up now. I will make it a few more years, but I am quitting being a cowboy in 1957 [three years more]. Hope to see all of you by that time. I will be in San Antonio January 15, 1957. Guess I had better bring this foolish letter to a close.

Best regards to all. Be glad to hear from Mr. Halsell, and you, any time. Have some money out on interest. Hope won't have to go to the poor house for awhile yet.

I am as ever yours truly,
John K. Skinner

This is the last communication in the Halsell Collection from John K. Skinner. He was a good cowman, certainly no ordinary cowboy. Under other circumstances he might have made it along with the Halsells, the Waggoners, the Burnetts, and others who had affiliations with the Indian Nations. By nature he was an individualist, a man of strong convictions who said what he thought even when others did not agree. Always he was true to himself.

His inability to get along with fellow workers with whom he had to compete is understandable. So he went through a long and active life as a loner. Had he been a conformist and played by the rules, he would have faded into oblivion with countless others who did the same jobs he did. But by his rugged individualism and steadfastness to his principles, he evolves as a character. Ewing Halsell understood all this and respected him for his intractable temperament and obstinacy. As Skinner would have said, ''But why bring that up now.''

Hands, Characters, Women   23

In recent years men who work on ranches have been called cowboys. Use of the name "cowboy" has been enhanced by the dime novels which came into vogue at the turn of the century, later by radio western serials and rodeo performances, and finally by television westerns. In the era of the origin and expansion of the cattle industry during the free range period from 1830–1884 and even during the age of the great enclosed ranches from the early 1880's to the early 1900's, the term cowboy was relatively unknown and unused in the ranching records. There were two designations; the owner, who was called the cattleman, and the man who did the work, who was designated a hand.

So it is ironical that during the free range era and later during the large enclosed ranch period, when men really lived with the cattle, spent most of the 24-hour day on horseback, and slept and ate in the open, they were classified on the payrolls as hands. No glamour or romance was associated with the business in that period. In more recent times, the popular nomenclature for the man who actually works with cattle has become cowboy. Ironically, he spends far more time driving a pickup or a truck than he does riding a horse. In this treatment we have used the terms interchangeably, but for statistical purposes we will use the original designation of hands. Some hands who started at fifteen to twenty dollars a month and keep, by hard work and crafty management and aided by lucky breaks in weather and prices, became cattlemen. Those men, many illiterate, or practically so, carried their records in their heads. The books they kept were a checkbook and a tally book. The stubs of the checkbooks and the tally books were seldom, if ever, preserved. When this generation passed, their records, except those dealing with land deeds and mortgages which were recorded in the courthouse, were buried with the men who made them. Few records, and they are exceedingly sketchy, of the free range era exist. For the big enclosed ranch span, the corporate ranches, foreign or domestic, such as the XIT, Matador, Spur, King, Adair, and others, kept definitive records.

W. E. Halsell belonged to the former group. During the twenty years, 1880–1900, while he was acquiring a fortune, some years handling as many as 40,000 cattle, he left no written records. The only item in the Halsell Collection before 1900 is a Day Book. The first item recorded was on October 1, 1898, and the last item was dated November 8, 1902. There are 98 pages devoted to money paid out. Wages, groceries, and incidentals are listed indiscriminately without any notation as to which is which. No entries appear as to income, number of cattle, taxes (which were few, if any), or liabilities. In a word, this sketchy record is all that was left by a man who accumulated something like a two million dollar fortune before any organized system of bookkeeping was implemented in his operation.

From this fragmentary account we can glean a few conclusions. It is to be remembered that W. E. Halsell was not a typical cattle operator of the 1880's and 1890's. He was not in the breeding business per se; although he had started a little herd with pureblood Hereford bulls at Bird Creek, he did not raise cattle nor trail them except from the open range to the nearest shipping point in the Cherokee Nation. While the cattle breeders were driving herds during the 1880's from South Texas to railheads in western Kansas and to grazing lands in Wyoming and Montana, W. E. was buying steers F.O.B. on the Katy in South Texas and unloading them on the bluestem grazing ranges of the Cherokee Nation. He had no fences to build or keep up and no physical outlay except for camping equipment. With the

exception of a few year-around hands at Bird Creek, he used a sizable crew of cow-hands only about four months a year. The operation in 1899–1902 was about the same as it had been since he began in 1881–1882. The Day Book indicated he employed from ten to twenty hands and paid them from $10 to $40 and keep a month.

It is of note that of all the names of hands recorded in the book, only one Cherokee name appears, Blue Jacket, which itself was an English appellation applied to a Cherokee. This does not mean that other Cherokees were not employed. However, the Cherokees, unlike the Comanches, were not a horse-riding people and as a rule did not take to cow work.

Unfortunately, no record exists of the names of the hands who were instrumental in helping W. E. Halsell accumulate a fortune between 1880 and 1899. The records* are extremely skimpy and scanty from 1899 to 1915, at which time Ewing got the Vinita office organized. From 1915 until Ewing's death, the records are full and definitive. Every penny of income and outgo is accounted for, and the name of every person who was paid any amount for any service is recorded for all of the ranches in Oklahoma, Texas, and Kansas. In addition to books which contain the names, dates, and wages of every hand since 1915, there are forty-four file

*These records consist mainly of four separate sources:
Only three account books exist in the Halsell Records dating before 1915. The entries were often made with no notation as to what they were, and they were not organized into broad categories. A good interpretation is difficult.

The several newspapers of Vinita, I.T., from 1882 until 1910 were used. Due to the nature of frontier journalism and W. E.'s status in Vinita, his business affairs were frequently noted. Cattle shipments, both into the bluestem country and later to market, could be followed from year to year through these accounts. Since Vinita was the center of the cattle country in the I.T., market prices appeared quite regularly and gave an understanding of W. E.'s overall operations. Mention was often made of additions to and changes in W. E.'s ranches. Whether it was a new $5,000 barn or the sale of a 100,000 acre ranch. These short, gossipy articles were also helpful in developing an understanding of his economic growth and social activity.

A number of legal documents available date from 1895. These included Mary Alice's will, agreements between Ewing and his father, land purchase agreements, deed records, various documents concerning W. E.'s transferring lands to his four children, records of land sales, contracts and similar documents. These records were scanty and incomplete considering the magnitude of W. E.'s deals and the scope of his business operations.

Finally, there are the very few letters and notes of W. E. himself. These are rare, difficult to read, and have only a limited value in obtaining an overall understanding of how he made his fortune.

drawers of correspondence and documents. These reveal the human aspects of the owners, the bosses, and the hands. Although very little in the written records concerns W. E.'s attitude towards the association with his hands, we have an abundance of material relating to Ewing's attitudes, policies, and relationships with those who worked with him and for him.

Ewing was a shrewd judge of men, cattle, and horses. He was a tolerant man without bigotry or prudery, but he was exacting and demanded full compliance with all agreements, whether it be a day's work or a $100,000 cattle deal.[1] He was aware of human frailties and shortcomings and realized he would seldom, if ever, find all desirable qualities in one person. This ascertainment was exemplified in the personalities of his three principal bosses; each had his deficiencies, but each in his own way got his job done. He tolerated their imperfections in order to acquire their loyalty and devotion to the jobs with which they were entrusted.

Ewing Halsell left to his foremen, or bosses, the employing of casual or transient labor. He personally approved of and took an interest in the regular employees. From time to time he tried out boys who showed signs of promise. With these, he requested the boss in charge to give special attention to the youth.[2] In 1939, he sent a lad named Johnny to the Big Creek ranch, and along with other duties he was to milk the cows which furnished milk for the people working on the ranch. On August 8, he wrote George Franklin in regard to the boy:

I want you to see if Johnny is milking his cows properly at the ranch. I do not want these milk cows to go dry, and just being a kid he might not milk them out well enough. See how he is getting along. He will make a good man if you will talk with him some and help him.

As previously indicated, Ewing was especially desirous of making his nephew Billy McCluskey into a good cowhand. While Billy was in his teens, Ewing sent him during summer vacations to one of the ranches.[3] He went to Spring Lake where Gaither was directed to spend considerable time explaining every facet of the operation of the ranch to Billy. Also, he was to put Billy on the payroll at $25 a month, and Billy was expected to assist Gaither full-time. At the end of the season, Gaither turned in a good report. The next summer, Billy was sent to Big Creek and placed under the tutelage of George Franklin. George sent in a progress report:

Billy McCluskey has been helping us burn fire guards with the exception of one night. He had something in his eye. It looked pretty bad and I was afraid he would have trouble with it so I would not let him go out. He has been cutting some cattle and I think he does pretty well. I think he has done exceedingly well at everything that he has worked at for a boy who never did any ranch work before.

Soon after this favorable appraisal, however, Billy's father went by the ranch, picked Billy up, and went on an extended vacation. When this was reported to Ewing, who was in his hay fever retreat in California, he was exasperated and expressed his reaction in a letter to the Vinita office August 26, 1939:

I do not like the idea of Mr. McCluskey coming by and taking Bill off just whenever it suits them. Little Bill has a job and he should stay with it. I hate very much to say anything about it, but if it continues too much I just can't work Bill.

Two weeks later he wrote again:

It sounds like Billy McCluskey doesn't intend to come back at all, since he said he would write you where he wanted his salary check sent. I want you to deduct for the time he has been away, both with his father and this trip to Kansas City. He will not have much of a pay check.

Ewing was appreciative of girls who helped out in emergencies. Keeping cooks for the four or five chuck houses was a most constant and annoying problem. For any of a variety of reasons they often left with little, or no, notice. Occasionally, a neighboring girl would volunteer to cook until a replacement could be found. An instance happened at the Big Creek ranch in September, 1943, while Ewing was in California. Helen Campbell, always the troubleshooter in such cases, secured Stella Barney, who took over the cook house and did an excellent job until a new cook could be found. Helen went to Santa Monica, as was her custom, to be with the Halsells. She told Ewing about the girl, and he was so grateful that he wrote her an appreciative letter and enclosed a sizable check as a bonus.[4] She replied with the kind of letter which made him feel good.

I received your check and nice letter. I thank you for the check. It will help out in school.

I am sorry I haven't answered sooner, but I've been busy with school work. I am taking typing and shorthand this year, and it takes a lot of time.

I enjoyed working for you, and am glad to know that you liked me. I hope you like your new cook, and glad to hear that you enjoyed your trip to California.[5]

Ewing kept informed about this girl. Had she ever needed help to attend a business school or college, she would no doubt have had it. However, she was independent and never asked for assistance. This quality no doubt enhanced Ewing's opinion of her all the more.

Rarely did a letter from a hand come to the Vinita office asking for a raise in wages. It seems that Harvey Sayles and one of his boys had been employed by one of the Oklahoma bosses for a collective wage of $50 a month and a promise of a raise if their work was satisfactory. Two or three months went by and no raise. Helen Campbell received the following letter:

Mis Cambile, yours truly, I just thought that I would right you a few Linds just to she if I cauld gat a raiz on my check fer I am not gating Enough money I thought you would raiz after the frist Month But I haven't got it Well Helen I thaink that you shud Pay me just Like I work and I dont Beleve that it wood Be oney more than right to gave no a $5.00 raiz I dont make enoug to Buy close for my flamly and I am Boarding My self it I cant get no more I will hav to quit an will from Harvey sayles and son.[6]

Helen replied:

I talked to Mr. Halsell about raising your salary and he thinks you are entitled to it. He is raising you to $55.00 and he says if you want to undertake to butcher a hog for your summer meat, you can have one at whatever the market is and pay it out at five or six dollars a month.

It may be that Carl would want to buy one also, and you two can take half a day off and dress these hogs. Mr. Halsell says it should be done right away if you do this.

Will let this $5.00 raise commence March 1st instead of April 1st.[7]

Requests such as these were handled on their merits.

Ewing Halsell always carried accident insurance for his hands. He took care of all bonafide accidents sustained in line of duty and, in many cases, personally paid the bills for illnesses sustained while in his service. Typical of such mishaps was the case of Bill Eden, son-in-law of Clyte Harlan.[8] Bill was a good-natured, outgoing cowboy with a sense of humor. The hands were loading at a railroad shipping point near the Big Creek ranch. A brahma steer got Bill hemmed up in the chute and broke his leg, not a square break, but a long slanting, spiraling one. The steer roughed him up pretty bad and tore his clothing. When they got Bill outside in the shade, he got sick. Ewing had the boys pour ice water on him. This was just before Bill and Sue Harlan were to marry. Sue was at the loading pen, and with help from the men she got Bill in the car and took him to Nowata where there were two doctors and a little hospital. The doctors set the leg the best they could.

Sue went back to get Bill's razor and other items he would need. On the ranch there was a fence which ran along a ridge, with an iron gate in the fence. Sue got out of the car, opened the gate, and drove through leaving the car in neutral. She had trouble with the fastener of the gate when she closed it. Looking around, she saw the car was rolling down the hill gathering speed. She took after it, but the car kept gaining. There was a curve in the road. The car did not turn but took out across the pasture heading for a deep gully. When Sue got there the car was standing on its front end in the gully. It was a ranch car. She had to walk several miles to borrow another car and get Bill's things to him. Later, they had to bring a tractor to pull the car out of the gully.

Two years later Bill needed to have specialized treatment for a back injury caused by a horse pitching him off. Ewing called for an ambulance and had him sent to Dr. N. S. Pickard, Ewing's nephew by marriage, a famous bone specialist in Kansas City. Later, Bill was moved from the hospital to a convalescent home, but time was never dull for Bill. Each day one of the McCluskeys, McDonalds, or the Holmes would come by and take him on a drive, to a show, or to dinner. Bill later claimed this was the best vacation he ever had. All the expenses were paid by Ewing Halsell.

Nearly every year an accident or two occurred on one or the other of the ranches, and Ewing took care of the bills. There were differences, however, in the attitudes of the recipients. One hand, a grown boy, got an ankle broken when his horse, while chasing a steer, stepped in a prairie dog hole which had grassed over.[9] The hand was sent to the doctor who put a cast on his leg. He could get around but could not ride a horse. Ewing paid the doctor and told the hand his wages would continue as if he were working, but he did not want him to work until his ankle was fully healed. At the end of the third month the boy was back in the saddle, and Ewing had saved a good cowhand.

One other example of Ewing's concern for his hands had to do with Buck Bloomfield's toothache.[10] Helen wrote to Ewing in California about it in one of her lengthy reports. In Ewing's next letter he devoted a half-page to Buck's tooth, naming "three good tooth extractors who had the proper equipment." Then he gave a sort of long distance, layman's diagnosis, pointing out what to expect "if the tooth had grown to the bone." In that case, "it would have to be dug out or sawed off." It would probably cost $5 for the x-ray and $5 for the extraction. Ewing suggested that Buck go first to Dr. Reed, a friend of his. If Buck needed the money, let him have it.

When Helen relayed Mr. Halsell's concern to Buck, he was delighted, and in Helen's next report to Ewing she included the following:

Buck was very happy that you had taken an interest in his tooth. He told me this morning that he did not realize what it meant to be working for an outfit that would suggest and insist that he take care of his health.

Dr. Reed had examined Buck's tooth and recommended that he go to Dr. Bowyer, who was equipped with the proper instruments. Dr. Reed told Buck to be sure to wear his old work clothes, and not tell Dr. Bowyer whom he worked for.[11]

Perhaps the most lamentable accident which occurred on the Halsell ranches happened to Blondie Goddard.[12] A horse fell with him, inflicting a brain concussion. He was never the same again. Both his mind and his speech were affected. Ewing spent several thousand dollars on treatments but to no avail. Blondie got to where he could ride, so Ewing had him ride the 6,000 acre Jarboe ranch and report anything that seemed to be wrong, such as the lack of water in the tanks, screwworms, and fences which needed mending. Also, he was a deterrent to cattle rustlers. It was just busy work, but he did help some by making known anything that was wrong. He lived about six years after the accident.

John Bennett, a common hand, lived in a line camp of one of the smaller ranches near Lenapah. He had an ankle injured while off the ranch and not on duty. He ran up a $150 doctor bill and was incapacitated for several months. He requested Ewing to pay the bill and asked other favors. Ewing was always willing to go all the way when he considered the injury resulted from performance of duty, but his letter to Bennett makes clear where he drew the line.

You had a very unfortunate accident, which was not any responsibility of mine, nor am I liable in any way for the accident, but you have been with me for some time and I knew you needed help so I have tried to help you, not from a sense of legal responsibility but just from the standpoint of friendship, but you are making it very difficult for me to continue.

Reports are that you are drinking and that you are dissatisfied with anything that you are told to do. I do not expect you to do anything that will hurt your ankle, but any work that you can do I want you to do and do it in just as good a way as you know how.

I have instructed Mr. Franklin to take you to your doctor and I am still willing to lend you one hundred fifty dollars to pay this doctor bill. You also owe several other debts that should be paid.

If you feel that you haven't been properly treated and are not being treated right, the best thing for you to do is to find another place to go. I want to hear from you, and I hope you are getting along all right and that the ankle is improving.[13]

Injuries were a part of ranch work. Most of them were not serious and could be doctored on the spot. Each headquarters and camp had simple remedies like antiseptics, bandages, liniments, aspirin, and purgatives. If a wound required stitches, the victim was taken to the nearest doctor. Hospitalization was rare but resorted to when needed.

Ewing Halsell was ever thoughtful of his office force and bosses. He always remembered them with presents at Christmas[14] and usually while away on his hay fever retreat in the later summer.[15] The following is a typical letter he always wrote to Helen before returning:

I wish you would send me the sizes of all the office force. For the men I want their neck, waist and coat size; for you girls I guess the size is in ages or bust sizes. Tell Ruth I would be glad to hear from her, and if she has some special thing she'd like, for her to write. I would like to hear from her anyway. And if you have anything that you would specially like Mrs. Halsell to get for you it would be lots of help if you would mention it. The same thing applies to Tom and Earnest. I also want Clyte's and Hie's neck, waist and coat size. Tell Ruth to get Miss Hale's size. She has changed.

Two days later he wrote again, maybe after having second thoughts:

If there are any little things that you girls would like to suggest to me about what I bring you, I would be awfully glad for you to tell me. You will note I said "little." This does not cover fur coats.

A month after this, he mentioned his shopping excursions:

I have been quite busy the last few days trying to get all of my little shopping done, and have had a nice time doing it. I think there are 36 different persons that I have bought gifts for and it did take quite a lot of time. Have finished with my shopping and am going to Long Beach today to try on some clothes, and then I will be thru with my work and ready to leave.

He always lost the list of measurements of the various employees, and each time he had to write to Helen for a new list.

At Christmas, bonuses were usually the rule, and on an exceptionally good year, checks would be for a month's extra salary. To Lester La Grange who helped him get the physical plant at Farias organized on a salary of $75 a month, he sent a bonus of $500 in 1945.[16]

Two faithful employees who gave Ewing much concern and anxiety were Mr. and Mrs. L. S. Price at the headquarters at Big Creek.[17] Mrs. Price was the cook, a good one, and Mr. Price did the chores, such as milking and gardening. In the late 1930's his health deteriorated, but he kept going, as he could get around. As he did less, Mrs. Price undertook to do more until she, herself, was worn out. Finally, on September 9, 1940, the Prices had to leave the ranch, much to the regret of everyone. Ewing and Helen Campbell assisted them in getting a small disability pension.

Although Ewing could be and was generous in both large and small measures, he would become penurious about a trivial transaction if he considered he was being duped.[18] Tom Walker, one of his top hands and a straw boss on one of the smaller ranches, paid a neighboring farmer $1.50 for driving some stray Diamond Tail steers back into the ranch pasture. Tom then included the amount in his expense account. Promptly Tom got a letter from Ewing, December 24, 1940:

See where we paid $1.50 for someone getting up some steers for us. I hate awfully bad for our neighbors to start doing us that way, and next time somebody gets some up, I would try awfully hard to talk them out of any charges. $1.50 is not much, but if this kind of work gets started, every neighbor you have will be picking up in the lanes or leaving your gates open so they can get them up. While I am paying this $1.50, I want you to tell this fellow we don't consider it a very neighborly act and am not in the habit of paying for holding our cattle. He wasn't out anything. Probably didn't take care of these cattle like he should have. So be as contrary about paying as you can and only pay when you have to.

If someone has really done us a favor, I would be glad to give them something for it, but I hate to have it demanded of me.

In the same vein, one Charlie Aren Hook, wrote from Kansas City to Helen Campbell, February 24, 1945:

I haven't herd from anyone at the ranch so thought I would drop you a few lines Miss Campbell. I don't know whether Mr. Franklin Sent in my time I have two days Coming and. If you want to you can pay me for 13 quarts of tomatoes and 3 qts of Pears and 2 qts of pear preserves.

I am not duning you for the money Miss Campbell. but thought I would write and tell you. Write us a letter.

Across the top of this letter were two words in Ewing's handwriting: Don't pay.

On the other hand, Ewing would go far out of his way to compensate for a favor he considered of merit. Helen wrote to Hie Spencer, November 4, 1939:

Mr. Halsell understood that you have had some trouble with your car, and he thought it might be in part due to your using it while on his business. He thought you were out quite a lot of money, and he wants to help you on this expense, especially if you were using the car to haul some of the hands.

Ewing Halsell had a policy concerning liquor on the ranches. He was convinced that liquor and ranch work did not mix. One of the cooks at Big Creek once asked him if he would object to her keeping some beer on hand. He replied,

I would rather you would not do it. It has always been my policy not to have any intoxicating liquors on the ranch except my own. I can control the occasion, the people involved, and the amounts. The occasions are social and the people are visitors. It is not good to have liquor available for hands who are working. When they are off the ranch and on their own time, it is then their business.[19]

The role which women played on the Halsell ranches is an interesting study. They went the full cycle of being necessary and essential to having no place at all and finally to becoming most essential again. During the late 1850's and early 1860's, as a boy W. E. teamed up with his oldest sister, Syclly Ann, and operated the kitchen in the Halsell Tavern in Decatur. When Syclly Ann married Dan Waggoner, she ran his house which was the headquarters of cattle operations for many years. She was an important factor in the Waggoner enterprise. She cooked, rode horseback, and was a member of the team. The same happened when W. E. married Mary Alice Crutchfield, and they headquartered at the stage stand west of Decatur. They were a team for several years. But when W. E. and his brother Glenn moved their rapidly increasing herd to the Cimarron River in Indian Territory and Mary Alice, Willie, and Ewing settled in Henrietta, W. E.'s world became a man's world where no woman fitted into the operation. It was during this period that W. E.'s philosophy concerning women and ranching was formulated: women were a disrupting influence on a ranch. When he and Glenn sold their Cimarron ranch and dissolved the partnership, W. E. moved his family to Vinita and he became a city-based rancher. He still did not want women on the ranch. As long as he managed the cattle operation he would not hire a married hand, or if he did, the wife could not live on the ranch. As he grew older he had to modify his policy a bit to allow his foreman to have a wife.[20]

When Ewing took over the cattle operation, the role of women on the Halsell ranches began to change. He was more oriented towards women. He grew up the only boy with his mother, three sisters, then later his stepmother. He established an office staffed almost entirely with capable and loyal women. During the latter part of his life his household consisted of himself and three women. So he was one man in a hundred who was surrounded all of his life by devoted females—and he loved it.

Ewing was convinced that women were better cooks than men, especially the kind of cowboy cooks he knew about, whose "repertoire" did not extend beyond sourdough, beans, and meat. It was Ewing who introduced husband and wife teams to run the chuck houses on the different ranches with the wife in charge of the cooking.[21] W. E., with reservations and a bit grudgingly, accepted the new order. Next, Ewing discovered that marriage was good for the hands, especially those living in isolated camps. It caused the men to be more stable, satisfied, and dependable. With creeping mechanization, women fitted more and more into the economic aspects of ranching. Some were good on horseback in emergencies. They could save manpower by making trips to town for supplies and needed parts. As time went on, Ewing, with considerable success, caused each ranch unit to become almost self-sufficient by means of gardens, orchards, canning, chickens, hogs, and dairy products. Only basic essentials, like flour, cornmeal, coffee, and sugar, had to be purchased. The cash outlay for food for the Halsell ranch units was amazingly low after Ewing had his system firmly established.[22] So the cycle of the role of women on the Halsell ranch operations came full circle.

When Ewing discovered the importance of having women on the ranches, he was confronted with the problem of keeping them satisfied.[23] One thing they all liked was indoor plumbing and a bathroom. Wherever possible, this would be provided. From first to last, he probably installed more than a hundred bathrooms.

Ewing was a person who loved to visit and made a point of visiting with the women when convenient. His remarkable memory helped immensely. He could meet the wife of a hand for the first time, and a year later, he would remember her name and recall something that was said or done the first time they met. This attention impressed the ladies and added to their feeling of importance. But it was always the cooks with whom he really established a rapport. There were Mrs. Clyte Harlan, Mrs. Robert Palmer, Mrs. L. S. Price, Mrs. Otis Langley, and a number of others. Ewing loved to write letters and get letters. He had plenty of secretarial help and time on his hands while on his hay fever retreat. He carried on a constant correspondence in an erratic manner with all of them. They were women of parts and wrote interesting and informative letters. Ewing had two reasons for keeping in touch with the ladies. He just liked to do it, and it gave him an additional means of keeping up with what was happening on the different ranches. Helen kept him well informed of business affairs and local news from the Vinita office, but the reports from the women cooks came right from the grass roots.

Mrs. Palmer was the most gifted of the letter writers. A considerable stack of her letters has been preserved in the Halsell Collection and to read them is to relive fragments of the history of the Spring Lake ranch. Her style was simple, easy, flowing, and gripping. One might be about the weather, another about the garden, another about the visitors. Whatever the subject matter, the recital was fascinating. Picking a letter at random indicates she knew Ewing was anxious to know if it had rained, and if so, how much. This letter has to do with rain. She never dated her letters other than the day of the week and the date of the month. This one was Saturday, 23:

Dear Mr. Halsell—I just had to write and tell you what wonderful rains we have had. I was afraid Mr. Gaither would not make it plain to you, so I am writing it.

Monday night we had a nice rain here, probably a half inch. Then Wednesday night is when we got the big rain. It was just a lake of water all over the place, the pasture from here to the farms [several miles to the east] and to the west side of Big Sand [pasture]. Mr. G. says Spring Lake is full and Soda Lake has more water than it has ever had since anyone can remember. The Alfalfa pasture and the Hog pasture are still under water. Muleshoe [ranch] had a good rain and East Camp got five inches. Mr. Gaither said the fields to the east were still under water yesterday. And it rained last night and is still raining now. Water is standing all over the yard. The boys are unloading a car of salt at Muleshoe and I have got to send them their lunch, but I just took time out to tell you about our wonderful rain and I know you will be very happy over it. We didn't lose but a very few chickens. Mrs. Palmer[24]

And again on Monday, Sept. 7:

Dear Mr. Halsell. Was glad to hear from you. Sorry I've waited so long to write, but we [have] been real busy since we got back. Seems like everything was out of place. I don't think Wilson took very good care of the hogs or the cows either, but Robert has fed the hogs good and they are looking a lot better now. They are feeding them green corn, stalks and all. And the cows and calves are gentle again. You know they were working on the pumps during that terrible heat wave and the garden just passed out, but we have turnips coming up since the rain, and I think sweet potatoes are going to make it just fine. We have had a mess already. Have a nice bunch of young turkeys, 31 in all. We have had a mighty nice rain, it is cool, everything looks good, and you are going to have a wonderful lot of feed, and your wheat is coming up nicely. We had several for dinner [at noon] yesterday. Rowland and a couple of their friends, Johnnie McMurtry, Mrs. McFall and Miss Mashburn. had fried chicken, peas, fried potatoes, and wished for you. let us hear from you again, and hurry up and come see us. hope Mrs. Halsell and Mrs. Ryder will stop to see us. Yours truly, Mrs. Palmer.[25]

Mrs. Palmer's letters give such vivid pictures of what went on at headquarters that we will add one more:

Friday

Dear Mr. Halsell. Got your letter. Was as usual very glad to hear from you. I wish you were here. Mr. Halsell this place is truly beautiful. I know it has been a long time since you have seen it like this. the native grass is seeded out all over this yard and all in the trap to the highway. and they say it is like that all over the Ranch. and I don't think you are any prouder of it than Mr. Gaither. he is so happy over the condition that is all he talks about. Wish you could see Mr. Rowland and Floyd crop. do hope you can come back before frost and see how very pretty it is. We are having lots of good eats out of the garden now. and I have put up six gallons of peach preserves since I got back, but that is all of them. I've lots of peppers, and have been canning them. and will make lots of relish next week. We have about 50 pounds of dried lima beans and I am proud of them. I have chickens of all sizes. several hens setting and eight small turkeys. We can have chickens, turkeys and squash when you come back. I am so glad the girls [Jean and Lucile] came and will be happy to have them any time. I love them all. I want you to know Mr. Halsell that I do think an awful lot of you and your family, and I appreciate all the good things you all have done for me. Any thing I can do for you I am happy to do it.

Robert has planted a turnip patch and some more beans since we came home. the turnips are up. We sure have to cut weeds. You never saw so many since the rains. but it is so pretty and cool. So hurry and come see us and bring all the family. Write us any time you can. We are always so glad to hear. Yours truly—Mrs. Palmer.[26]

Below is one typical letter from Ewing. His prose is not so florid or embellished as her's, but he knew exactly how to keep her letters coming. Each one for him was the equivalent to a brief visit to the beloved Spring Lake ranch:

I wish you would write me about your garden and chickens and cows. I like to see this ranch make all of the garden that they can use. The last dinner I had with you was just fine.

Are you going to have any watermellons? Sometime this fall I think I will try to plan out a different system for the chickens. I don't like to see just one old hen leading one chicken around, and think maybe it would be a good plan to build a chicken yard some place and try to get these hens where we can get to them.

A Ranching Saga

I hope Jimmy Rogers [son of Will Rogers] and his wife come by for a visit with us, and that you will be able to give them some of those good fried chickens and fresh vegetables that we have.

Look after my houses and keep the mice out of them, and write me now and then.[27]

This was Ewing Halsell keeping up with how things were going on the ranch in a way that he could not have learned from any man. A warm and close friendship existed between him and all of the principal working women on the ranches. All of them were not as articulate as Mrs. Palmer, but each had something worthy to write about.

While interviewing old hands who had worked on the ranches, the question was frequently asked as to how the hands living in the close quarters of the bunk houses got along together. Newt Robison, who was on the Spring Lake ranch several years in the early 1930's while Ernest Huffman was boss, said:

Of all the time I spent living in bunk houses and cow camps with sometimes as many as 25 or 30 men I heard mighty few arguments and saw only one fight. The boys had a grudge and finally decided to fight it out. They went outside and fought with fists until they gave out. We were all out in a circle watching. Finally they had enough, made up, and stood side by side on the porch and washed the blood off. After that they got along pretty good.

When asked how the hands got along with the neighbors he answered:

We got along good. We did not associate with them much. Some of them did not like Ernest Huffman on account of how he would not let them hunt on the ranch, but that was the least of his troubles. He kind of enjoyed his reputation, which was not very good with the hunters.

Of the thirty or more old hands interviewed, who had worked for the Mashed O or the Diamond Tail, one of the most poignant was Doc Watt Vann, a black man in his 80's when the author met him.[28] Small of stature, lean, bowlegged, he had an air of distinction, and his narration was moving and arresting. He was the son of a freedman, who, in turn, had been a slave of the Vann family, a name well-known in Cherokee history. Doc was totally illiterate, but had a dignity and sincerity which set him apart and compelled respect. His diction was fluent, disregarding grammatical niceties, and, when he had finished, he left lumps in our throats. A recital of his story without meeting him personally leaves something amiss.

He had been with the Halsells in some capacity since 1926. Once, when Ewing was having to rotate his crews from one ranch to another because of labor shortage, Gaither had been helping at Big Creek. When the work was finished and Gaither was ready to start back to Spring Lake, he said to George Franklin, "You only have one real cowboy in your entire crew." Franklin asked, "Which one?" Gaither replied, "The colored boy." This was an accepted fact by all the hands, and, strangely, there was no jealousy. Gaither, Franklin, and Ewing considered him the best bronc buster who had ever been on their ranches or any others they had heard about.

Another aspect of Doc's character was that by his own choice, he was never integrated. He was universally respected and loved and would have been welcome by those who knew him at any table or in any drawing room. With quiet dignity, he refused and ate in the kitchen or to himself in the camps. He lived the way he was raised as a child among the Cherokees and did what he thought was proper. He was superstitious. Ewing Halsell trusted him as much as he did any man and sent him alone on various important missions. Once he was to make a trip from Big Creek to Spring Lake in a car by himself. He got up early and started. An hour or so down the road it occurred to him that it was Friday, the 13th. He turned around and went back to Big Creek. The next morning he got up extra early and started again.

He was married to Corine, whom he adored, and they had a daughter they called Izetta.

Now for Doc's story:

In 1926, I was farming Tom Miller's allotment, about 20 acres, on the shares. Tom sold it to Mr. Halsell, and then he was my landlord. The allotment was a field inside the Big Creek ranch. My corn crop which I had made with a mule and a Georgia stock [a one-horse walking plow] was pretty good. Mr. Halsell's cows broke down the fence and ruined the crop. Miss Helen heard about it and told Mr. Halsell. The next time he was at the ranch he came to see me and paid me for the corn, a very fair price, and said he could use me on the ranch. That is the way I got started. I learned to do all kinds of things from Mr. Halsell and Tom Miller. They were my teachers, and I guess Mr. Halsell was pleased with the way I learned. Whatever there was to do I would do it, farm, work cattle, break horses, drive a truck, pull pipe, just about anything there is to do on a ranch. One day Mr. Halsell came to the ranch and sent for me. He was setting on the porch of his house. He told me to set in another chair, but I didn't. I sat on the edge of the porch. He said he wanted to make a feed boy out of me. He wanted to put 390 big steers in a feed lot east of the barns and feed them all they could eat for three months. He was putting me in complete charge from beginning to the end. Then he wrote out a list of the kinds of feed, how much by weight and how to mix them. I did not have any education, and I could not read or figure. I could count. So I had him read [the instructions] over and over until I memorized it. He was very patient, kept on until I had it all in my mind. I was to have a wagon and a team of mules to haul with.

We got the steers in the pens, and Tom Miller showed me how to run the grinder and mixer. Part of the feed was bundles stacked in various places near the barns. Then there was corn in the shuck and stored in the cribs, and cottonseed cake, salt, and minerals in the barns.

I lived at the little house on the allotment about four miles away and I went and came horseback. We started the feeding in December and it went on through the coldest part of the winter. Many times I had to break the ice on the pond so the steers could drink. I fed twice a day. The last thing I did in the late afternoon was to grind enough for the first feeding next morning. It was hard to get the engine started early on a cold morning. After the feed was put in the troughs I ground feed for the afternoon feeding. Then before leaving I ground for the next morning.

When we put the steers in the pens, Mr. Halsell sent 200 half-grown hogs and put them in with the steers. The grinder did not crack the corn very good and it went through the steers. So the hogs rooted the unused corn from the manure. I think they call this recycling now.

The work was not so hard, but the days were just not long enough. After several weeks I got some help. Two colored boys about 15 came to see us and I got them helping me. One was named Carl, and he later married my daughter. He had a little education. We had to be very particular with the mixing and I kept count by making marks on the ground with a stick. Carl could figure, so that made it easier to keep count. With the boys we could get the work done and get home before dark.

I guess we did pretty good. In March we started shipping. We would send out two loads of steers and one of hogs all at the same time. The hogs weighed about 200 pounds each. Mr. Halsell told me later those steers topped the market in Kansas City and brought $300 apiece.

In going and coming Mr. Halsell had me to ride a different horse every day so as to keep them sort of tame. It was a pretty wild bunch sent up from Texas. Each horse thought he had to pitch when I got on him before daylight, and the amount of pitching was according to how cold it was.

When the steers were gone, Mr. Halsell put me to looking after the cattle on that part of the ranch, and my Corine would help me. She would ride a gentle horse, and she was the best help I ever had. We could go all day and never say a word. Just by the wave of a hand or a nod of the head and she knew what to do. When they needed extra help in the kitchen at the headquarters during canning season she worked there. One day when she was there and the hands were eating dinner [noon] the telephone rang. Mr. Franklin answered, and it was Mr. Halsell. They talked a bit and then Mr. Franklin called to Corine, "Mr. Halsell wants Doc to go to Texas for a while, he wants to know if you will let him go." She said, "Yes. He has never been to Texas, and I would like for him to go." That was the way Corine was. She always thought of me before she did of herself. Mr. Franklin said to me, "He wants you to leave Saturday and go back with Mr. Gaither." So I went to Texas, and many times after that.

Our daughter married Carl and they went to California and had pretty good jobs. After a few years, my Corine went out to see them. While there she took sick and died real quick, and they telephoned about it. I could hardly stand it, but I knew I had to go. I didn't have any money. I was at Bird Creek, and Clyte Harlan phoned Miss Helen at Vinita. Next morning there was a check there for $450 from Mr. Halsell. I went out there and put my Corine away.

Here Doc choked up and with misty eyes looked out of the window until he could get control again. Then, he added in a whisper, "Life has never been the same since." We changed the subject and got him talking about horses for awhile. This brought him out of his mood because he loved horses and knew so much about them. Then we talked about the outlaws he had known about. He had heard of many of them and told about a trip he made once with Tom Miller to Blue Canyon, a well known hideout used by outlaws. He didn't really enjoy the trip because he thought the place was haunted. Finally, we got back to discussing Ewing Halsell:

He was the best man I ever knew. He treated everybody as an equal. The money he sent me to bury Corine, I told him I wanted to pay it all back. He said "No, I wanted to do that for you and her." But I did manage to pay back every cent. I just had to do it.

Doc lives now in a house on the highway which goes to Lenapah. He has social security and lives comfortably. He said, "Every time I come here [we were at the headquarters at Big Creek seven years after Ewing's death], I see Mr. Halsell setting in his rocking chair on the front porch, and motioning to me to come talk to him," and again his emotions took over. "I just can't come here without it makes me awfully sad," he finally added.

Helen Campbell said that at Mr. Halsell's funeral at Vinita the family had Doc to sit near them. The service nearly broke him up. He sat with bowed head repeating

over and over in a scarcely audible voice, ''The Massa's gone! The Massa's gone!''
After the funeral he went back to his little house and sat on a bench in the yard and
mourned for days before he could bring himself to do anything. His job was to saddle a horse when he felt like it and ride about the pastures to see if all was well. He
had strict orders never to try to fix anything himself, but to report the matter to Clyte
Harlan.[29]

Buttermilk Smith was an itinerant cowhand who came and went, and he either
worked on or stopped at every sizable ranch in Texas, New Mexico, and Oklahoma. Practically on every ranch one visits he encounters a legend of Buttermilk's having been there. He was a wit, a clown, a show off, and, incidentally, a
good cowhand. His main trouble was that he just would not stay put—for long. He
was ever in search of new audiences, the kind he found at the bunk houses on the
ranches. Some of his jokes and pranks were pretty raw, resulting in his getting beat
up, something he did not seem to mind very much. He worked awhile on the Bird
Creek ranch. There is a story of his being on a drive of a herd from the stalk fields
south of Tulsa to Bird Creek. The cattle were a little unruly.[30] A part of the drive
was down a lane with farmers' fields on either side. Occasionally, the steers would
break over a fence into a corn field. Then there was a problem of getting the cattle
out and making peace with the farmer. Buttermilk had been assigned to the rear to
take care of the damages. One irate farmer came storming out, doing all the talking,
giving Buttermilk a cussing, and not allowing him a chance to explain. ''Get off
that horse and I'll beat hell out of you!'' Buttermilk with irritating calmness replied,
''I had a better offer back down the road. That fellow offered to take me off.'' Then
he rode on leaving the farmer to take care of his own fence.

On another occasion, a big ruffian had him down astraddle of him and was beating him unmercifully. Buttermilk took it for awhile and then said, ''Hurry up and
get through. The sun is in my eyes.'' The spectators all roared, and the assailant
looked about sheepishly and got up.[31]

Later, Buttermilk was working for a spell on the Spring Lake ranch. Will Rogers
came by for a couple of days. He nearly always came when they were working cattle because he loved to team up with Ewing and rope calves for the branding. This
time he dropped by when only routine chores were being done. With two cowboy
wits in camp, all work ceased and the hands gathered under the shade of a tree in

the yard near the chuck house to listen to the professional and the amateur wits carry on a dialogue. The two were about equally good, even though one was internationally known and the other only a regional character. Mrs. Palmer was in the kitchen cooking. They were out of coal and wood, and she was using corncobs. She came to the door and called out to her husband, Robert, "I am out of cobs!" As quick as a lightning flash, Buttermilk shouted back, "Can't you use paper for once?" That nearly broke up the meeting.

For the better part of two days the cowboys on the Mashed O were treated to a show that they would have paid many dollars to have seen and heard in New York. The second day the audience was much larger because the news had spread to the adjoining farms and ranches.[32]

Tooyah Bean was a hand who worked on the Spring Lake ranch.[33] He was half-Negro and half-Cherokee. The rumor was that he had killed his stepfather for beating up his mother. He had worked on the Bird Creek ranch many years and was a good hand, able to do any kind of ranch and farm work. W. E. Halsell had taken him to the Spring Lake ranch to keep him from going to prison.

He was a privileged character on the Spring Lake ranch.[34] He was silent, reserved, dignified, and did just what he pleased. Gaither did not pretend to direct him. Neither did Ewing. He left everybody else alone and no one dared cross him. George Kuykendall, who ran the bank at Muleshoe from 1913 to 1917, remembered how about once a month Tooyah would ride into Muleshoe, tie his horse to the hitching rack by the depot, get on the train, and go to Clovis. He would be gone from three days to a week. He would leave the horse without a word to anyone. George would get the horse and feed and water him until Tooyah finally showed up. He would get off the train with two bottles of whiskey, one in each coat pocket. He seemed to know where he would find his horse. He saddled up and rode back to the ranch without a word.

One time after a spree in Clovis, Tooyah returned to the ranch to find the crew was at a roundup. He did like to work cattle, so he headed for the roundup still drunk. He got to the camp at mealtime. He got off his horse, fixed his eyes on the big coffee pot on the fire, still full of coffee. He walked slowly to it, but instead of picking it up and pouring a cup full, he whammed away and kicked it just as far as he could. Ewing was there. For the first time, Ewing really blew up; he told Tooyah

J. CISNEROS

he was fired and to get off the ranch and never come back. Tooyah got on his horse and rode away. Three days later Ewing went to the roundup in another pasture. There was Tooyah, sober, and working as usual. Ewing said, "I thought I fired you!" Tooyah replied, "I decided I did not want to be fired."

Tooyah did not live very long after that. The bottle finally got him. When they called W. E. in California about his death, W. E. directed that he be given the best of burial equipment and shipped to Vinita. He was buried at Fairlawn Cemetery, Vinita.[35] Tooyah was completely loyal to W. E. He had sold W. E. his Cherokee allotment, but, fearing the deed might not be valid, left W. E. the land in his will.

Mathilda Elbe was a young woman of uncertain attainments, but she did have opinions and was not lacking in frankness. She may have been motivated by some romantic impulse to try working on a ranch. She was certainly disillusioned. In July 1940, she wrote Ewing a letter, which, to use one of her own terms, was a "humdinger":

Dear Mr. Halsell, I worked for 3 weeks this summer on your ranch in Tulsa, Okla. Well, it was on your ranch in Tulsa County near Owasso and Mr. and Mrs. Clyte Harlan run it, or I better say managed it. I worked there during thrashing in July. I helped Mrs. Harlan can peas, beans and corn.

One thing I wanted to talk to you about was the idea about things being "spic and span." I think it is a nice idea, but the BUNK HOUSE looked as if it never saw new. Most of the men usually quit there in a short time. Mrs. Harlan really works and still don't notice everything. I know there are no two people alike and so very much cannot be done about some things.

Well any how I only got $4.00 a week for working there and room and board, and the Harlans seemed to think I was playing instead of working. She (Mrs. Harlan) says she don't pay a girl to let her have time off during the time they work there, but I think a girl needs time to do a little personal shopping for herself. I quit working there especially on that account. Otherwise I liked it around there even if the work was longer than one should expect. Also, I liked Mr. and Mrs. Harlan and Clyte Jr. and Leona Wilma. They call Leona Suzzanna, or Sue. Even I liked the men who worked there.

I am not really complaining and I don't think I should, because after I got the "supper" (or "dinner") dishes finished, Mrs. Harlan let me ride the bicycle that was the little boy's, if the weather was agreeable.

I really think it would be nice to have the bunk house cleaned a little more frequently than

A Ranching Saga

it is kept (or was kept while I was there). You ought to see it! It's a "Humdinger," if you would class it with a "Squatter town."

You ought to talk with me some time and let me tell you how things go on your ranch. My real home is in Edna, Kansas, not very far from Vinita.

Mrs. Harlan thought I didn't know anything about working out much, but I have, and I am real good at it too. She shouldn't expect too much for only $4.00 a week and room and board, especially if she paid a colored girl $1.00 a day and her dinner at the same time during thrashing.

I am working in Wichita now and all I have to do is clean the house, get the meals, wash the dishes, and the work is finished by 7:00 P.M. I get $5.00 per week and room and board. Mr. Halsell, I worked one Sunday at your place, and I cut eight large washtubs of corn off the cob, and you certainly don't call that playing and fooling. I don't mind work, and I don't intend for anyone to think I'm grouchy or too dignified for a farm or ranch, but I wouldn't mind if they knew I worked 16 hours a day, from 4:30 A.M. to 9:30 P.M. That isn't play, is it? (Remember, if you would like to get things clearer, write me.)

Well, I hope you don't misunderstand me. I mean write me and get it straight.

I wouldn't mind if you would work it some way that I may work on one of your ranches somewhere [else] in Oklahoma or Texas. I wasn't running your ranch down 10 miles northeast of Tulsa, and I did appreciate working there.

Well, my paper is full, and I am sleepy, so I will say bye, bye, and good luck to you all. Thank you for reading this. From Mathilda Elbe. My address is 1633 Saline Ave. Wichita, Kansas.[36]

There is no evidence in the records that Ewing Halsell answered this no doubt well-meaning letter—and what a pity! Perhaps, she might have made some cowboy happy and could even have become a boss's wife. At least she had ideas.

Ewing corresponded with the children of some of his hands. In addition to those of Clyte and Mabel Harlan, there were several others in whom he took a particular interest. One was Billy Ray Walker, son of Tom Walker, a straw boss on one of the Big Creek divisions. On September 2, 1940, he got a letter from Billy:

Dear Mr. Halsell—How are you getting along. I am just fine. I still think I got the top horse on the ranch. I've had a good time since school was out helping with the cattle. I have been with them every time they have shipped.

Mr. Franklin promised that he would give me another horse when school is out next year, and I have a rather good promise from daddy that if I do my school work good he might buy me a new saddle. I was very proud of my check of ten dollars which Mr. Franklin give me. I have bought my school books and some clothes, and I will be in the seventh grade this year.

Goodbye.

Ewing replied the day he got Billy's letter:

Dear Billy—I am glad to have your letter and know that you are pleased with your check, and that you have had a good time working this summer.

I am sure your father will be looking out for a good saddle, because I know you are going to work hard in school. Get a good education so that you can run a ranch some day. . . .[37]

Billy got the saddle with some help from Ewing. The correspondence went on for two years.[38] Billy kept Ewing informed about the rain, the grass, condition of the cattle, and other items Ewing loved to hear about from whatever source. Billy's letters were as informative as those from Gaither or George Franklin. Some of the office force got to referring to Billy as "the little foreman."

Through the years since 1937, Helen Campbell liked nothing better when time and occasion permitted than to get on her boots and spurs and take part in a cattle drive. Recently she wrote:

I am sitting on the porch [1972] at Farias thinking about Ewing Halsell and trying to recall more of his stories:

One which he loved to tell was the Bobby Murrell Story. Bobby is the son of Oma Pearl and T. V. Murrell of Earth. One fall when he was about 6 years old, he, Mr. Halsell and I were riding the drag on a bunch of old cows and calves that had been cut to go to town. This was after we had delivered the Spring Lake calves, and it was part of the regular clean up work in preparation for winter. An old cow came out of the herd and started to run off. Bobby was riding Santa Claus, a shetland. He made a wide circle and brought the old cow back to the herd with no help from anyone. Mr. Halsell told him, "Bobby, that was a good job. I think you know what you are doing." Bobby replied, "Well I orter, I been working for this outfit for four years."[39]

The hand at Farias who endeared himself to the Halsell family more than any other was a teenaged boy who came across the Rio Grande at El Indio when he was fourteen.[40] His name was Lupe Garza. His father had been a talented Japanese gardener with a surname which was unpronounceable in Spanish; and so Lupe used his Mexican mother's last name.[41] He was found in the pasture by Richard Thomas who worked for Joe Ferguson. Lupe was bright, willing, and quickly learned English. In 1945, he started working for Ewing Halsell who developed a fondness for the boy, took a personal interest in his career, and taught him, with help from various old hands, how to do practically everything there was to do about a ranch.[42] Lupe was agile with his hands as well as with his brain. He learned to cook, ride, rope, repair windmills and machinery, build and repair fences, and do carpentry work. Lupe caught on quickly and, with a willing, cheerful disposition, by the time he was twenty became about the most valuable man on the ranch. By his own efforts he learned to read, write, and figure. Furthermore, he was scrupulously honest and trustworthy.

In 1953, 1954, and 1955, an enormous cotton crop was raised on the farms at the Spring Lake ranch which required many cotton pickers, mostly Mexicans. Lupe, who had just married, was sent to Spring Lake to oversee the gathering of the cotton. This was a considerable responsibility, finding hands, weighing, ginning, and keeping accounts. Lupe's disposition was such he could get along well with the cotton pickers, and he did an excellent job.[43]

Ewing was having troubles with the operation of the irrigated, 2,000-acre farm at Farias. He brought Lupe back and put him in charge. This involved overseeing twice as many men as were doing ranch work. Lupe's ability to get along with the Mexican workers impressed Ewing all the more, and he placed the grinding of the grain and the feed lot under his supervision. Also, he counseled him about his future: "The best way to have a good life is to work. The best way to get ahead is to watch your pennies, and pennies grow into dollars. The best place to put your dollars is in the bank." Ewing began putting part of Lupe's wages in a special education fund to send his daughters to college.[44]

Lupe stayed with the Farias ranch from 1945 to 1967. He got along with everybody, even Gaither. His success was observed with interest by a neighboring cattleman, David Cannon, who raised registered Hereford. Mr. Cannon employed Lupe for $650 a month, a modern house, and expenses. Ewing Halsell was proud of him and justifiably took a little credit for Lupe's success.[45]

The transient cowboys had problems ranging from ration books to marriage. If Ewing Halsell was not available, Helen Campbell had to cope. The following letter is typical of many affairs which were directed to her:

May 27, 1944

Dear Hellen Camell

I will try and write a few lines to let you know that I am all right and I hope you are the same. Please excuse my handwriting as I am not feeling very good today. Hellen I went off from the ranch with George Franklin into Vinita. I forgot and left my ration books out at [the] ranch and I [am] wondering if you would get them and send them down to me here as I need them very bad. Please do. My address is: Mr. Jim William Spencer. Mr. Tom Gilbert, Route # 1, Morrison, Okla.

He is the Guy that I am staying with, and I sure do need my ration book. very bad. Hellen [when] I get married will you find an opening for Me and wife, or is it I didn't do my work the way the right way to suit you all. Or what was wrong. I would like to know I done to make youall and them up at the ranch Mad at Me. for I'd like to know them [so that] I [can] make up for what it was and apolize to all of you. Have you had much rain. We have down here. And we are going to start shipping cattle the first day [of] June. There will be four or five months of it. Is George Franklin still working at the ranch. Tell him I've been going out every night with a different woman and haven't Missed a Night in the week, and wont. Well tell him if he wanted me to ride for him, to come down to the Tulsa rodeo right away because they got My Name the second on the list from the top and I wont fail either when I start hookin My bronco. Well I dont know when I am getting married because I haven't set the date, but I can tell you this it isn't very long off. I dont know much to write so I will ring off. I will write more next time, and Please dont forget to send me my ration books. I need them very bad. Ask George Franklin [if] they was left in the bunk house. I will be expecting you to send my books and write me both. Give My regards and blessings and tell them hello for Me. Write soon. From your Lovingest and Best, and Truest Friend.

Mr. Jim William Spencer

Adios and Farewell, Hellen.

Cattle Rustlers, Outlaws, Lawsuits

24

W. E. Halsell, a man without fear, grew up during the troubled era before, during, and after the Civil War, when differences were settled by individual action or mob violence. The story is told of the time just after the War when W. E. was a trail boss taking a herd of Dan Waggoner's cattle to Saint Louis; one late afternoon his outfit came up to another herd which had stopped for the night.[1] W. E. recognized the crew in charge as a notorious gang of rustlers. He stopped his herd far enough back so the herds would not mix, stationed two men to hold the Waggoner cattle, and told the other hands he was going over to cut the other herd for Waggoner "strays which may have got in it." This was a generally accepted procedure on the trail. He told the remainder of his men about the reputation of the other outfit, and he wanted his men to follow him at a reasonable distance and back him up. W. E. rode to the wagon of the other outfit and confronted the boss, a burly ruffian, and told him he wished to cut his herd for Three D. cattle. The other boss, letting go a big squirt of tobacco juice, said, "By god, no man ever cut my herd. I will kill the first man who tries it." W. E. looked him steadily in the eye and said, "My name is

Bill Halsell, and I have some brothers over there, and I am going to cut your herd.'' The big bully had evidently heard of the Halsells and their reputation with handgun and rifle. He stood there and watched W. E. ride in and, deliberately, cut the herd, yielding about fifty Three D steers. In this manner W. E. recovered property belonging to his employer. There was no sheriff, no marshal, and no court action. It was man against man.

This kind of an age and an environment created such individualists, and W. E. remained one as long as he lived. During his career in the Indian Territory he dealt with problems and people firsthand, man to man. This he did in cattle deals, with the Cherokee officials at Tahlequah, and in Washington. Laws and rules were vague and confusing and the law enforcers were far away. He personally handled affairs which directly affected him, whether it be with Cherokee authorities, neighbors, or outlaws. As long as he rode horseback he wore a pistol at all times. Later, after his ''heart attack'' in his mid-forties, while riding the range in a buggy, he always carried a Winchester on his lap.[2] After he gave up active ranch supervision and before he moved from Vinita, he hired a chauffeur and companion.[3] This rugged individualism remained a part of his nature as long as he lived. In the latter part of his life he grudgingly made some concessions to law and order and occasionally employed a lawyer.

Ewing, on the other hand, grew up during the transition period when differences which could not be compromised by the parties concerned were settled in the courts. He had a pistol which he wore during his earlier days at Bird Creek and Spring Lake, but there is no record of his ever having flourished it or even having drawn it.[4] He was a law and order man, but, in a way, he spanned the transition period. He always wanted to settle disagreements or differences in business deals himself, to his own interest if possible, but if all else failed he resorted to lawyers and courts.

Many of the differences and acts of violence during W. E.'s period have been mentioned in previous chapters. Illustrative of the more or less accepted mode of redress during territorial days are listed items from the *Vinita Indian Chieftain*:

August 4, 1887. J. M. Rumm was shot by William Smith with a Winchester. There were 20 witnesses. After the shooting Smith got on his horse and rode away.

December 8, 1887. Deputy Marshal Ed Stockley was shot by the same man who shot Frank Dalton the week before. He was Will Towerly. A posse headed by Stockley went to get Towerly, who was ordered to surrender. He replied with a shot which struck Stockley in the heart. He died in ten seconds but not before he recovered enough to shoot Towerly dead.

May 3, 1888. The following were hanged at Fort Smith: Owen D. Hill, for cutting his wife's throat. George Moss, for killing a Mr. Taff. Jack Crow, for shooting C. B. Wilson. All three were of Negro extraction.

August 23, 1888. Jim Martin shot Louise Dickerson in a row about Martin's wife. No problem.

November 10, 1888. John Crutchfield shot through the foot by Bill Canahan. Crutchfield went to town for treatment. Canahan went to jail.

April 21, 1889. U.S. Marshal W. A. Moody was killed by William Bruner. Bruner was arrested.

December 2, 1891. Alec Choteau was shot and killed by John Davis. The latter will plead self defense (the usual plea which about nine times out of ten was effective).

February 20, 1896. Jim Chandler was killed by Dave Petty.

November 19, 1896. W. O. Wright was killed by Tom Terrell.

September 9, 1901. U.S. Marshall was shot by B. W. Taylor.

September 26, 1902. Two outlaws killed and two wounded in shoot out with U.S. Deputies.

April 21, 1902. Four cattlemen, two on either side were killed in a duel resulting from a feud of long standing.

January 2, 1904. Katy depot agent killed by Dr. Black, a dentist.

December 4, 1906. Ad Reeves was killed by Hardy Smith in a street fight.

With the exception of the three freedmen hung at Fort Smith and about two of the others listed above who were acquitted on self-defense, the other incidents including shootouts with marshals, were pretty much private feuds, and retribution, if any, was later privately extracted. Indian Territory, because of its scattered Anglo population, its dual system of laws and courts, its lack of law enforcement personnel, became a haven for outlaw gangs, cattle rustlers, escaped convicts, and criminal refugees from the states. It was, in fact, the reason W. E. always carried a gun with him.

Among the more famous outlaw gangs which operated in Indian Territory, and to a lesser extent Oklahoma Territory, were the Daltons, the Youngers, and the Starrs. The Halsells were, in a small way, acquainted with the Daltons.[5] They did not contrive with the outlaws, but did accommodate them on occasions. The Dalton family had lived near Vinita when the boys were little and was regarded as an average poor family. Four of the boys grew up and became lawmen. Frank was a deputy U.S. marshal and was killed in action while attempting to capture some bootleggers. The government was more concerned about keeping whiskey from the Indians than anything else pertaining to their welfare. Grat was appointed to take Frank's place. Bob and Emmett were prisoner guards. Bob was later a deputy. So for several years all the Dalton boys were on the side of the law. The hours were long and the pay was poor, based on the number of miles traveled, and it was always months in arrears. Eventually, after some unfortunate and unpleasant experiences with government officials, they decided it would be a lot more adventurous and profitable to be on the other side from the law. Then followed several years of holding up banks and trains. Most of their activities were in the Cherokee Nation. The U.S. marshals were constantly after them. Much of their going and coming was through the Halsell range. They had two situations in their favor. Many of the local people had known them when they were law-abiding. Some had gone to school with them. Generally the Daltons were considered "good boys gone wrong," and they did have friends among the local people.[6] The other factor was that the boys had many friends among the marshals and deputies with whom they had previously served. These men really tried to avoid a clash with the Daltons. A sort of truce existed between them and these old fellow deputies. It happened that during the time the Daltons were at the height of their outlaw careers, W. E. had a foreman at Bird Creek by the name of Thompson. He was friendly with the Daltons and with their old deputy buddies.[7] Both groups felt free to stop by the chuck house for a meal. One day a posse of deputies came by and were in the chuck house eating. The Daltons rode up, recognized the deputies' horses, circled around, and stopped at the barn to wait for the deputies to leave. In a little while they saw Thompson come out of the chuck house. One of the Daltons hollered at him, "Tell those guys to hurry, get through eating, and get gone. We are hungry, too." The deputies came out and rode away in the opposite direction, and the Daltons headed for the chuck house.

W. E. instructed his men to give the Daltons what they needed, whether food or change of horses. In return, the Daltons never bothered anything that belonged to the Bird Creek ranch. They might have killed a calf or yearling for food, but never took a horse unless they left one in return. Also, they never made a raid in Vinita.

Billy McCluskey, Ewing Halsell's nephew, tells a story he remembers having heard his Uncle Ewing relate.[8] When Ewing was about 15, he rode a freight train from Vinita to Tulsa. He climbed in an empty boxcar which had three or four men in it. They looked him over and inquired who he was. He told them, and they seemed satisfied and said they were the Daltons and had eaten many a meal at the Bird Creek chuck house. They were loaded with ammunition and spent most of the day as the train moved along at 20 to 25 miles an hour target shooting at insulators on the telegraph posts, rabbits, and at most anything that moved, except cattle and horses. The train stopped at the switch with shipping pens nearest the Bird Creek ranch house, and Ewing got off. That was the last he ever saw of the Daltons. Shortly after that all the remaining Daltons, except Emmett, were exterminated while trying to rob a bank in Coffeyville. Emmett, seriously wounded, was sent to the penitentiary, finally pardoned, married, lived a respectable life, and wrote a book about the Dalton escapades.

Another outlaw band not so well known was the Rogers gang.[9] They headquartered in what later became part of the Big Creek ranch. They lived near a hill known today as Rogers Mound. They were tough, stole cattle, bootlegged whiskey, and engaged in a few minor holdups. The federal marshals tracked them down, stormed their house when they were drunk or asleep, or both, and killed all of them except a boy. Somehow, they never got into the outlaw literature of the period, and all that is left to their memory is Rogers Mound.

Al Spencer was born and raised in the Big Creek area; he was a lone operator and had better luck than the Rogers.[10] He robbed a few banks and trains. Locally, he was known as a good bad man, a sort of Robin Hood. Tom Miller and Clyte Harlan liked him and befriended him. He, too, never bothered Halsell cattle or horses.

He was finally caught, tried, and sent to the penitentiary for 25 years. He did not live to serve them all. He was buried in the local cemetery near the Big Creek ranch. His escapades are well known in northeastern Oklahoma, but his fame has not spread like that of Billy the Kid.

W. E. sustained few, if any, cattle thefts prior to 1910. Cattle stealing was reported in the Vinita newspapers, but interestingly none from W. E. His reputation may have been such that thieves shied away from cattle with the Mashed O brand. He did have a thoroughbred horse stolen, but he got it back before he missed it.[11] John Gore, a friend, recognized the horse among a number in a livery stable in Adair and brought it home. The livery stable man reported he had bought the horse from what he thought was a passing cowhand.

W. E. did help capture an outlaw.[12] He had a Negro and his wife living in a line camp on his range in the Cherokee Nation. The outlaw, upon whom there was a reward, sometimes stopped at the camp for food. W. E. made a deal with the hand to capture the man. The next time the outlaw came by, when he stooped over to light a cigarette in the fireplace, the hand hit him on the back of the head with a poker and knocked him out. He tied him securely and sent word to W. E., who with a deputy marshal went out and brought the man into town. W. E. collected the reward and split it with his accomplice.

W. E. Halsell was implicated in only a few lawsuits; in one he, Nat Skinner, and others, were named defendants in a case for breaking a Cherokee law which required white cattlemen within the Nation to employ Cherokee cowboys.[13] The cowmen had not complied because Cherokees were not adept at handling cattle on horseback. They could have been trained had they been taught when they were young as was the case with whites and some Negroes. The next issue of the *Vinita Indian Chieftain* carried a two-line item: the case against the cattlemen had been dropped by the judge.

W. E. did have a nonlegal controversy with the *Vinita Indian Chieftain* in 1899.[14] It came up during a Board meeting of the First National Bank, of which W. E. was the biggest stockholder. The manager of the newspaper, M. E. Milford, was also a director, but a small stockholder. The editorial policy of the *Chieftain* was pro-Cherokee and anti-cattleman when the latter did not observe all the laws and regulations of the Cherokee Nation. At an explosive board meeting, October

19, 1899, J. O. Hall, a close friend of W. E., introduced a resolution to the effect that the bank withdraw all connection with the *Chieftain* until the paper changed its policy towards the bank, 80 per cent of whose stock was owned by cattlemen. The resolution provided that all stockholders cancel their subscriptions, and that the bank withhold all advertising, printing contracts, and cease all connection whatever, including loans to the *Chieftain*. It further stated that Mr. Milford be expelled from the Board. Mr. W. H. Kornegay, a lawyer and member of the Board observed that Milford could not be dropped until his term expired several months later. Then a hot argument ensued largely between Halsell and Milford. Milford asked W. E. just why he was so opposed to the policy of the paper. W. E. came to the point: "Because it is against my interest. Me and my son, Ewing, are threatened with a 50 cent tax per head for all the cattle we bring in from Texas. You and your paper are being disloyal to the cattlemen." Milford replied he was not so much trying to be disloyal to the cattlemen but loyal to the Cherokees who owned the land rather than those who got the profits from it. Mr. Hall, as reported in the *Chieftain*, turned ashen and Mr. Halsell red. The vote was taken, eight for the resolution and one against. It was not long until Mr. Milford was not only off the Board of Directors, but out of the newspaper business.

W. E. and Ewing Halsell and William R. McCluskey were indirectly connected with a killing which took place in 1917 at the old Spring Lake store which was located five or six miles northeast of the Spring Lake headquarters.[15] A family by the name of Keller had a section of land adjoining the Spring Lake pasture. The family was composed of an old lady and several sons, all of whom were big fellows. The mother owned a land note due her for $12,000 and a quarter section of land. The oldest son's name was Earl, a huge, overbearing man with a mean disposition. He had a herd of about 100 cows. He was in constant conflict with his neighbors. W. R. McCluskey was the manager of the Spring Lake ranch at the time. He conferred with W. E. and Ewing about keeping a check on Earl Keller. According to Cleve Hamilton, a close friend of W. E.'s and manager of the adjoining Flag ranch, the Halsells had a neighbor by the name of Watts who farmed in the Spring Lake Store community. The Kellers became convinced that Watts was spying on them.

There was some kind of a sale in the neighborhood, and nearly everybody attended. Watts was there, and the Keller men picked a quarrel with him. He was a small man and unoffensive in disposition. The Kellers had evidently gone prepared for a fight. Each one had a two-by-four piece of lumber about three feet long. Earl started the fight by clobbering Watts on the head, knocking him down and temporarily out. Then he jumped on Watts and beat him unmercifully. Cleve Hamilton was at the sale and witnessed the fight. He said, "I knew Watts was Ewing's man, and several of us wanted to pull Earl off of him. But the brothers surrounded him with their clubs and kept us back. We could not do a thing."

Watts recovered but did not leave the country as the Kellers had warned him. Instead, the Halsells let him have a pistol which he kept under the bib of his overalls. Also, W. E. and Will McCluskey made a practice of going by the store every day. Watts made his headquarters at the store. Forty days after the fight, Watts was going out of the store just as Earl Keller was coming in. According to one account, Earl made a lunge at Watts, and Watts stepped back, drew the pistol and shot Earl dead. The Halsells hurried Watts to a place of concealment, fearing that the brothers would be after him.

George Kuykendall had been privy to all that was going on.[16] While operating the bank at Muleshoe, both the Halsells and the Kellers had been customers of his. Mrs. Keller, the mother, had placed the $12,000 land note in his keeping and told him it would be collateral for any money her son, Earl, might need to borrow. After this, George had moved to Clovis where he had an interest in a bank. Immediately after the killing he had a call from Will McCluskey asking if he could meet Will and Ewing Halsell at a certain place on a country road in the sandhills within an hour. George had not heard about the killing but knew something unusual was happening or had happened. He met them at the designated place, and they told George about the killing, and how apprehensive they were as to what the Keller brothers might do. Ewing asked George if he would go to Mrs. Keller's home and try to ascertain what the family's reaction was to the killing.

George went to the Keller home and spent the night sitting up with the corpse and visiting with the family. He had a long talk with the mother, who was both sturdy and sensible. She called the boys in, and in essence said, "We have had a lot of trouble, and Earl is dead. I want you boys to quit your meanness. You have done things you should not have done, and you have not done some of the things you have been accused of. I want this to be the end of this trouble. There must not be any more killing.'' The boys promised they would not retaliate.

George had agreed to meet Ewing and Will the next morning at the same place at 9 o'clock. They were there waiting and were tremendously relieved with George's report. However, they had already sent Watts to a safe place where he would remain until the trial which was sure to follow.

Cleve Hamilton was not at the store at the time of the killing but did go there shortly after it happened.[17] Later, he was a witness at the trial which was held at Tulia. The tenor of the trial was that Earl Keller was a dangerous man and had beaten up Watts without mercy. The defense had a perfect case: that Watts feared for his life, and what he did was in self-defense.[18]

Notwithstanding the pledges made to their mother by the Keller boys, the Halsells kept Watts closely guarded at the trial and whisked him out of the country as soon as it was over. Also, the Halsell family was concerned about the safety of Will McCluskey and arranged to transfer him back to Kansas City.[19]

The Halsell family, descendants of Electious and Elizabeth Jane, was more closely knit than most. Some disagreement and friction developed from time to time but nothing serious. All went well until time came to probate the will of Syclly Ann Halsell Waggoner.* Mrs. Dan Waggoner died May 29, 1928.[20] When the provisions of the will were made known, the fat was in the fire for a period of two months, June and July, 1928.[21]

It was a good will, filling thirteen legal-length pages, executed by a most knowledgeable lawyer, and was as near breakproof as a will could be drawn.[22] Although the value of the estate was not given, it involved several hundred thousand dollars. Since most of the estate of Dan Waggoner, who had died in 1906, had been left to the Waggoner side of the family, Syclly Ann left a considerable part of her estate to the Halsell line of the family. She left legacies for twenty-five members of the family, a brother, a sister, twenty-three nieces and nephews, the nurse, and the companions of her last years. The amounts ranged from $500 to $60,000. Her youngest brother, Ed, was completely omitted. The will provided $10,000 for a building for Texas Womens College in Fort Worth (now Texas Wesleyan College). The residue

*In the Halsell Records Mrs. Waggoner's name was usually spelled Syclly, but in the will it appeared spelled Sicily.

of the estate was placed in a trust, the income to be used to help needy girls attend any Methodist college.

The will contained thirty-four items. The one which caused most of the furor was number eleven: "I give and bequeath to my beloved brother, W. E. Halsell, of Kansas City, Missouri, two hundred shares of stock of the First National Bank of Fort Worth, Texas, with the request that at his death, he give the same to his son, my beloved nephew, Ewing Halsell; that the said W. E. Halsell do so, however, being only a request."

W. E., after the death of Dan Waggoner in 1906,[23] had been his sister's adviser and counselor regarding her investments. According to her lawyer, Bruce Young, she had always given W. E. credit for the growth of her estate.[24] Some three months before Mrs. Waggoner died, W. E., who knew in a general way his sister's wishes about the disposal of her property, wrote to Bruce Young, requesting him to insist that Syclly Ann change her will and leave him out of it and treat his children in the same manner as the other nieces and nephews. On March 26, 1928, Mr. Young wrote W. E. that he had prepared the codicil as requested, and had repeatedly telephoned the house to see if Mrs. Waggoner felt like conferring and signing the document. Each day she put him off until she felt better. That day never came, and the codicil was not signed.

When the will was read after Syclly Ann's death, all the members of the family seemed satisfied, except her brother Ed, who was left out completely, and the three sons of her deceased brother, Roswell Keach Halsell: Claud, Milton, and Roswell, Jr., to each of whom she left only $500. A great silence followed the reading of the will, and each member of the family departed to rejoice or brood according to the treatment each had received. Ed was furious and, being an outspoken, vociferous person, began uttering threats about breaking the will. This he never actually attempted, because the will was so well-executed and airtight that no lawyer would take the case.

W. E.'s first reaction when he learned that Syclly Ann had left him the 200 shares of bank stock was to execute a Bill of Sale, June 8, 1928, transferring to Ewing Halsell, Eva Halsell McCluskey, Clarence Halsell Holmes, and Mary Halsell Combs "all my claim and interest in 200 shares of First National Bank [of Fort

Worth] to come to me from the estate of Mrs. Dan Waggoner, and any other part of the estate which may come into my possession."[25]

He did not have this document recorded but sent it to Ewing to be handled by him in the most appropriate manner. Ewing immediately sent it to Judge Bruce Young for his advice as to how and when it should be used.

He received a prompt reply from Judge Young advising that it would be unwise to record the Bill of Sale until after Mrs. Waggoner's will was probated and title to the stocks had been legally transferred to W. E. Halsell. Any premature action would be questionable and might hold up the probate process. Luckily, as things turned out later, Ewing did not record the Bill of Sale.[26]

After a period, the first dissent to surface came from an unexpected quarter, W. E.'s youngest sister, Ella, Mrs. W. T. Waggoner. This was surprising for two reasons: first, paragraph number nine in the will left to her one hundred shares of the First National Bank of Fort Worth; and, second, the estate of W. T. Waggoner at that time was worth much more than all the Halsells combined. On June 9, 1928, she wrote to W. E. who was in poor health in California:

Dear Brother:

As we have all settled down again in life since our sister passed away, I want to write that I did everything I could for her. I was with her everyday for ten weeks and finished up most of the eleventh trying to adjust the home the best I knew how. She raised me and was the only mother I had since I was nine years old. I never crossed her in any way. I have been with her most since she has been a cripple. I am glad I can say this, as no other member of the family can. Now, Brother, what I want you to do, and I know you will, I want you and Ewing to sign over to me the First National Bank stock which our sister [left to you] . . . she told Tommy [Ella's husband] twice long ago that she was going to leave all the First National stock to me. . . .

It was a great shock to me when I heard the news. . . .

I do not want to hurt your feelings in any way or your health, for it keeps us all busy just [trying] to live. . . .

With love,
Your sister

W. E. was appalled when he received the letter and the more he thought about it, the more agitated he became. He sent the letter to Ewing in Vinita and told him to handle the matter.[27] Ewing's careful, diplomatic, and meticulous treatment of the affair demonstrated one facet of his nature which differed radically from that of his volatile father. He drafted a long letter to Aunt Ella, then rewrote it two or three times, and before sending it to her, he mailed a copy to Judge Bruce Young with the following accompanying letter:

June 20, 1928

Dear Judge Young:

I need help. I received a letter from father enclosing a letter from Aunt Ella which he asked me to answer.

I am enclosing a copy of Aunt Ella's letter with a copy of my proposed reply. I am not going to mail this until I hear from you. Do you think I said too much or too little?

I have not taken this matter up with my attorney here but have written just what I felt about it. If there is anything in it that would have an adverse effect upon our interest from a legal standpoint, I would be glad to have any suggestions you care to make.

Ewing's letter to Ella Halsell Waggoner:

(no date)

Dear Aunt Ella:

Your letter to my father was sent me with the request that I answer or look after it as my father's condition is such that he attends to no business and we do not want him to have any worries that can be avoided. In regard to his giving you the stock which Aunt Ann left him I can at this time give no answer, of course he would have no title to it until the will has been finally upheld and the executor's have turned it over to him. We know that Aunt Ann left him this stock because she loved him dearly and more as a token of her love than for the value of the stock. She always felt and said that my father and Tom Yarborough were largely responsible for her having as much property as she had and my father told her he did not need what she had and did not expect her to give him anything. Of course we all know that Aunt Ann had a mind of her own and knew what she was doing and what she wanted to do, and I know my father did not expect anything and would not have felt hurt and would not have had one bit less love for her and her memory if she had not given or left him anything. We all know that Aunt Ann loved you very dearly and I think you are making a mistake in feeling that Aunt Ann slighted you in not willing you more property. I feel sure that she felt that you had more worldly goods than you could possibly need or use and that you would value more the bank stock which had been in your family so long and her personal effects and that she did not have in mind the money value of the things she left you or my father and I am truly sorry that you look at it differently and feel hurt. Of course we hope there will be no contest or squabble but we hear all kinds of rumors as to who will contest and who are urging it on and backing them. However we know Aunt Ann did just what she wanted to do with her property and we are willing to fight to carry out her wishes if it is necessary to do so.

So far as I am concerned although the will requests my father to leave the bank stock to me at his death, if he wants to give it to you or to anyone else, I will make no objection as my love for him will always be too great for me to have any hard feelings over what he does with property or money.

When the will is finally disposed of and my father's condition improves he will write you fully.

All send much love to you and yours, Ewing[28]

Ewing was worried about the claim in his Aunt Ella's letter about Aunt Ann's having promised her the bank stock. Should Ed Halsell and some of the dissatisfied nephews undertake to break the will, Ella's testimony would have a bearing on the court. On June 21, Judge Young, who had prepared Syclly Ann's will and had worked with her for a number of years, reassured Ewing in a letter:

. . . Mrs. Waggoner told me upon several occasions that she wanted to give all she had to your father, but he had refused to permit her to do it, and he had told her he did not want her to leave him anything. I heard such a conversation myself upon one occasion. It would not be a bad idea in your letter to her [Ella] to state [these facts]. You may also remind her that until the will is probated that your father has no legal right to transfer the stocks to anyone.

In the meanwhile Claud Halsell, son of Roswell Keach Halsell, went to California to confer with W. E. Claud hoped to be able to persuade his uncle to give from his share enough to bring his and his two brothers' parts up to the amount that the nieces received; that is, $10,000 each. This was a questionable procedure on Claud's part because W. E. had had dealings with him before and his uncle's opinion of him was not good. W. E. refused to see him. He stayed around a day or two and then sent W. E. a telegram: "Am leaving tomorrow night for Texas to contest Aunt Ann's will. Do you want to see me before I leave. Answer."[29]

Immediately W. E. wired Ewing, "Claud Halsell just notified me he leaves for Texas tomorrow night to contest the will. Plans to mention me as having used undue influence. He said I could fix it if [I] really wanted to, and he is coming here tomorrow to see me before he leaves. Am all right."[30]

W. E. must have spent most of the night fuming about how he would receive Claud and what he would tell him. When Claud arrived W. E. was already at the boiling point and when his nephew entered the room, he forgot the logical sequence he had planned and burst out with a string of expletives, all of which was what he really wanted to say anyway. These shortly became the part of a legal document. After his tirade he ordered Claud out of his house, leaving not the slightest doubt that he never wanted to lay eyes on his nephew again.

The very next day he was served with a copy of a lawsuit filed against him for slander. The document is so replete as to what really happened the day before, it is set forth in full below:

IN THE SUPERIOR COURT OF THE STATE OF CALIFORNIA
IN AND FOR THE COUNTY OF LOS ANGELES

— — —

CLAUD E. HALSELL,	)
	) No.
Plaintiff,)	
	) *COMPLAINT FOR SLANDER*
vs.)	
	)
	)
WILLIAM E. HALSELL,	
	)
Defendant)	

— — —

The Plaintiff, complaining of the defendant, alleges:

I.

Plaintiff and defendant are each residents of the County of Los Angeles, State of California.

II.

On June 10, 1928, the plaintiff, by invitation from defendant, called upon plaintiff at the latter's residence in Long Beach, California. The defendant had invited plaintiff to his residence for the purpose of discussing with him the matter of the estate of defendant's deceased sister, who was plaintiff's aunt.

III.

Immediately upon plaintiff's arrival at the residence of the defendant the following slanderous words were uttered by defendant to plaintiff in the presence and hearing of plaintiff's family and of the defendant's family and of diverse acquaintances of plaintiff:

"You have come here to rob me"; "You are a dirty liar, a dirty crook, and a thief"; "You have stolen money from me, and you have stolen twenty-five head of cattle from me"; "You have stolen from your sister and from your brothers"; "I will kill you, you crooked son-of-a-bitch."

All of the foregoing slanderous words and expressions were maliciously uttered by the defendant to the plaintiff in the presence and hearing of the foregoing mentioned persons and were uttered with the purpose and intent of defaming, slandering and injuring plaintiff's character and reputation.

During the last seventeen years, on diverse occasions, the dates of which are not known to the plaintiff, the defendant has said to diverse relatives and acquaintances of the plaintiff: "Claud Halsell is a crook, a liar and a thief, and he has stolen money and cattle from me." Said slanderous words were uttered by defendant to diverse friends and acquaintances of plaintiff maliciously and with the intent and purpose to defame, slander and injure plaintiff's character and reputation.

IV.

All of the foregoing slanderous words and expressions were false and were known to the defendant at the time of their utterance to be false.

V.

Prior to their utterance the plaintiff possessed a good reputation among his friends, relatives and acquaintances, but since said utterances by the defendant the reputation of plaintiff among his relatives, friends and acquaintances has been damaged and injured.

VI.

By reason of all of the foregoing the plaintiff has been generally damaged in the sum of $50,000.00; and by reason of said slanderous words and expressions having been uttered by defendant with malice, the plaintiff is entitled to exemplary damages in the sum of $25,000.00.

WHEREFORE, plaintiff prays judgment against the defendant for Fifty Thousand and no/100 ($50,000.00) Dollars as actual damage; for Twenty-Five Thousand and no/100 ($25,000.00) exemplary damage; for costs of this action and for all other proper relief.

(Signed)   WHITNEY SMITH
                        Attorney for Plaintiff

STATE OF CALIFORNIA   )

                             (ss.

COUNTY OF LOS ANGELES   )

I, Kendra K. Hamilton, a Notary Public in and for the County of Los Angeles, State of California, residing therein, duly commissioned and sworn, do hereby certify that the foregoing document is a true copy of the original complaint filed in the Superior Court of the State of California in and for the County of Los Angeles entitled "Claud E. Halsell, Plaintiff, vs. William E. Halsell, Defendant No. 254361" and served upon defendant William E. Halsell on June 11, 1928.

IN WITNESS WHEREOF, I have hereunto set my hand and affixed my official seal in said county this 18th day of June, 1928.

(Signed)   Kendra K. Hamilton
                Notary Public in and for the County
                of Los Angeles, State of California

After Ewing became fully informed about the status of the situation in California, and bearing in mind that paragraph Thirty-two in Ann Waggoner's will would act as strong deterrent to other beneficiaries attempting to contest the will, he wrote a second letter to Aunt Ella.[31] He had decided to ignore the Bill of Sale his father had written, transferring his 200 shares to him and his sisters.

(no date)

Dear Aunt Ella:

As you know, in Aunt Ann's will bequeathing to my Father 200 shares of the stock of the First National Bank of Ft. Worth, which you have asked him to give you, Aunt Ann expressed a wish in her will that Father turn this stock over to me, but stated that the stock was his to do as he pleased with and her expressed wish was not binding on him.

It is my Father's wish that this stock go to me and he has given me a transfer of his expectancy under Aunt Ann's will.

I am very anxious to keep any worry or annoyance from my Father that I possibly can.

There is no doubt in my mind but Aunt Ann willed her property as she wanted it to go and it is our right to accept it and to defend it; but, from a desire and wish to stop the worry, annoyance and disgrace of a family row, and with my Father's consent, I am willing to give up the 200 shares of stock of First National Bank of Ft. Worth.

I know that it is not the value of this stock that is bothering you, and, while I lack a great deal of being extremely wealthy, I think that I would rather do without this stock than have my Father or myself go through two or three years annoyance and bother over it.

If all contests of this will can be avoided and the consent obtained of all legal heirs to the distribution of this estate in accordance with the will, I am willing to sell this stock and distribute the proceeds as follows: $10,000.00 each to Claud Halsell's two brothers, Roswell and Milton Halsell; $5,000.00 each to Oscar Halsell, Harry Halsell and Forrest Halsell, which would raise the amount going to them from Aunt Ann's estate to the same amount as Claud's two brothers would receive; $5,000.00 to Thusa Reed; $2,500.00 to Katie Reed; $2,500.00 to Mrs. Regan.

As I have stated, I am making this offer in an effort to stop all suits and worries and this offer is made subject, in addition to avoiding all contests on the will, to the withdrawal by Claud Halsell of his suit in California against my Father. If my Father is going to be annoyed by a lawsuit in California, I would just as soon fight a lawsuit in Texas also.

I am not suggesting this proposed settlement through any feeling of criticism of Aunt Ann as to the distribution she made of her estate, nor as a recognition or an admission of the righteousness of any claim or claims now being urged, or that may be urged, but purely as a matter of trying to save a family from being torn to pieces and save annoyance to my Father, myself and the beneficiaries of this estate.

Soon after writing the second letter to Aunt Ella, Ewing and family went to Hotel Virginia where his father and wife were staying in Long Beach, California. He had three reasons for going: first, his father was in a state about the lawsuit and was threatening to countersue Claud and Ed (he thought the latter was behind the whole movement against him); second, he was convinced his cousins, Oscar and Furd, and Judge Young could handle the complaining beneficiaries in Texas better than he; and third, he had to convince his father to accept the compromise he had suggested in his second letter to Aunt Ella. When he arrived in California he learned that Thusa Reed and Kate Reed, two relatives, and a Mrs. Regan, a nurse and companion, had been with Aunt Ann for several years and had nursed her around the clock for her last ten weeks, were dissatisfied because of oral commitments they claimed Mrs. Waggoner had made to them.[32]

In California he found out indirectly that Aunt Ella was agreeable to dropping her claim to the 200 bank shares. This left him free to concentrate on the lawsuit. He had to calm his father, but it took a lot of persuasion to get him to agree to the compromise he had suggested to Aunt Ella. W. E. finally agreed to a modified version of Ewing's proposal.[33] It was:

Canty, Hanger and McMahan, attorneys' fees	$ 1,000
Milton Halsell	10,000
Roswell Halsell	10,000
Oscar, Harry and Forrest $5,000 each	15,000
Thusa Reed	4,000
Kate Reed	2,500
Mrs. Regan	2,500
$1,000 each for six Whitehead children	6,000
$1,000 each for eight Walcott children	8,000
$1,000 for attorney fees in California	1,000
Total	$60,000

This took care of everybody with a claim except Ed and Claud. W. E. made it very clear that he would see them in hell before he would give either of them a cent. News came that an extra $10,000 had been privately raised to pay Claud.[34] The records do not reveal from whom this money came. W. E. was not apprised of this, and negotiations moved along.

Specific provisions were set forth regarding the distribution of the $60,000 from the sale of 200 shares of bank stock.

W. E. specified that:

(1) An agreement would have to be signed by every beneficiary of the Ann Waggoner will, except himself. He would sign one later, (a) accepting the terms of the will, (b) acknowledging the legality of the gifts, (c) the withdrawal of the suit filed by Claud, (d) payment of all legal claims by Claud, and (e) acknowledgment of satisfaction of all claims set forth by Claud.

W. E. sent Oscar his power of attorney to secure the agreements and to pay off the claimant.[35] Oscar, Furd, and Judge Young had a meeting with the principals. They were all agreeable except Ed who was still left with nothing. But the threat of W. E. to have him included in a suit as a troublemaker and spreader of slanderous remarks caused him and Claud to require an agreement by W. E. that he would drop any thought of bringing suit against them. Ewing expended the last ounce of his endurance to get his father to sign such a document.[36]

In this manner, the case of Ann Waggoner's will was brought to an end. W. E. lost his bank stock. Claud Halsell lost his lawsuit, and everybody was pleased and happy except Ed. The estate was settled without a legal contest. But it all was not as simple as set forth herein. Hundreds of pages of letters were exchanged. The telegraph wires were kept hot for more than a month. Stacks of telegrams accumulated. For weeks it was like a cloak and dagger novel.

Ewing Halsell had a fondness for fishing. Not that he enjoyed catching fish himself, but he loved to raise fish for his family and friends to catch. For this purpose he needed a large, permanent lake. There were hundreds of small, playa lakes on the Spring Lake ranch, which were dry most of the time, but only two permanent lakes, Spring Lake, for which the ranch was named, and Soda Lake. These were fed by springs but the water level varied with wet and dry periods, and neither was adapted to supplying a constant source of fishing. However, he did have an ideal situation for constructing artificial lakes. Black Water draw entered the ranch at the northwest corner and went out almost at the exact southeast corner.[37] With its meandering, there were about 25 miles of the channel on the ranch. It was normally an intermittent stream, but with dams across it, enormous lakes could be created, supplied largely with surface flood waters. So he had a dam built across the draw about eight miles north of Littlefield. The dam was constructed so that the water would stand about six feet deep at the dam. The survey indicated the water would back up in the draw about two miles, but would stay within the main channel. A spillway, or locally called a run around, was provided at one end of the dam to insure the water would not flood adjoining lands. The government supplied the fish, and they did very well.[38]

The surveyor made a slight error, and when the rains came and the reservoir filled, the water did flood about thirty-two acres of land belonging to a Mr. Vinther, who had purchased the labor from Halsell Farms. There was a windmill and water trough on the east side of Vinther's land, and when the area was flooded the water stood about two feet deep at the windmill. The land was in grass and used for sheep. Not long after the dam was installed a flood caught 360 sheep between the lake and the east fence of Vinther's pasture and they drowned. This occurrence started a controversy between Mr. Vinther and Ewing Halsell which lasted for years. Vinther not only wanted damages for the sheep but for the land which would be periodically flooded.

Ewing at first offered what he considered a reasonable settlement; that is, pay for the sheep and buy the land subject to flood back from Vinther at thirty dollars an acre. Vinther wanted more.[39] Soon the two were at loggerheads, and the matter dragged on with threats and counter threats. W. F. Rowland, as Ewing's representative, was the middle man in the dispute.[40] Scores of letters were written back and forth about the matter over a period of seven years. On November 21, 1939, Ewing wrote to Rowland:

Dear Bill:

In regard to the damage to Vinther, I do not think anyone would say that he has been damaged. He has more grass on this place than he has ever had. Am not going to pay him any fancy price for his place or anything like what it has cost him, and I think the best thing for us to do is to have a tank man, Albert Taylor, come by and cut this down to where it will not overflow this place and get it off our minds. So if you can get in touch with Taylor, ask him to come by there and run his levels properly or take Jeff Williams' survey, if we have it, and run stakes for it.

Vinther realizes that he paid entirely too much for this place and is just trying to pay for it this way. I am not going to pay any damages for what has been done and we will try to prevent it recurring. You can tell him this. I will give him $30.00 an acre for this land that overflows if he wants it and can sell it to me.

What Vinther is trying to do is to make us take something off the $1,000.00 he owes us, but if he doesn't pay it, we will just start foreclosure and let him file his claim for damages. And I wish you would tell him this when you see him so that there will not be any misunderstanding about this matter. In fact, you can read him this letter if you think it is necessary. Don't want to make him mad unless you are sure that he is trying to hold us up.

Vinther was also stubborn, employed a lawyer, and informed Rowland he was going to court.[41] The year 1941 was unusually wet, with almost three times the average rainfall. On May 26 Ewing wrote to Rowland, instructing him to look over the dam situation and get some good witnesses. He was sure Vinther was going to sue.[42] He added, "I don't want to be forced to buy this place at the price he paid for it."

Rowland employed a Littlefield lawyer by the name of Martin, and Vinther secured a Mr. Bills, also from Littlefield.[43] The two lawyers got together with the officials of the Amherst bank and arrived at a compromise proposal: that Vinther sell Ewing the labor of land and drop the damage charges for $6,000.[44] This information was relayed by Rowland to Ewing, who promptly rejected the proposal, restating that the most he would pay would be $25 an acre plus $1,000 damages for the loss of the sheep. Then Vinther's lawyer said they would try the lawsuit in court in February, asking $10,000 for damages.[45] The lawsuit never came to court, and the records are vague as to what happened after that. However, nature was probably the deciding factor. The wet year of 1941 was followed by four average years, with no appreciable floods, and in 1946 a flash flood upstream of Black Water Draw took out the dam, removing the cause of the trouble in the first place.[46]

In 1942, Ewing Halsell sustained considerable loss when several cattle cars jumped the track. He sued the railroad in 1942, and his lawyers tangled with the railroad lawyers who were experts in tactical delays. This, in addition to clogged court dockets, stretched the case out for five years. In 1947, it was dropped with the condition that the railroad pay all court costs, which presumably included the fees for Ewing's lawyers.[47]

In 1955, Clyte Harlan, foreman at Bird Creek ranch, sent three trucks of steers from the Bird Creek feed lot to Oklahoma City. The trucks were owned by Ewing Halsell and driven by three of his cowboys, Sam Wilsey, John Bennett, and Arthur Inman. They traveled on the Oklahoma Turnpike between Tulsa and Oklahoma City.[48]

On the way, Sam Wilsey had some trouble with his tail-lights and stopped on the side of the road to work on them. Arthur, who was following Sam, realized the difficulty, and pulled up behind Sam's truck. The two of them repaired the tail-lights. Then, as was their custom, looked up and down the road before moving into the right-hand traffic lane. Sam made it without incident, but Arthur did not quite make it. Three cars, drag racing, came roaring up from behind at great speed, one attempting to pass another. The front car swerved just enough to clip the corner of the cattle truck, doing little damage to the truck but sending the car out of control. The three cars piled up, killing two of the drivers and seriously injuring the third one. The truck driver was not injured.

Ewing Halsell was faced with a half-million dollar lawsuit. The trucks were insured by the Maryland Casualty Company. The company hired a firm of Tulsa lawyers, which with the company's regular lawyers, assisted by Halsell's lawyer from Vinita, R. L. Wheatly, defended Mr. Halsell. The trial was at Sapulpa, Creek County, Oklahoma. This particular county had a bad reputation for damage suits, with juries being oriented in favor of the claimants. The defense team presented an excellent case with evidence and legal opinions. When the lawyers had finished and the judge was giving instructions to the jury, one juror stood up and asked one question, ''Was this an insurance case?'' The judge did not answer, but the question indicated clearly what was in the minds of the jurors, and the size of the battery of lawyers for the defense probably left little doubt in their minds.

The jury retired for a very short time and returned. The verdict was for the claimants for the full amount. Ewing Halsell's lawyer held that the question asked by the juror was ample grounds for a mistrial. However, since a second trial would have to be held in the same court, it was decided by the defense that another trial would be useless.[49]

The trial had taken a week and Ewing Halsell, assisted by Helen Campbell, had been present at every moment the court was in session. When it was over, they were anxious to get home but paused to talk to the three truck drivers who had also been in constant attendance. Three of the lady members of the jury came to them and explained to the cowboys that the jury did not think they were in any way responsible for the accident but that the widows and their children needed the money. The insurance company paid off but severed all future relations with Ewing Halsell.[50]

All in all, the Halsells, father and son, whose many and various operations spanned a century, had amazingly few lawsuits. Other than routine legal procedures for regaining titles due to default of payments, they spent very little time in courthouses. Their good fortune in this respect was due in large measure to their foresight and perception in conducting their business affairs. They were cautious in their commitments and contracts. Believing in the old adage "that an ounce of caution is worth a pound of cure," they contemplated all eventualities and left few loose ends which might later become bones of contention. Their record in avoiding lawsuits was no doubt a factor in W. E.'s becoming so agitated and worried when confronted so late in life with Claud Halsell's lawsuit. Even this was settled, out of court, by Ewing Halsell's ability to negotiate and compromise.

Horses   25

Both W. E. and Ewing Halsell appreciated horseflesh, but in different ways. To W. E. the horse had an all-enveloping connotation. It was the means of travel, transportation, power, and economic and social status. He judged his fellowman more by the kind of horse he rode, or drove, than by the type of house he lived in. To Ewing, the horse had more of a utilitarian significance. He admired the conformation of a horse in the same manner he did that of a bull or a cow, but his estimation of the horse did not extend beyond the effectiveness of the animal in handling cattle. Some were more alert, quicker in action, and more intelligent in judgment than others. These he cherished and rewarded more than the average or sub-average animals, just as he did the people who worked for him. To him, the horse was a necessary adjunct for carrying on his business and was never a social status factor.

These different attitudes were due in large measure to the roles which horses played during the periods when each of the two men lived. During W. E.'s youth and early manhood, the horse was the most indispensable creature for the man who lived off the soil, whether he tilled it or utilized the grass which grew on its surface. The horse was the only means of getting from here to there other than on foot. He carried or pulled the loads, generated power where water or steam was not available, and without him the cattle industry could never have developed beyond the herding on foot stage. Man's utter dependence on the horse left a lasting impression on W. E. As he became more and more affluent, the horse was not only a beast of burden, and essential for handling cattle, but became to him and his generation a symbol of status. A successful cattleman needed fine horses to pull his elegant carriages and to carry his magnificent saddle. Good-looking, well-proportioned horse-flesh represented that intangible status that a graceful, expensive yacht, or a costly automobile or jet plane, does today.

Mrs. Eva Halsell McCluskey, in 1973, recalled that her father ''liked horses; plow horses, cow horses, carriage horses, polo horses, and racehorses. He always had a few close at hand.''[1] His special horses were always of sufficient importance to be mentioned in the local newspapers:

October 18, 1888. W. E. Halsell bought the Dustin span of blacks from Southwest City.[2]

September 27, 1898. W. E. Halsell bought two high stepping, driving horses.[3]

May 24, 1906, L. P. Isbell arrived with a $200 buggy horse for Mrs. W. E. Halsell.[4]

May 18, 1907. W. E. Halsell bought team of matched black horses in Kansas City, ''Finest team in Kansas City,'' just arrived.[5]

The newspapers also took note of W. E.'s blooded horses:

March 31, 1887. W. E. Halsell traded for good looking stallion. One he had on ranch died recently.[6]

September 28, 1893. W. E. Halsell's horse, McKinney, rode to death in a race at the Fair [in Vinita]. The jockey rode horse over a seven wire fence.[7]

May 28, 1896. W. E. Halsell received a carload of blooded stallions.[8]

September 30, 1897. W. E. Halsell is the possessor of what, without doubt, is the finest string of thoroughbred race horses ever brought to the Indian Territory. Six of the finest of them are now at the fair ground in this city in the hands of Dave Duty, the well known horse trainer. Duty is too experienced a horse man to boast or talk a great deal about stock that

he is handling, but it's evident from the care he is giving these horses that he knows he has a prize.

The first horse shown the reporter for THE CHIEFTAIN was Bonny Dundee, a splendid four year old red sorrel stallion, sixteen hands high, weighing eleven hundred pounds. Dundee is a mile horse and looks like a greyhound.

Murondo, a blooded bay with a single stocking leg, was the next animal shown. He is also a mile horse, four years old and weighing nearly eleven hundred pounds; a noble animal. Then came Oelio, a three year old coal black with a blaze face, fifteen hands high and weighing about nine hundred pounds. Oelio is also a thoroughbred and runs three quarters of a mile, and is as pretty as a bird. We then went over to another stable and looked at a horse called Polkadot, another red sorrel fifteen hands high and three years old. This horse shows that he is being handled with more than usual care, and when Duty was asked about the horse's record he looked knowingly and whistled a snatch of a tune as though he didn't want to tell. Polkadot runs a mile and a quarter and looks like he might go a good deal farther than that. Then a fine little two year old sorrel weighing 700 pounds was brought out. This horse is being trained for mile heats and is a good one. Another seven year old bay gelding, a mile horse that has every appearance of being fast was shown.

In addition to these six thoroughbred horses, Mr. Halsell has recently purchased twenty thoroughbred mares and last week shipped them from St. Louis. They will be sent to his stock ranch on Bird Creek.[9]

January 25, 1900. W. E. Halsell is wintering a lot of his thoroughbred colts in Vinita.[10]

June 26, 1902. W. E. Halsell shipped race horse by express to Zack Mulhall, Frisco livestock agent at Saint Louis last week.[11]

His fascination for fine horses prompted W. E., who seldom ever wrote a letter about anything, to write the following to the local newspaper:

Nantasket, Mass., August 21, 1903
Daily Chieftain, Vinita, I.T.

Dear Sirs:

Am sending you in the mail today a copy of the *Boston Herald* in which you will see an account of lowering the world's record for trotting by Lou Dillon. I had the pleasure of seeing this record made and it was the finest race I ever saw in my life—a wonderful race, wonderfully well run. The weather here is quite perfect and we are enjoying it very much. We receive the *Chieftain* regularly and it is a welcome visitor.

Very truly,
W. E. Halsell

W. E. took the initiative in organizing the local Chapter 176 of the national organization of the American Horse Trainers Association.[12] This gave him connections with other horse fanciers throughout the country, allowing him to keep abreast of the expanding business of horse racing. Also, the inauguration of the local chapter marked the beginning of an economic and social aristocracy in Vinita. The old adage, "horse racing is the sport of kings," had a measure of application. Racehorse trainers have never been a basic necessity in the cattle business. Racehorses and trainers constituted a barometer which testified to the success of men who had made fortunes in the ranching industry and could afford an expensive hobby. In more recent years, oil beneath the land sometimes augmented the grass on the surface, and it hastened the creation of fortunes sufficient to afford the "sport of kings." W. E. Halsell was well on his way towards becoming a racehorse raiser and operator when his health and domestic problems caused him to taper off and utilize his blooded mares and stallions to upgrade the working horses on the Halsell ranches.

No records exist as to how W. E. and his brother, Glenn, started their remuda of cow horses. Probably their original complement came from the horse surplus of Dan Waggoner.[13] Dan's generation collected its cow horses from wherever it could find them. Some came from the states, others were of Spanish origin from Mexico, and some were the mustangs running wild on the unsettled prairies to the west. So great was the demand for horses when the cattle industry spread up the Great Plains to Canada in the 1870's and 1880's that a new type of frontiersman, called the mustanger, appeared to catch and market the mustangs. However, the first generation of captured mustangs seldom made usable plow or cow horses. The offspring of mustang mares when bred to domesticated stallions made good cow horses. Horse ranches, started in this way, helped to supply the increasing demand. By the time W. E. and Glenn Halsell located on the Cimarron River west of Tulsa in the late 1870's, their horses were no doubt a mixture whose antecedents had come from the States, from Mexico, and from the mustangs. This was pretty much the type of cow horses W. E. set about upgrading with the "carload of blooded stallions" and the "twenty blooded mares." This upgrading was continued by Ewing after 1920, by purchasing blooded mares from the Waggoner ranch and stallions from the King ranch.

It is significant that nowhere in the file of the Vinita newspapers or the Halsell records is any mention made of W. E. buying or owning an automobile. When questioned about this, Mrs. Eva Halsell McCluskey said that her father purchased the first car ever owned in Vinita, and that as cars improved he bought better ones and always the best available.[14] It is obvious that as long as W. E. lived in Vinita, carriages and matched horses were the status symbol and not Packards or Cadillacs.

Ewing Halsell grew up during the horse period and accepted it. He liked horses for the sake of horses, but there is no evidence that he followed his father's regard for them as a status symbol. Probably there were several reasons for his attitude. Because his father was a successful cattleman from Ewing's earliest memory and because he was naturally a modest person, he felt no need to seek a symbol. More important, perhaps, his active career coincided with the development of the mechanization of farming and ranching. With the advent of the automobile, the truck, and the tractor, the role of the horse declined. To the last day of his long life, Ewing was a man who adapted quickly to change.

The number of horses needed for a constant number of cattle declined with mechanization. The pickup and jeep replaced much pasture riding, and the truck replaced trail driving and wagon freighting. Ewing tailored the remudas strictly for cow work—gathering, holding at the roundup, roping, and cutting. Until recent years, draft horses were used for pulling the chuck wagon and plowing garden plots at the various headquarters and camps. He never participated in horse shows or rodeos. On rare occasions he permitted a few of his cowboys to ride ranch horses in the parade at county fairs but seldom permitted them to enter races or rodeo contests, wanting to take no chances of getting a good cow pony injured.

Ewing's only connection with horse racing was as an occasional onlooker. Being a gambler at heart, he did love to bet on the horses, but always in a cautious manner, often hedging his bets.[15] In his later years he made use of bookies, but never without carefully studying the forms and records of the horses participating.

Dr. Merton Minter, the family physician in San Antonio, tells this story:

Mr. Halsell loved to bet. He and Sid Katz used to bet on horse races. One day Sid said, "Mr. Halsell which horse are you going to bet on tomorrow?" Ewing replied, "I am not going to tell you. You want to cash in on my knowledge. I pay forty cents a week for the forms and put in several hours figuring out the dope with Miss Campbell's help, and all you do is to call up and ask which horses I am going to bet on. You win just as much as I do. You buy your own racing forms and do your own figuring." Sid said they used the same bookie. After he left he called the bookie and told him, "I want to bet five dollars each on the same two horses Mr. Halsell bets on." Both won. That evening Sid saw the Halsells at dinner. Mr. Halsell said, "Sid, did you bet today?" Sid replied, "Yes, I bet on two horses." "Which ones? How did they come out?" "They both won." "You must have bet on the same ones I bet on." Sid gave their names. Mr. Halsell said, "I don't see how anybody who does not know any more about horses than you do could possibly pick those horses!" Sid replied, "Well, I just figured it out." Mr. Halsell said, "If you are that good, I won't mind helping you. Maybe we had better work together."[16]

Dr. Minter had another story about Ewing's proclivity for betting on most any sport event about to take place. This one occurred during the football season when the horses were not running:

I knew the Halsells for fifteen years. All of them were my patients. I dropped by their apartment nearly every day. All three were people who loved life. I never had patients I enjoyed more. Mr. Ewing used to bet on football games, always on the University of Texas. After Royal went there the team nearly always won. Mr. Ewing wanted to bet on points. So I gave points, and won by one point. He paid. Next week it happened again, and I won by one point. The third week, by some odd coincidence, I did it again. He paid off and said, "Next week, you need not come by, I will just send you the money."

After Ewing Halsell took over the management of the Spring Lake ranch, owned by the Halsell Cattle Company, which he ran in conjunction with his own ranches, horse breeding was concentrated there for replacements for all the ranches and with a few to sell. In 1940, while the main office was still in Vinita, he wrote George Franklin at the Big Creek ranch:

Go over your saddle horses and see what you think we have to fit the Army needs. I think some of the Frank Little horses would be what they would want. I don't want to sell any of the Mashed O horses which we think will make good cow horses, but would sell the horse named Sock, and maybe two or three others. We can bring plenty of horses from Spring Lake to take care of all our needs.[17]

It is evident in this letter that Ewing considered the Mashed O horses superior to some he had obtained in a horse deal with Frank Little. Five years later, 1945, Ewing, in a letter to George Franklin, again demonstrated his horse sense:

I don't think we have any horses there that are good enough to rope on with possible exception of Old Ginger. If some good roper wants to use him, it might help sell him. If he is good enough to rope on, he ought to bring two hundred dollars.[18]

When Helen Campbell, who was also a lover of horses, was asked about Ewing Halsell's favorite horses, she wrote:

He had a favorite cutting horse at each ranch. At Big Creek it was Gotch. He had been trained by George Franklin, a superb trainer of cow horses. Gotch was a big bay and one of the smartest horses I ever saw. He seemed to know just what an old cow was thinking.

Rex was a coal black horse Mr. Halsell rode at the Spring Lake ranch. He was deathly afraid of a little Shetland pony named Santa Claus, owned by the son of one of the hands on the ranch. When Santa Claus would come near him, Rex would try to get away from him. If that were not possible, Rex would just stand and tremble. No one could ever explain the reason for Rex's behavior. Other than that, he was a fine cow horse and Mr. Halsell was very fond of him.

After the demise of Gotch, Buddy was Mr. Halsell's favorite horse at Big Creek. He was out of Richard, a famous King Ranch stud, and was a sorrel sixteen and a half hands high. This made it difficult for Mr. Halsell to mount him, but once he was on him, they made a working team that was hard to beat.

In later years Mr. Halsell had his favorite horse hauled in a trailer to the herd instead of riding him. The hand at Spring Lake who was assigned this chore was George Turner, a very witty cowboy. On one occasion Mr. Halsell brought George a new leather jacket when he returned from California. George looked at it, and said, "Mr. Halsell, I will have to have this jacket altered. One of my arms is longer than the other. You see it got that way while dragging your old horse to so many roundups."

There is the story of Mazie, a mare, which was a good cutting horse, but unpredictable. One time when Mr. Halsell mounted her, for no discernible reason, she started pitching and threw him off. Mr. Halsell was in his late 70's, and the cowboys went running, expecting to find him badly injured. He got up on his own, and one asked, "Are you hurt?" He replied, "No. I can think better than I did before."

Once when holding a roundup at the Big Creek ranch, Doc Vann, the colored cowboy, was helping hold the herd on a young horse. When Mr. Halsell cut a contrary cow out of the herd, Doc had trouble getting her to the cut. Mr. Halsell went out to help him. When the

cow was taken care of, Mr. Halsell asked Doc about the horse he was riding. Doc said, "Mr. Halsell, if this pony lives to be 30 years old, he still won't know what business you are in."

Mr. Halsell had a deep affection for his favorite horses and never sold one. When they were too old to work, he had them put in the Brush pasture where they grazed and took their ease and were allowed to die in peace.[19]

The high regard for horses on the part of men outlaws, and men within the law, is revealed back in the days of the early 1890's when the Daltons were active.[20] It was one of those occasions when the Daltons and the United States marshals had a near confrontation at the Bird Creek headquarters. The Daltons were at the corral and the marshals were near the cook house. Bob Lynch came in from riding the pasture on Old Chili. The horse was already a legend, well-known to the Daltons and the marshals. Bob rode into "no man's land" before he was aware of the confrontation. When he realized his precarious position, he yelled at the top of his voice, "Don't shoot! You will kill Old Chili!" It worked. Not a shot was fired and he rode out of danger unmolested. Later one of the Daltons told Bob, likely with tongue in cheek, that Old Chili had saved him; that had he been there without Old Chili they probably would have let go at the marshals without regard to Bob's situation, but they did not want to endanger Old Chili.

Clyte Harlan's comment on the Bird Creek horses is terse and graphic:

We have had some good horses on our ranches. They knew more about working cattle than we did. All we had to do was to show them what we wanted done, and they did the rest. Mr. Halsell's horse could be looking at anything, but when Mr. Halsell showed him the steer he wanted, the horse would go after him. Regardless of what the steer did, the horse never took his eye off of him. He was always quicker than the steer and the steer never had a chance. That was Buddy and he came from Spring Lake.[21]

Clyte told about Pigeon, which he had bought for the Halsells from the Robertson ranch for $40.[22] Pigeon was young and not an outstanding looking horse. He developed into a wonderful cutting horse. His disposition was not too good. He had kicked his former owner, which was the reason the horse had been sold. The Bird Creek cowboys respected Pigeon's temperament, stayed clear of his heels, and never had any trouble. In time, Pigeon mellowed and was quite companionable.

J. CISNEROS

When it came to working cattle, he was one of the best. Mr. Halsell rode him often and thought highly of him. He was not showy, but he did what he had to do, using his head with a lot of judgment. When the rider showed him the steer he wanted, Pigeon did it his own way. Regardless of how the steer turned or twisted, Pigeon without loss of motion or undue exertion, anticipated every move of the steer and, apparently without effort, got the steer out of the herd, one of the finest examples of "horse sense."

Buck Bloomfield also had an affinity with Pigeon which was reciprocated.[23] Once, when working cattle at Bird Creek, Buck was riding Pigeon. An old cow was nervous and kept trying to leave the herd. Clyte told Buck to rope the cow as she made a dash from the herd. Buck made a loop, and Pigeon bore down on the cow. Buck made his catch and had his end of the rope tied to the saddle horn. Pigeon, knowing what to do, stopped short and braced himself for the impact. It happened that Buck's saddle did not have a flank girth. When the cow hit the end of the rope the back of the saddle turned up throwing Buck over Pigeon's head. Pigeon did not move but held firm. The cow was thrown heels over head, but she recovered and got up before Buck did. She was on the prod, saw Buck on the ground on his hands and knees, and took a dead aim at him. Buck saw her coming but was too addled or did not have time to get up. So he started crawling back toward Pigeon, who was still standing rigid. Clyte was observing from a distance, watching Buck trying to outcrawl the foaming cow. He held his breath until he saw Buck was going to make it. What saved Buck was Pigeon who seemed to understand the situation. As the cow came nearer he backed his ears and showed his teeth. The cow took notice and veered off to one side. When Clyte saw Buck was out of danger he exploded with laughter at the sight of Buck's trying to outcrawl the cow. This scene was so vivid with Clyte that thirty years after it happened he could not tell about it without laughing until he had to wipe tears from his eyes. Both Buck and Clyte gave Pigeon credit for preventing Buck's getting horned and trampled.

Soon after this episode, Clyte and Buck wanted to enter Pigeon in the calf roping event at a rodeo in Tulsa.[24] It cost ten dollars to enter. They did not have ten dollars but did have an idea. Sometime before, someone had dumped an old car on the ranch near the highway. Buck proposed they sell the car. A man came along and bought it for ten dollars. So they went to town and entered the calf roping event.

When the time came Buck was the rider. The boys did not know the rules, and they assumed it was like roping at a roundup. When the calf emerged from the chute, Pigeon knew what to do. Buck made an easy catch and tied his calf. When the event was over Buck and Pigeon held the time record by several seconds, but they were disqualified because the judges said Buck flapped his chaps, whatever that meant. Anyway Clyte and Buck were told a rider was not supposed "to flap his chaps." They never did quite figure out just how one "flaps one's chaps."

Pigeon became a sort of living legend. He was hauled from Kansas to Texas and back again several times. Helen Campbell, like Buck, had a fondness for Pigeon and rode him often. Pigeon liked her and was always gentle and responsive with her. When he was too old to work, Ewing gave him to Helen. She retired him to her farm near Vinita where he was a beloved and privileged character as long as he lived. When he died, she said, it was like losing a member of the family.[25]

Clyte told how Ewing Halsell liked to ride.[26] When he was 84, he had Clyte saddle a horse. The animal was impatient and would not stand still. Clyte was uneasy and fearful of the outcome and suggested that they get a more stable horse. Ewing would not hear of it. Instead he said firmly, "Clyte, hold this horse." Thereupon, he mounted unassisted. Once in the saddle he was in control.

Doc Vann's favorite horse was Gotch, previously mentioned by Helen Campbell. Doc told of the following incident:

We were working cattle in the Osage Nation. There was a fellow there taking pictures. Mr. Halsell was riding Gotch. The picture man asked Mr. Halsell to cut a steer out of the herd. He did, and the steer tried to turn back to the herd, but Gotch said, "No, No," and I never saw a horse perform better. It was beautiful. The picture was later in the *Cattleman*, and no picture ever got in the *Cattleman* unless it was good.[27]

Paul Howe, a hermit-type bachelor, started working for the Halsells in 1936 and has been with them in one way or another for 38 years.[28] When asked about horses he said he had never had many good ones but had named a lot of the ordinary horses. He recalled Peaches, Geronimo, Coe, and Speck as being fairly good. He especially remembered the mean ones and always put "old" in front of the ones he did not like. There was Old Badger, Old Buck, who always had to pitch a little, Old Fox, Old Floxy, Old Browny, and Old Hawk.

Paul was a quiet, reserved stay-at-home who did the chores that no one else wanted to do. Never a broncbusting, swashbuckling, hell-for-leather cowboy, he stayed at Big Creek during the winter, fed cattle, broke the ice, plowed the garden, fixed the fence, and made repairs.[29] For caking the cattle in the pasture, he used a wagon and a team of mules, Punch and Judy. They were two of a kind, ornery, temperamental, and smart in a dumb sort of way. They were the bane of Paul's existence. He stayed mad at them all the time, and yet they were a sort of therapy for him, a challenge, somehow to be outwitted. They kept him going.

When Paul loaded the wagon with cake or bundles and started from the barn to the pasture the mules walked slow and stopped dead still at every pretext. If there was no pretext, they would stop anyway. Paul would whip, beat, and cuss, but they had been through all that before and paid little heed. He had to go through a gate to get into another pasture. This was always a battle. They pulled up just enough to leave the wagon in the gate. It took another battle to get the wagon through so he could shut the gate. Then he made a big circle while pitching the feed out on the grass. The mules did a little better on the circle because they knew it was about time to start back. When they headed back towards the barn, the mules wanted to run. They would stop at the gate. He opened the gate and the mules of their own accord went through but did not stop while he shut the gate. Instead, they took the bits in their mouths and started home on the run. He dropped the gate and took after the wagon on foot but never caught up. The mules swung into their accustomed place at the barn and with total innocence waited for him to come up, unhitch them, and take the harness off. When he arrived, out of breath, he wanted to kill them, but he had to settle for a good cussing, using every expletive in his vocabulary. When he had finished with them, he saddled a horse and rode back to shut the gate. He spent every waking moment that night thinking how he could outwit those mules. The next day, when they got back to the gate after distributing the feed, he set the brake on the wagon so tight that the hind wheels dragged and tied the reins up short. Opening the gate he yelled at the mules to go through. They did, dragging the hind wheels. He yelled "Whoa!," and they kept moving, but at a slow pace. This gave him time to shut the gate, run about a hundred yards, catch the back end of the wagon, climb in, untie the reins, undo the brake, and let them run back to the barn. This was the method Paul used the remainder of the winter.

A Ranching Saga

These mules knew when six o'clock came in the evening. Whatever they were doing, they would stop, balk, and refuse to budge. The only motion they would make was to start to the barn. When time came to eat they would jump the fence, if necessary, to get to the trough.[30] Paul would use cuss words to give vent to his feelings. Ewing and Helen went to the ranch occasionally to see about Paul and check on the condition of the cattle and would catch Paul unaware and hear him cussing the mules. Helen remonstrated with Paul one day for using so much profanity. Paul, one of the gentlest of men, replied in a soft, contrite voice, "I know, Miss Helen, I shouldn't do it, but [with rising accent] that's the only language those goddamn mules understand!"[31]

On one trip in late spring Ewing took along a bushel of potatoes. He had Paul cut the potatoes into quarters to plant in the garden behind the barn. In the afternoon he put Paul to planting the potatoes. Paul hitched Punch and Judy to a plow to make the furrows into which he would drop the potato quarters by hand and then cover with the plow. After Paul had been working sometime, Ewing sent Helen over to the garden to see how Paul was doing. When Helen arrived, Paul was so busy with his walking plow and talking to the mules he did not know she was there. Judy kept pulling off to the left side. Paul, holding the handles of the plow with both hands, with the reins around his shoulders, let go with his left hand and jerked Judy back, and with gritted teeth, growled, "Judy, if I had another mule, I would kill you, you old son-of-a-bitch!" Helen quietly returned to the house without Paul's knowing she had been there. Ewing was sitting on the front porch. He had not been feeling well that day. When Helen told him what she had seen and heard, he laughed as he had never laughed before. It made him feel better. It made his day.[32]

The stories of Paul and his mules were many. Punch and Judy have been dead for a long time, and Paul, now a beat-up broken old cowboy, tells the yarns about them with real feeling and nostalgia. Once he wanted nothing more than to kill them. Now he speaks of them with fondness and affection. He ends each story with "Those mules were sure smart."[33]

The methods of breaking horses to the saddle differed during Ewing's time from those used in W. E.'s day. In the earlier period, cow horses were not handled until they were two to three years old. They were wild and skittish. When time came to break them, they were rounded up, penned in a corral, roped, snubbed down, sad-

dled, and mounted by a professional broncbuster. When the snubber let go, the horse downed his head and went into bucking convulsions. He had just one purpose in mind—to get rid of the rider and the saddle. Horses bucked in different ways, each with his own style. Some pitched in a straight line. That was the easiest for the rider. Others pitched in circles. This was harder for the buster because it threw him more off balance, especially when the horse whirled and changed directions. The worst of all to stay on was the sun-fisher. This was a horse which jumped and twisted while in the air. There was an old saying on the ranches, "There never was a horse which could not be rode and never a puncher who could not be throwed." The ones thrown were usually riding sun-fishers.

The same horse would be ridden by the broncbuster on successive days until the horse was convinced he could not get rid of the man and the saddle. Each day his pitches were of shorter duration until finally he was considered saddle broke. It was essential that he be used regularly by the cowhands. Otherwise, if he were not ridden for a considerable period, it would have to be done over again.

Ewing Halsell, along with many of his contemporaries, changed the method of breaking horses.[34] It began when they were colts. All the hands participated in the process. The mares had been gentled. The colts were handled, rubbed, and taught not to be afraid of people. When weaned, they were accustomed to the halter, and later the bridle. By the time they were a year old, they would have saddles placed on their backs but were not ridden. When they were two, a man could slip into the saddle. Seldom did one try to pitch. It did not take long to teach the young horse to be rein-wise.

When Ewing purchased the Farias ranch, he took over the Mexican vaqueros with it, some of whom had been raised on the ranch. He learned that his method of breaking colts had long been used by the Mexicans, and the vaqueros were experts at it. Jean Holmes McDonald, Ewing's niece, grew up spending summer vacations on the different Halsell ranches. She became an avid and accomplished horsewoman. She says that of all the horses she has ever ridden, the Mexican-trained horses at Farias were the smoothest and easiest to ride.[35]

Newt Robison spent several years as a hand at Spring Lake during the transition from the old method of breaking horses to the new way. In response to our inquiry, he wrote in a recent letter how they did it in the late 1920's and early 1930's.

500

About the time I went to the Mashed O they got 100 wild mares from the Waggoner ranch. They had good stallions from the King ranch. Also they had a big jack and a Percheron stud. With these they raised mules and draft horses. There was a market for both because the tractor had not yet replaced horsepower on the farms.

The Waggoner mares were good ones but had not been gentled or broke. Their first crop of colts were as wild as their mothers. Another hand and I were put to breaking the two-year-old colts and doing what we could to tame the mothers. We were selected because of our ability to ride bucking horses. This is a gift one either has or doesn't. It is not something that one learns.

We had to use the old-fashioned methods in breaking the older ones. We would get ten or twelve in a corral, rope one, ear him down, put a hackamore or bridle on, and one of us would hold while the other put the saddle on. Sometimes with an unruly animal we would have to tie a hind foot up to the saddle. When all was ready one of us mounted and the other turned the horse loose. Then the pitching began. We did not have a rider to come along-side after ten seconds and lift us off like they do today in the rodeo. It was stay on, or hit the ground. We usually stayed on. After a horse has his pitch finished he wants to run. At this stage the man on the ground opened the gate, and away we would go for a big circle in the pasture. When the run was over the rider got the animal headed back towards the corral. When we got there the horse was usually in a lather and considerably chastened. On the next horse the other man did the riding. We alternated until we finished with that batch of horses.

Mr. Ewing was in process of putting in a new system of breaking horses. For the young colts he had us to catch and handle them and get them used to the halter, to lead, and to have light burdens on their backs.[36]

In a letter to George Franklin, December 27, 1940, Ewing Halsell said:

Don't forget to send the colts to the Wallen place for this man to handle. Want him to put a rope halter on them and lead them around for the time being.

He sent similar instructions over and over to his several foremen and straw bosses. He became adamant about having horses broke without going through the pitching stage.

Today, instead of horses carrying the men to work, the men carry them—in trailers pulled by pickups. A cattle working day on the average ranch now goes something like this: The ranch has been cross fenced in pastures, each of which accommodates about the right number of cattle to constitute a day's work for a crew. Usually, each pasture has access to a working corral. Just before daylight the hands arrive in pickups at the headquarters chuck house. Few, if any, live at the headquarters any more. They come from other houses located on the ranch, or from nearby towns, sometimes twenty to thirty miles away. The cook has breakfast for those who did not eat before leaving home. All of them play the coffee pot. At daybreak each goes to the barn, saddles a horse, and leads him to a trailer behind a pickup. Some ranches have trailers which carry several horses. The procession takes off to the corral of the pasture to be worked, which could be from five to twenty miles away. There the horses are unloaded and the men mount and gather around the foreman or straw boss. He explains and lays out the procedure for gathering the cattle in that particular pasture. By this time the sun is coming up, and the men scatter out as directed and proceed at a brisk walk or pace—never in a dead heat as portrayed in the movies. All is done quietly and smoothly. The men circle the perimeter of the pasture and start drifting all cattle towards the corral. About noon they converge driving the herd into the corral. Only rarely does any horse have to make a dash to intercept a nervous cow or calf trying to turn back. By this time the cook has arrived from the headquarters chuck house in a pickup equipped with containers for keeping food and coffee hot, or, in warm weather, with iced tea. The

meal consists of everything from soup to dessert. Even the biscuits are warm. The men eat with relish. For most of the horses the day's work is over.

The afternoon is devoted to working the cattle, most of it on foot. There are still two ways of processing the calves. One is the old-fashioned method of roping and dragging the calf to the place where the branding irons are heated. This necessitates a roping horse and cutting horse. If this method is used this horse has been resting all morning. Such horses are extremely rare and highly prized, and they seem to enjoy the work. The more modern method consists of putting the calves down a chute. At the end is an apparatus, called a branding table, which clamps the calf rigid and lays him on his side. By either method the same operation takes place, all in about two minutes. The calf is branded, dehorned, swabbed with horn paint, ears marked, and in case of the males, castrated and the scrotum swabbed with horn paint to stop bleeding and keep the screwworm flies away. The Halsell ranches in Oklahoma used the chute method. The two in Texas made use of the rope and drag.

A crew consists of from eight to twelve men depending on the number of cattle to be worked. When finished, the cattle are turned back into the pasture, the horses are placed in the trailers and carried back to headquarters. Here they are unsaddled and rubbed down if they need it. Most of them have not raised a sweat all day. In the lot there will be grain, forage, and water.[37]

Mechanization has greatly reduced the number of horses needed on a ranch. The same ranch which used 300 horses in W. E.'s time now can operate with about 30.[38] For the moment the great horse period in ranching lies in the past. But with the rapidly declining petroleum resources, the transportation modes of the future are in for a drastic change. There is a possibility that the horse may come into his own again as the backbone of the ranching industry. If so, the spirit of W. E. Halsell will be mighty pleased.

Benevolences **26**

W. E. Halsell and his son, Ewing, had one particular trait in common. Both were generous in their support of what they considered worthy persons or causes, but both wished their generosity to remain anonymous. A close friend characterized them in this manner: "What they did they did quietly, without drumbeating. Most people did not know about their philanthropic activities."[1]

In his heyday, W. E. was constantly helping on some nonsectarian, public project. He contributed to church building programs but did not participate in their promotion, with two exceptions: he, on his own, built little non-denominational churches when he founded Amherst and Earth. He did such things for Vinita as buying furniture for the courthouse and building an opera house for entertainment. The local newspapers repeatedly mentioned drives and individual undertakings. If it was a public solicitation, over which W. E. had no control, he would be listed at the top as the largest contributor. If it were something he had done alone, like buying turkey dinners for prisoners or books for the school library or paying off the mortgage on a church, the newspapers respected his demand for anonymity by saying it was done by a "wealthy patron," "a local citizen," or "an interested person." However, in a small town, the word got around, and soon everyone knew who the donor was.

The fact that W. E. never wanted credit for his many contributions was a bit out of character with his style of living. His physical appearance, his dress, his horses and carriages, and his home were tastefully flamboyant, but with his philanthropic activities he was sincerely modest. His bestowals were personal and individualistic. He did what he did of his own volition and not in conjunction with others.

Ewing was equally as modest and sought anonymity also, but he was more farsighted and encompassing in his benevolences. Many of the charitable things Ewing did were in cooperation with other people. He could, and did, often work as a member of a team. It might be with his wife, his sisters, with Helen Campbell, or with a committee or a commission. An example of the latter was the Will Rogers Memorial Commission of which he was a very important member for thirty years.

Will Rogers, a beloved national figure and an international celebrity, crashed on Point Barrow, Alaska, August 15, 1935, while flying with Wiley Post. Fourteen days later, August 29, Ewing, who was at the Miramar Hotel, Santa Monica, California, received the following telegram from J. M. Milam in Chelsea, Oklahoma:

Wiring you at the suggestion of Aunt Sally [Will's sister] who concurs in this request. The Rogers County Committee on the Will Rogers Memorial with headquarters at Claremore requests that you see Mrs. Rogers earnestly and sincerely asking that they be remembered in the disposition of Will's personal effects and articles from his collection. They feel sure a Memorial in the form of a Museum costing two million dollars will be erected at Claremore. Yesterday our Committee met with Governor Marland who [had] secured the cooperation of Amon Carter of Fort Worth, and we hope to get this movement consolidated under one organization. The plans are to purchase the twenty acres overlooking Claremore that Will bought some years ago on which he expected to make his home in later years. Dr. Bushyhead, George Davis and Bill Sunday are cooperating with Governor Marland.

This was the beginning of the memorial movement. The following day, Mr. Milam wrote Ewing Halsell a lengthy letter in which he enlarged on the overall plan:

Yesterday morning, as I have for several days, I was out to see Aunt Sally and in talking

this over she stated that Will felt closer to you, Irwin Cobb, Ed Borine and Mr. Vail, as you had each been cowboys and fitted into Will's idea of a real, free, American life, and probably next was Amon Carter. Anyway, following Aunt Sally's suggestion we wired you as outlined.

This morning Mr. Carter talked with Dr. Bushyhead and we feel that all efforts will be consolidated under one general committee, and that a monument will be erected on the Capitol grounds at Oklahoma City, the purchase of his ranch in California, his ranch in Oklahoma, and a memorial at Claremore in the form of a Museum, costing probably two million dollars.

About a year ago Mrs. Lawson together with Miss Ada Robinson, who designed the Boston Avenue Church and other buildings in Tulsa, drove to Chelsea to see Aunt Sally and asked her cooperation in securing Will's permission to build a memorial for him at that time. This was to have been in the form of a Museum to house mainly Indian Relics and Relics of the old Indian Territory, together with a small library covering Indian books, records and anything pertaining to the early days of this country. And, according to Aunt Sally there was to be seven columns on which there would be a light, and this was to burn continuously and was representative of the seven clans of the Cherokees. Aunt Sally approved of the sketch and the proposition generally, except she with Will objected to a Memorial at that time. It never went farther, but Aunt Sally suggests that that would be very acceptable. And too, the local committee thought that this should be located on the twenty acres that Will purchased a few years ago. This is just North of the Oklahoma Military Academy overlooking Claremore. They of course have other things in mind regarding the ranch that can be worked out.

Again thanking you and asking that you convey to Mrs. Rogers, if you see her again, our most sincere wishes.[2]

The plan did not work out just as it was envisioned.[3] Mrs. Rogers did give the land, a fraction over twenty-one acres. The Oklahoma promoters induced Congress to pass a $500,000 appropriation for a Memorial at Claremore, but President Franklin D. Roosevelt vetoed it. He said that if it had been for a children's hospital instead of a museum he would have signed it. This action made the state legislature so mad that it passed a $200,000 bill which was promptly signed by Governor Marland. The bill provided that the implementing of the project would be under a committee of fifteen, including Ewing Halsell.[4] For the selection of architects, a nationwide contest was inaugurated.[5] The results were that a hundred or more designs were submitted. Some of them were weird, horrible, and grotesque, like Egyptian pyramids and western ranch house affairs with lots of windows and porches. John Duncan Forsythe, architect and protégé of Governor Marland, and Robert West came up with the design accepted.

The committee went ahead with the building without knowing what Mrs. Rogers was going to do. Several other groups over the nation seemed to have a similar idea and were after her for Will's paraphernalia. She was noncommittal.

The committee did have two or three people trying to act as go-betweens with the Rogers family, but they were getting nowhere. Ewing Halsell, in deference to the family, had been reluctant to intercede. The building was almost finished, but with nothing to go in it. The Commission, in the summer of 1938, pleaded with Ewing Halsell to go to Beverly Hills and use his personal influence with Betty Rogers. He agreed to go. He found that Betty, though uncommitted, was most interested in the Claremore project. She wanted to know what assurance there was concerning the permanent upkeep of the Memorial. Who would be in charge of the installations? Who would direct the policies, the operation, and the maintenance? These were the items with which she was concerned before deciding where to commit Will Rogers' personal effects. She did not intend to let them go until her conditions were complied with beyond a reasonable doubt.

Ewing must have laid to rest all of her reservations. It so happened that living in Chelsea was a niece of Will's, Paula McSpadden Love, daughter of Will's sister, Sallie McSpadden. She was a special favorite of both Will and Betty Rogers. Paula was married to Robert W. Love, also highly regarded by the Rogers. There is little doubt that the Loves, unbeknown and unsuspected by them, were discussed at length by Betty Rogers and Ewing Halsell.[6]

As to what happened next was revealed in a recent interview with Bob Love:

We were vaguely aware that the Commission was looking for a director. It never occurred to us that we might be involved. Neither of us knew anything about museums or memorials. One night we had a call from Morton Harrison. He wanted to know if we would meet with a committee of the Commission. We were at a loss as to a reason for their wanting to see us, but we agreed. We met and the committee asked if we would be interested in taking charge of the Memorial. We asked for time to consider it. I was then the area architect for the W.P.A. and had charge of the projects in thirteen counties. Paula was teaching school in Chelsea, and we were doing pretty well. We realized our complete lack of knowledge and training required to operate a memorial museum. Like everyone else around Claremore we had been interested in the construction progress of the building and frequently drove by to see how it was getting along. We asked for time to consider the offer, and were on the verge of turning it down when Mr. Harrison called up and asked what we decided. We began to explain our decision, and he interrupted and in a businesslike fashion came right to the point: ''I will just give it to you in a nut shell. We are not going to get any of the Rogers' exhibits from California unless Mrs. Rogers knows who is going to run the Memorial. She has intimated that Paula and Bob Love would be a good team and would be most acceptable to her. That's the reason we are urging you to take the job with Bob as manager and Paula as curator.''

We accepted on the spot. Mrs. Rogers called us up, and we went to Beverly Hills and arranged to get a considerable amount of memorabilia. I told Paula that it would just be a summer operation, and we would be there only three months of the year, and that for the other nine months we would have to find other jobs to keep going. That was thirty-six years ago in the summer of 1938. We have not been off the job a day since.[7]

So the understanding Ewing Halsell had with Betty Rogers in 1938 had lasting effects. However, that occasion was just the beginning of a long series of crises for which solutions were worked out by Ewing and Betty. The Memorial was opened November 4, 1938, in a modest way with objects and documents displayed in a temporary manner. The bigger than life bronze statue of Will Rogers, which dominates the foyer, had been completed and put in place in time for the dedication.

In 1939, the Legislature replaced the committee of fifteen with a commission of seven.[8] Ewing Halsell was one of the persons appointed to the Commission.* The most important concern for the Commission was to build a tomb and arrange, if possible, to bring Will's body from California to be placed in it. Just as the Commission had done with the museum building, it proceeded with plans for the tomb without any commitment from the Rogers family that the body would be made available. This proved to be a sticky problem. The Commission had been after Betty from the beginning, but she could not bring herself to talk about it. At the time there was no crypt or tomb in or connected with the memorial building. The matter was being complicated by the aggressive efforts of Forest Lawn Cemetery

*Other members were: N. G. Henthorne, Tulsa; Lew Wentz, Ponca City; W. M. Harrison, Oklahoma City; Dr. J. C. Bushyhead, Claremore; W. E. Sunday, Claremore; Bill Rogers (Will Rogers' son), Beverly Hills.

in Glendale to keep the body there. It was still in a holding crypt in the Wee Kirk of the Heather Church in Forest Lawn. A movement was on in California to build a magnificent tomb and make it a feature of the cemetery. Even the Governor of California had interceded.[9]

After the dedication of the Memorial, Betty Rogers made periodic visits to Claremore and stayed with the Loves. In a year or two she got to where she could talk with Paula and Bob about a permanent repository for Will's body. The only other person she would discuss it with was Ewing Halsell. Still no definite decision was made. She finally brought herself to look at the plan which the architect had prepared. It was a tomb which projected back into a hillside, patterned after the Washington tomb at Mount Vernon. Betty did not like it. So the architect tried again. She did not approve of that either. When the third plan was ready, Betty was in Beverly Hills. A committee of three from the Commission, including Ewing, went there to show the concept and try to get a commitment. Realizing how delicate the negotiations were, the other two members of the Committee insisted again on making Ewing the liaison, and he went alone to visit with Betty and show the plan. She liked it and the way was cleared for the other two members of the Committee to meet with her.[10]

Next was the matter of financing. Originally, Ewing Halsell and Lew Wentz wanted to share the costs. But several others wanted in on it.[11] In the end, $42,000 was raised from five individuals.* How the money was to be handled became an issue with Betty. If it were turned over to the State to be dispensed it would go through the State Treasurer, making it technically a State installation. Betty contended that Will was so dedicated to free enterprise that he, if alive, would never have consented to having the government provide his grave. So it took some special arrangements to handle the funds in a way satisfactory to Betty.[12]

Considerable time was consumed in constructing the tomb because of the scarcity of certain building materials and the rationing during World War II. The tomb was located just south of the Memorial building and was so constructed that it would accommodate other members of the family. After it was finished, some time

*The donors were Lew Wentz, Ewing Halsell, John Mabee, Frank Phillips, and Waite Phillips.

elapsed before the body was moved.* In the meanwhile, the Forest Lawn people were, according to Bob Love, resorting to "dirty tricks." They had someone in Claremore who sent, from time to time, derogatory reports about the treatment of the tomb and memorial: people were writing on the walls, the roof was leaking, peanut hulls were scattered all around, and there was mold on the walls. Such rumors kept Betty worried and caused her to delay giving her permission to move the body. She would call Ewing and ask him to investigate. He made several trips to Claremore for personal inspections. Each time he called, or wrote, that there was absolutely no basis for the derogatory allegations about the Memorial and the tomb.[13]

The restrictions imposed by World War II delayed moving Will Rogers' body. Transportation of all kinds, rail, air, overland, was practically stopped except for war purposes. Finally, Jesse Jones of Houston, who was high in the echelons of power in Washington, arranged to send his private railroad car to Los Angeles to bring the body and family to Claremore in May 1944. Ewing Halsell was the only person outside the family whom Betty Rogers insisted accompany the body.[15] Ewing was the arranger and expediter. The body was in an express car placed adjacent to the private car.

When the funeral cortège reached Claremore, the arrival was without previous announcement or fanfare. The two coaches were sidetracked. Ewing had called Helen Campbell from Los Angeles and told her how many automobiles would be needed to take the family to the Memorial. The only warning which the townspeople in Claremore had of the event was when several cars and a hearse unobtrusively converged at the depot. The little procession made its way to the Memorial, entered, and the gates were locked.

*During this period, after the tomb was finished and before the body was transferred, an amusing incident occurred in Claremore. Bob Love was in military service in the South Pacific in World War II. Paula, who was in charge of the Memorial, had a dinner party. The Ewing Halsells came from Vinita, driven by their black chauffeur, Clarence. A few guests, including Governor Kerr, came. The house was small, and the dining area was part of the living room. Mrs. Halsell told Paula that Clarence could help with the serving, something at which he was rather good. Paula told him he should always serve the Governor first. Then she was amazed that when Clarence brought the rolls and the desserts, he always served Mr. Halsell first. Then it dawned on her that to Clarence Mr. Halsell was "the governor."[14]

A Ranching Saga

The funeral service was private. Only relatives and close friends had been invited. The coffin was placed in front of the large, bronze statue of Will in the foyer. Betty's family were Christian Scientists. Will had once said that he had been born and raised a Methodist, but that he himself belonged to the big church, the one which embraced all mankind. The service was conducted by a Christian Science reader, a lady who lived in Claremore. When she had finished, the coffin was carried to the tomb and placed in the crypt and sealed. At last Will Rogers had come home to Claremore as he had long intended to do. He was now within a short ride, horseback, of the spot where he was born.[16]

In June 1944, Betty Blake Rogers passed away. Her body was brought back to Claremore in November 1944, and, after a simple Christian Science ceremony, was placed in the Will Rogers Memorial tomb beside her illustrious husband.[17]

The Ewing Halsell family's close relations with the Rogers' family had continued as long as the principals lived, with much visiting back and forth. Next to Betty, Paula was the one who was nearest and dearest to Ewing and Lucile Halsell. Paula was a gentle, lovely, sensitive, outgoing, compassionate person, and they could not do all that they really wished to do for her. In spite of all they could do, they could never repay the love, affection, and encouragement which emanated from her unselfish and radiant personality.

Paula's family were of modest circumstances but blessed with those indefinable qualities which collectively produced Will Rogers. Paula's brother, Herb, was a prototype of his Uncle Will, lacking only the flair which made Will a beloved citizen of the world.

The correspondence between Paula and the Halsells makes fascinating reading. The three following letters will give an insight into the relationship. On May 26, 1939, Ewing wrote to Paula. It is to be borne in mind that when he said that the "Memorial Commission" wishes to do so and so, he really means Ewing Halsell was going to do it:

Dear Paula:

I made reservations to leave on the 3rd of June on the Frisco to St. Louis and the B & O to Washington, arriving in Washington the morning of the 5th. If you and your mother would like to be there a day early, I think this is probably the best time to leave. You would probably have to come to Vinita to take this 9:23 train. I made my own reservations at the Raleigh Hotel, where I understand most of the Oklahoma crowd will be.

My understanding is that the King and Queen will be in Washington on the 7th. I am sure you and your mother will want to stay over that day. I think the commission wants to entertain the Rogers family, the Governor, and your mother and yourself. The dinner and the tentative plans were for the night of the 5th, as there is going to be quite a lot of entertainment on the 6th.

This is quite an expensive trip and your mother has been called on so much for this kind of service that I think that it is nothing more than right that the commission should take care of both of your expenses and I want them to do this, and I am sure they will be glad to do it.

Do you think your mother would like to go on to New York while she is in the East? If she does I think it would be a good idea to buy your tickets on to New York as I think the cost is very little more on to New York. If you will tell me what your wishes are, I will arrange for transportation and make reservations for Pullman, and if you will tell me where you would like to stay I will make reservations for your hotel. Would you and your mother occupy the same room?

If you have attended to these matters that is fine, but if I can do anything to help please let me know.

The trip to Washington had to do with the unveiling of a bronze statue of Will Rogers in the Capitol Building. It was a duplicate of the statue in the Will Rogers Memorial at Claremore. Paula's reply is charged with her anticipation and excitement at contemplating the trip.

May 28, 1939

Dear, dear, Mr. Halsell,

I have never read anything as sweet as your letter which came yesterday morning. You are wonderful to think of Mother and me . . . just like Uncle Will . . . and I can't tell you how much we both appreciate it. I went up home yesterday evening and took your letter to read to Mother and she shed a few tears for your extreme thoughtfulness.

It is so sweet of you to want to do so much for us, but Mother and I are so very, very happy to be able to go that we don't want the Commission to do anything. You have so many expenses and it is only right that we should take care of our own. It is such a privilege for me to work for such men as you are, that I consider myself the most fortunate person in Oklahoma.

I have written to the Raleigh Hotel and asked for a room for us. Yes, we shall stay together. I have also contacted the agent and he is looking after our reservations. The little one-horse-power man at Chelsea got busy and is having the train stop for Mother and Mr. Milam in Chelsea. We are planning to leave the 3rd., on the same train with you. Mother said to tell you she was so happy you were going to be there, that it made the entire prospect of the trip the brightest ever.

I was in Tulsa Friday morning to get some of the invitations that Mr. Henthorne had ready to mail. At that time an agent for one of the R.R. companies came in to see Mr. Henthorne. He afterwards called Claremore, and Bob told him to make our reservations along with the others, so I think everything is coming along nicely. However, if anything goes wrong, I shall feel perfectly free to call you and ask for your help. I think all the Oklahoma people are going to be placed in the same car and that will be so pleasant.

I had a wire from Bill [Rogers] saying he would see us in Washington, so I suppose he will fly from the coast. I am so excited about the whole thing that I can hardly sleep nights. I should love to go on to N. Y. but don't know whether Mother will be willing to do so. I have talked it over with her and she will tell me tomorrow.

Thank you for everything, dear Mr. Halsell. I can't put into words what I feel for you but I hope you know that I am grateful more than I can ever express. We shall see you Saturday if you don't hear from us before then.

> Fondly,
> Paula

After her return she wrote again to Ewing. Although Paula died April 28, 1973, her endearing presence lives on in the pages of the hundreds of letters she wrote and the books she published:

June 26, 1939

Dear, dear Mr. Halsell,

I wish I could tell you how very much I enjoyed every minute of my wonderful trip. I wish I could tell you how deeply I appreciate all the sweet things you did for Mother and me and how much you contributed to our happiness. You are such a dear that it is no wonder so many of us have such a claim on you!

Mother and I talked about you so much and could you have heard all we said you would know that each little act and thought you gave us was more than appreciated.

My trip was perfectly wonderful from beginning to end. I did, however, miss all the fun on the way home for you men have a way of pepping up a party that a poor lone traveler cannot produce.

I moved to the Shoreham hotel with Aunt Betty after Mother left on Thursday—the same day the king and queen were there. We went to Mr. Pat Hurley's home for a night and a day and returned to Washington on Friday. That night we had dinner with Mr. and Mrs. Jesse Jones on the terrace, and we spent much time talking about the Memorial. Mr. Jones is so interested!

From there I went to N. Y., and tried to see and do all I could in the short time I had. I went to the fair and by as many museums as I could locate. Before I left Aunt Betty came, and I spent another day and night with her. I enjoyed the day on the Hudson and spent another day in St. Louis—waiting for a train for Oklahoma—so went out to the Jefferson Memorial to see the Lindbergh trophies again. Every place I looked I saw nothing as appealing or as lovely as our Memorial right here.

Of course, there's lots more to tell you but nothing very important. Bill was by the 21st for a meeting and presumably ALONE. He seemed in a big hurry but the Commission asked him to go by Colorado Springs to see Mr. Forsythe before returning home. (I'll send you a copy of the minutes as soon as I have Mr. Henthorne's okay.)

With a heart full of love and deep gratitude for everything you did for Mother and me.

Affectionately,
Paula

An extract from a letter from Bob Love to Ewing Halsell, June 28, 1953, reveals the frustration and plight of the dedicated people who found and undertake to operate most museums:

The legislature wound up by cutting our request back to what it was the past two years, $21,000.00 for each year. This would be all right if all we had to do was operate, but we've got to have some of the above equipment so it means I am going to have to cut down on the routine operation some place.

I haven't had a chance to take it up with Mr. Henthorne yet, but I have some definite ideas so will write to you again before long.

What makes me so mad about the above is we were just about the only place the legislature made a cut. They spent more money this time than ever before, and a lot of it for some very foolish things.

I am afraid the time has come when the Commission should give some serious thought to what will happen to the Memorial in the years to come. When it ceases to have the backing of men like you and Mr. Henthorne no telling what those people in the legislature would do.

As for Paula and me, we won't live forever, and I have to make this statement, but I am afraid no one else could or would operate it for what we have in money, nor on the same plane.

I hadn't intended to devote but one paragraph to the above but I see I've gone overboard.

By 1973, the legislature had grudgingly raised the appropriation to $71,000. Ewing Halsell remained on the Commission and continued his personal interest as long as he lived.

In Vinita, Lucile Halsell gave the old Halsell homeplace with about two city blocks of land to the public school system.[18] When W. E. and Josie moved to Kansas City in 1910, W. E. had given the place to Ewing. Later, for some justifiable reason, Ewing deeded the property to Lucile. They moved into the house, and after a period, decided to have the house redecorated. They employed an interior decorator to advise and supervise and left the actual work to be done while they were away during the hay fever season. Bob Love, then nineteen, was a member of the crew.[19] He had been raised in Vinita, but in the opposite part of town. He had seen the Halsells at a distance but never got to know them until he started working on the house. He was the only native in the crew of more than thirty workers. He did get to know the Halsell family, and, as he said, "because I was a jack-of-all-trades, they always called me [after the work was completed] when anything went wrong." In that way a friendship began which he cherished ever afterwards.

The house, after it was redone, still had three stories. Downstairs was a spacious living room, large library with fireplace, breakfast room, dining room, and Chinese room,* kitchen and pantry. On the second floor were four large bedrooms, each with bath, a sewing room, and a large sleeping porch. The third floor, which had been the playroom and ballroom while W. E.'s children were growing up, was left pretty much as it was, other than fresh paint.

When, for reasons of health and climate, Ewing and Lucile decided to move to

---

*So named because that was where Josie had kept her extensive collection of oriental furniture before moving to Kansas City.

the St. Anthony Hotel in San Antonio in 1945, the fine old house in Vinita became a vexing problem.[20] Times and modes of living had changed. No one who could afford to purchase and cherish it could be found. So it stood vacant for seven years. The Halsells tried to give it to some responsible organization to be used for some worthwhile social purpose.[21] First, they offered it to the Oklahoma Methodist Conference who might use it as a home for elderly people, including retired preachers. The Conference had architects make an exhaustive study of the feasibility. They reported that the cost of modernization and adaptation would exceed that of beginning anew. The three stories did not lend themselves for use by old people and also there was a considerable fire hazard. So the Methodists turned it down.

The same proposal was made to the Baptists, and they, after investigation, arrived at the same decision. The Halsells also offered it as a public library. After this Lucile and Ewing decided that it would be better to have the house torn down than to let it become a victim of vandals and the elements, augmented by the shaking of the diesel engines of the Frisco which pounded by only a block away. They started negotiations with the Vinita School Board in 1956.[22] An arrangement was made whereby the Board would tear the house down for the salvage value, with the Halsells reserving the right to take such things as fireplace mantels, leaded windows, and other similar items. The land was to be deeded to the School Board.

Prior to this time Lucile had taken all the art and some of the furniture to use in their apartment. Also, Ewing had built family houses at Big Creek and Farias ranches. These houses were furnished largely from the old home. The wooden mantel from the ballroom was taken to Farias and reassembled for the living room of the new house there.[23]

When the ground was cleared of the old house, stables, and other buildings, the School Board built a new high school on the land. The members insisted on calling it the Ewing Halsell High School. Ewing objected vigorously, urging that it be called the Mary Alice Halsell High School for his mother. The Board stood firm and pointed out that Mary Alice had been gone for sixty-five years and only those over seventy who were living in Vinita before 1893 would remember her, probably not more than a half-dozen persons, if that many; whereas, the name of Ewing Halsell was a household word. So, with the board's determination and Lucile Halsell's support, the school became the Ewing Halsell High School. From time to time the Halsells made cash donations for special needs of the school.[24]

The citizens of Vinita have been grateful and appreciative. A letter from Mrs. Mamie Adams, wife of Dr. Felix Adams, expressed the attitude and feelings of the people at large in the town:

My Dear Mr. "H":

How sorry I was busy "Baby Sitting" when you called. I am becoming if "practice makes perfect" rather efficient in that line, and of course enjoy helping with the grandchildren. However, I sometimes wonder where the "sitting" part comes in. However, if at any time in your line of work you have need of such I am available,—after these months of experience I am positive I could handle baby calves just as well or maybe better. No joking, the babies are adorable (I think). With two graduating this spring (I might modestly add, beautiful girls) gives one a slight "?" feeling of growing maturity. Mercy I have eight grandchildren! "Mr. H." I was so pleased my Sally was in the first graduating class of The Ewing Halsell High School. I had such a personal feeling. Truly I have always been deeply proud, humble and most thankful to have you as our friend. You meant so much to Dad and me and now to me and my children and to so many others. The first visit I had at the school was when the play "The Robe" was being given and most effectively with our Sally as one of the stars. Part of the time was there, another part, happy part, was with you wonderful ones in the beautiful old home so filled with friendships, hospitality so genuine. Happy times, memories I never want to forget. But we know change is inevitable and usually brings some sadness. But "Mr. H" as I saw the play so well portrayed by the promising young people—so happy, the appreciative audience of seven hundred, later hearing so many compliments on the spacious building—from the exterior you can't imagine the capabilities of the interior—with the many expressions of gratitude and appreciation, for the generosity and heavenly kindness and foresight of the one who gave for the coming generations, I stopped my introspective thoughts and became elated, thankful even to know you and yours—beyond that our happy friendship. Well I could no longer have a feeling of remorse. Beyond this I know of so many (by no means all) deeds you have so quietly and humbly given. I know the little song you sing (or hum) as you walk along will ever be in your heart. "Mr. H," you are much beloved—May God bless you and keep you always.

The following story told by Helen Campbell deals with one of the Halsell benevolences. It also shows that at 87, when Ewing Halsell would not stoop down and tie his own shoes, he still had a little of the "Old Nick" in him:

Ewing had mentioned to Dr. Walter Browers, the popular pastor of the Travis Park Methodist Church, that he had some money to give to a worthy cause. He called a few days later and said his church had started a Home for Unwed Mothers [a rather worthy project], and they could certainly use funds, but he thought Mr. Halsell should visit the Home first to see for himself if he thought it worthy of his support. I made a date with Dr. Browers for him to take us to the Home the next day. When Mr. Halsell woke up and I was tying his shoelaces, I told him about Dr. Browers' call, and that he was to pick us up the next day. He looked at me with an impish grin, and said, "No, Helen, I can't do that. Some of those little girls might recognize me, even though it was dark."[25]

Anyway, the "little girls" got the money.

Lucile Halsell was a devoted Methodist and had been all her life. When they moved to the St. Anthony, she affiliated with the Travis Park Methodist Church, largely because it was just across the street. Already she was suffering from a type of lung disease. How she had contracted the disease was a mystery to the medical profession because she had never smoked and had lived an exemplary life. The malady caused an increasing shortness of breath and restricted her physical exertion. More and more, trips to the ranches exhausted her. To compensate she concentrated on the affairs of the grey stone church across the street. Outside her home, it became the most important factor in her life. She was one of the most generous donors to its support, and Ewing, not yet a member, gave in her behalf a very sizable check every Christmas.[26]

On October 24, 1955, the church burned, leaving only the bare stone walls. The question arose as to whether the congregation would rebuild it, or sell the lot, which was located in the heart of the city and was very valuable, and move to a less expensive site. A meeting of the congregation was called in a nearby auditorium to discuss the matter and, if possible, come to a decision. Lucile was anxious to attend and Ewing and Helen took her to the meeting. Much pro and con discussion ensued. At length, the pastor called on Ewing Halsell for his opinion. Before he could reply a woman with a carrying voice interrupted, "Don't listen to him. He doesn't even belong to the church." The preacher, who felt that Ewing was one of the biggest of potential givers, turned red. Ewing, instead of walking out in a huff, was amused. He was very fond of the pastor and to relieve the tension, he said, "The lady is correct. I am not a member, but the old church is very dear to my wife,

and she is anxious to have it restored. If that is the wish of the membership, she and I will contribute $50,000 toward its restoration.'' This simple announcement was the turning point in the decision. There was no further discussion of moving but simply how quick they could get the restoration started. The church was rebuilt, more beautiful than before.[27]

Lucile wanted Ewing to join the church very much, and in 1961 Ewing proposed that he and Helen join as a Mother's Day surprise for Lucile. J. Walter Browers, minister of Travis Park Methodist Church at that time, describes the event,

Mrs. Halsell was ill a great deal of the time and my visits with her in the Nix Hospital, and at their suite in the St. Anthony Hotel, gave me many opportunities to hear the stories of her life with Ewing in Oklahoma and West Texas in the early days. She told me of days filled with some hardships but love strong enough to overcome whatever trials they faced. Many times Mrs. Halsell expressed to me her desire that Mr. Halsell would unite with the Church before she died. On Thursday, May 11th, before Mother's Day of 1961, Mr. Halsell called me to come to his office. He told me that he wanted to unite with the church the following Sunday. This decision was not impulsive but one he had considered and pondered. He mentioned his bad habits, as he referred to them, and one of his confessions was his love for playing ''Penny-Ante.'' After a serious discussion of the requirements of Church membership, we knelt down by his desk and had prayer together.

I can never forget that Sunday morning, May 14, 1961, when Mr. and Mrs. Halsell, Mrs. Rider, and the Halsell's faithful and invaluable secretary, Miss Helen Campbell, came into the sanctuary and sat near the front, to my right of the Church. When the invitation was given Mr. and Mrs. Halsell and Helen came forward. Helen transferred her membership from a Church in Vinita, Oklahoma. Mr. and Mrs. Halsell knelt at the altar as he presented himself for baptism and the church vows. This took courage and nobility for a man of eighty-four years of age. What a glorious experience for Mrs. Halsell on her last opportunity to attend her church. On September 9, 1963 she transferred her membership to the Church Eternal. I conducted her memorial service from the altar at which she had knelt with her husband only twenty-eight months earlier.[28]

Ewing's affiliation with the church was in large measure to please Lucile. However, added to that incentive as he grew older, was the recurring memory of what a devoted member his mother, Mary Alice, had been, and by family tradition his grandmother Halsell, Elizabeth Jane. He recalled that his father, W. E., had been so moved while passing a Methodist church in Kansas City at hearing the congre-

A Ranching Saga

gation singing an old hymn he had heard Elizabeth Jane sing when he was a child that he stopped, went back, and paid off the mortgage on the church building. Although the father and son took little part in church affairs, the religious tradition in the family had an influence on both of them. After he joined the church, Ewing's Christmas donations became larger.[29]

Dr. Browers writes, "No one knows how many times Mr. Halsell helped me meet the needs that would otherwise have gone unheeded. There were many times when I turned to him for help and he never failed me."[30]

Ewing was also interested in a Catholic Mission, San Juan de Los Lagos. It was in the small, remote village of El Indio, located between the Farias ranch and the Rio Grande River. It was attended by the families of the cowboys on the Farias and the adjoining ranch and administered by a circuit-riding priest who came by about once a month. Ewing gave fifty dollars a year to the congregation. When the ladies needed something extra for their kitchen, or a special occasion, they let it be known to Mr. Halsell, and they always got it. Ewing derived as much pleasure from this participation as he did from Travis Park Methodist Church.[31]

Dr. Merton Minter, the Halsell family physician, was Chairman of the Board of Regents of the University of Texas which was establishing a medical school in San Antonio. To get the medical school started, it was necessary to establish a medical center on about one thousand acres of land on the northwestern edge of San Antonio.[32] There had been a lot of bad feeling engendered by the selection of the site. Many downtown merchants, supported by a goodly number of medical doctors, wanted to locate the medical complex downtown. Dr. Minter sought Ewing's advice as a practical businessman. Ewing studied the alternatives and advised by all means it should be placed out at the edge of town where plenty of room could take care of expansion for a hundred years to come. His opinion had considerable weight in the final decision. The land would cost $3,000 an acre.* Although Dr. Minter was not able to persuade Ewing to be on the Finance Committee, he was very active in the launching of the project. After pledging $100,000, he felt no compunction about going after others. He was not physically able to pad the sidewalk, twist arms, and ask for money. What he did was more effective. Dr.

*It is in 1974 valued at $100,000 an acre.

Minter arranged for him to team up with Sid Katz, who also lived at the St. Anthony Hotel. Ewing thought of the potential donors and the approach to each, and Sid would make the contacts. The routine went something like this. Ewing would go down to breakfast in the morning, and there would be Sid in the lobby looking dejected. Ewing would buy Sid's breakfast and listen to his troubles. Ewing would say, "You go out and tell your prospects that if they will give so much I will match it." This approach was used only on the toughest cases, but often worked. In one way or another, the money was raised, and Dr. Minter gives Ewing Halsell credit for a large part of it.

In addition to helping secure the site for the Medical Center, Ewing Halsell was active in promoting the building of the Methodist Hospital on the new location.[33] In 1961, he was presented with an appreciation testimonial.[34] It read:

The Board of the Southwest Texas Methodist Hospital extends to you, Mr. Halsell, our sincere thanks for what you did to make possible the gigantic task Mr. Katz started. Only through the efforts of friends such as you, Mr. Halsell, could the task have been done. This Board wants you to know that it recognizes your unselfish devotion to the task of making this a truly great institution where we can in fact "Serve Man to honor God."

Later Lucile and her sister, Grace Rider, equipped a surgical suite in this hospital in memory of their mother and of their father, the pioneer doctor Benjamin Franklin Fortner and Lucy Jane Fortner.[35]

Ewing did not live to see the full results of his vision and efforts. Already on the site, in 1974, are the University of Texas Schools of Medicine, Nursing and Pharmacy, Veteran's Hospital, a Methodist Hospital, a Psychiatric Hospital, a Lutheran Hospital, a Radiation Center, and many others. There still exists hundreds of acres for further expansion. While the medical centers in Houston and Dallas are hampered by lack of adjacent land, the future growth for the one in San Antonio seems assured. Ewing Halsell was recognized after his death by having a street in the medical complex named Ewing Halsell Drive.[36]

The Christmas season was the time of year Ewing Halsell enjoyed most. He loved to give and to share. For the regular hands, if it had been a good year, it was an extra month's wages.[37] Not all years were good. Occasionally there was one when the annual loss was measured in six digits. Even then the bonuses were only reduced in size, they were not omitted. For the family, the office helpers, domestic help, and a host of friends, Ewing shopped for appropriate gifts, spending several hours a day, for a week or two. This was a chore he did not delegate. He received much pleasure doing it himself. In his latter years when walking became more difficult, Helen Campbell accompanied him.

Helen Campbell recalls a small incident that was, in a measure, indicative of Ewing Halsell's philosophy of life:

I remember one Christmas Eve he and I had gone to the office to check the mail. All of the help was off, so we did not stay long. As we walked home there was a beggar by the Vogue store. Mr. Halsell dropped a $20.00 bill in his box. I said "Mr. Halsell, that is wonderful! You have made that man's Christmas."

That night as Mrs. Halsell and I were getting him ready for bed, I told her about the beggar and the twenty dollar bill. Mr. Halsell added, "I want to tell you something. Unless you make a sacrifice when you do things you don't light a candle in heaven. You know better than anyone that I did not make a sacrifice when I gave the beggar that $20.00, so don't give me credit." I consider this typical of his attitude toward life.[38]

Perhaps the most important gifts Ewing Halsell gave were intangible, a part of himself. He was interested in people, their welfare, and their happiness. A statement from Emerson Price in Vinita exemplified this quality: "He helped me in many ways. He had confidence in me, and that gave me confidence in myself."[39] This statement was expressed by scores of others who were interviewed during the preparation of this narrative.

The Last Hunt 27

In 1961, several of Ewing Halsell's close friends were together on a social occasion in San Antonio.[1] Johnny Murrell from the Spring Lake ranch and Helen
Campbell were there. They all had had a few toddies and were feeling sentimental
and nostalgic and talking about what a wonderful person Ewing Halsell was. Someone said, "We ought to give him a big birthday party." Everyone thought that was
a great idea. Helen Campbell pointed out it was really not his birthday but that did
not make any difference. Any old day could be celebrated as a birthday. So they
got on with the plans. Helen said she had often thought how nice it would be to
have a surprise party at the Big Creek ranch. Everybody agreed, but no definite
plans were formed, other than vague suggestions that it should be a big barbecue
and include Ewing's friends from South Texas, Spring Lake, and Oklahoma.
Whether it was the result of the mellowing effects of toddies wearing off, or the
rush of pressing business, or both, no further mention was made of the party for
a couple of weeks.

But Johnny Murrell went back to the Spring Lake ranch and did not forget about the proposed party. One night he called Helen and said he had invited twenty-five or thirty old Mashed O hands and friends from Muleshoe, Amherst, Spring Lake (town), and Earth to the Big Creek party and would like to know the date it was to be. Helen, who never was nonplussed about any emergency or crisis pertaining to business, was overwhelmed by the thought of organizing a social affair of such magnitude. She did not sleep much that night but did decide on one step to take. It happened that two of Ewing Halsell's closest friends, Gus Lowrance and Horace Barnard, had been present the night the project had been discussed. She was fortunate next morning to contact both by telephone in their respective offices, Mr. Lowrance in the Gunter Hotel and Mr. Barnard in the Drew Building, Tulsa. She asked each their advice about what to do. When they realized her perturbed state of mind, they reassured her in a fatherly, comforting, and slightly amused manner that there was no problem. They would just get busy and work it out. Mr. Barnard said he would arrange for a caterer to provide the barbecue with all the fixings at the Big Creek ranch. He would lure Ewing up there on some pretext of having some kind of a gathering at Barnard's Oklahoma ranch which was located in the same general vicinity as the Big Creek ranch. Gus and other invited guests would fly to Tulsa, where cars would be waiting, and would detour briefly by Big Creek so that Ewing might get a glimpse of the condition of the grass and cattle. When they drove up to the headquarters, there would be the party, with everything ready and everybody waiting. It worked.

A planeload of friends flew from San Antonio. A special private luncheon at the Mayo Hotel in Tulsa did not cause Ewing to suspect anything unusual. It was just a jolly good bunch of fellows and Helen, going up to help Horace celebrate some occasion. Lucile was the hostess for the luncheon. Although she was ill and unable to attend, she wanted to participate in some way. Then the party took off in automobiles to the north, detouring by the Big Creek ranch. Clouds were gathering and getting thicker and darker. This caused no concern, because ranch people were always, or nearly always, ready for a good rain. All went well, with Ewing riding with Gus Lowrance, Horace Barnard, and the driver. The road winds down a long hill, circles a large earthen tank, and goes up a slope to the headquarters. Ewing had not noticed a half-acre of cars near the headquarters and nearly 200 people milling about, waiting. But he did see smoke from the barbecue pit, and said, "I can't

science News
192:6 J14
192

J. CISNEROS
EL PASO

imagine why Clyte is burning trash in the rain at this time of year." When the car started up the slope, he saw the people, the cars, and the pickups. Everyone in the car with him was watching his reaction. It was surprise, amazement, and bewilderment. He looked from one to another for the meaning. Then Mr. Barnard said, "This is it, Ewing. This is your Birthday Party. All of these people have gathered to wish you many more of them." The surprise was complete.

As Ewing greeted more than 200 of his good and cherished friends, men and women, from South Texas, West Texas, and Oklahoma, he was overcome. Tears mixed with smiles of joy. The ladies placed an orchid lei around his neck. A bar, attended by old cowboys Ewing was fond of, dispensed a variety of liquids which enhanced the warmth of fellowship.

It was a great party. The threatening clouds, as if in collusion, held off until the barbecue was served and eaten and then the bottom fell out and rain poured in torrents. All guests who could moved into the main house, others took refuge in other houses. Some undertook to go home. The creeks were up. All roads to the highway were impassable except one, and it was flooded with about two feet of water. Cars could not get through without the motors drowning out. The cowboys spent most of the night pulling cars across with a tractor. For those who stayed at the ranch, the whiskey held out, and no one seemed to mind. Helen saw to it that Ewing got to bed.

All this took place in 1961. Twelve years later, Helen Campbell had an all-day gathering at the same ranch for the purpose of interviewing many of the people who were at the Birthday Party. They came from Tulsa, Bartlesville, Nowata, and all around. The long dining table was loaded with food and the bar with drinks. The Birthday Party of 1961, which they had come to talk about, was now a fond memory, but was as vivid to all of them as if it had happened the night before. Ewing lived five years after it took place, and it was one of the highlights of his later years.

Ewing's only regret about the birthday party was that Lucile had been unable to make the trip and share with him the outpouring of affection and friendship the occasion afforded him. Before her health began to decline, Lucile loved to entertain. Especially did she like to entertain her women friends at luncheons. About twice a year she repaid all her social obligations with beautiful luncheons at the St.

Anthony Hotel. She would decorate with flowers and place cards, would always supply musicians, and the women would come in their finest clothes.

Lucile herself was a talented pianist, having studied at the Cincinnati Conservatory of Music, and she had many books on classical music, opera, and related subjects. She always loved music and enjoyed attending concerts. After the Halsells moved to the St. Anthony, she sat in the lobby every day at noon and before dinner to hear the string quartet play light classical music.

Ewing and Lucile traveled each year until her health prohibited it. Her favorite travel spots were California and Honolulu. Helen Campbell remembers that Mrs. Halsell always wore a hat and gloves on her travels and among her luggage was a large hat trunk, carrying her various hats for the trip.

The years after her illness began in 1960 were to be saddened by the slow decline of Lucile's health.[2] She was in and out of the hospital a number of times that year with a respiratory problem. It was not exactly emphysema. She could breathe air into her lungs with no trouble but had difficulty expelling it. Its origin was unaccountable. In August 1961, she became seriously ill but did not want to go to the hospital. She hated being a patient in a hospital, although she supported hospitals in general with her money.[3] Ewing was the opposite. He loved the treatment he received in hospitals. So she remained in the apartment, and the family put nurses on around the clock. They stayed on for two years and one month. Dr. Minter came by every day. When the spells were serious they placed an oxygen tent over her. She did not mind it. In this she also differed from her husband. He could not stand a tent. In his later years when he needed oxygen, he would take it from a little device over his nose.

Her condition fluctuated from fair to worse. The following extracts from Ewing's letter to his sisters indicate her gradual decline:[4]

January 2, 1962

Lucile is not showing much improvement in the last week or ten days. I am afraid for her to walk without a nurse or someone to hold her. She does come down to lunch everyday. She eats fairly well, but not as much as to improve her strength. She is very seldom despondent, but does have bad days and thinks she will never be any better, but most of the time she is rather cheerful. She sleeps well, enjoys television and can read some.

We had to have another nurse with Lucile while we had to be gone. She is just not able to get up off the sofa where she likes to listen to television and get to the bathroom and bedroom. We had been doing without one from 3:00 P.M. to 7:00 P.M., and [we have] one for [the] twelve hour duty 7:00 P.M. to 7:00 A.M., and another to 3:00 P.M. I am very much disappointed at her lack of improvement.

July 18, 1962

Lucile is doing much better. I doubt she will ever be strong enough to go to parties or take drives. But she is comfortable and dresses each day and goes to lunch downstairs.

January 1, 1963

Lucile shows more interest in what is going on. She dresses one day out of four and goes down for lunch. Our morning and afternoon nurses are good cooks, and they prepare food for her when she does not go downstairs. She is eating better.

August 6, 1963

Lucile is slipping pretty fast. We went to the ranch this past week and left her in high spirits, but on my return I found she had definitely weakened. I am very concerned about her, and fear she will never recover.

If she dies, I do not think it would be best for you girls to try to come here. We will have to take her to Vinita, and you can meet us there.

August 13, 1963

Lucile is very seriously ill. She has almost quit eating, and we keep her under an oxygen tent. She still knows who is in the room, but she is gradually weaker, and we cannot predict how long she can last.

It was not long. On Monday evening, September 7, 1963, Ewing and Helen, as was their custom after the 10 o'clock news, went in to tell her "Good Night."[5] The nurse detained Helen after Ewing left and told her that Mrs. Halsell's pulse was slowing down rapidly, and she asked Helen to leave her door open so she could call her quickly if needed. Next morning, September 8, at about 4:00, the nurse called her. Lucile's pulse had all but stopped. The two debated if they should call Mr. Halsell and Mrs. Rider, and decided against it. About 5:15 the pulse stopped completely. At 7:00 Helen awakened Mr. Halsell and told him. His one question was "When did it happen?" "At 5:15." He said, "That's very strange. Something caused me to wake up at 5:15. I looked at the clock."

A little more than two months before, on June 28, Ewing and Lucile had celebrated their sixty-fourth wedding anniversary. Although Ewing was braced for her death, after all the happy years together the sense of loss was almost overpowering.

A funeral service was held in Travis Park Methodist Church.[6] Dr. Browers conducted the service and later wrote, "Never had 'Lead Kindly Light' held more meaning as the grand finale was played for one who had walked by faith—'one step enough for me' was the essence of her trust." After the San Antonio service, the body was sent overland in a hearse to Vinita. Mrs. Rider was not able to make the trip. Ewing, Helen, and Mrs. Eva McCluskey flew to Tulsa where they were met and taken to Vinita in a car. The extended family had converged there, and another service was held in the Methodist Church which Lucile had attended from early childhood until 1945, when she and Ewing moved to San Antonio. Burial was in a lot Ewing had long before purchased adjoining the lot of his father. After the funeral, Ewing, Helen, and Red Murrell went to the Big Creek ranch where they had a quiet week.[7]

When Ewing and Helen returned to San Antonio and to Mrs. Rider, hundreds of letters of consolation awaited them. One sentence expressed the message of them all, "You have had a great loss, plus two years of watching a lovely flower die."[8]

Lucile's illness was paralleled by that of William R. McCluskey, Eva Halsell's husband, referred to by the family as Billy Mac.[9] In the exchange of letters between Ewing and his three sisters during 1962 and early 1963, comments frequently were made on the state of health of both Lucile and Billy Mac. Lucile outlived him by about four months.*

After Lucile died in 1963, Ewing, Mrs. Grace Rider, and Helen continued living in the apartment in the St. Anthony Hotel.[10] Mrs. Rider was in delicate health and seldom left the hotel except for an occasional party or function outside, a drive

*After leaving the Spring Lake ranch in 1918 following the Keller killing, Billy McCluskey returned with his wife and two children to Kansas City and engaged successfully in the automobile business. He left a sizable estate which aside from a number of small gifts, went to his daughter, Eva Ann, and his son, Billy.

about the city, or to attend Travis Park Church across the street. Ewing was 86 when his wife passed away. Mentally he was as alert as ever, but physically he had slowed down perceptibly. His gait was unhurried, his steps short and carefully placed, he could not stoop, he was a little overweight, his breath was short, his heart was giving him trouble, and he was a diabetic. Helen, who accompanied him everywhere as secretary, nurse, and companion, always carried in her purse a vial of nitroglycerin tablets for the heart, sticks of peppermint candy for instant use when his blood sugar dropped, and her little black book to make notes for instructions which constantly emerged from his nimble mind. In the apartment she had large cylinders of oxygen, and in the car small cylinders, all equipped for instant use. He had occasional bad days when he did not feel like leaving the apartment, but for the most part he carried on his schedule of going to the office and the ranches. Dr. Minter had instructed Helen as to how to detect symptoms and what medication or treatment to administer.[11]

For more than two years Ewing carried on his business, as alert as ever. Helen tells this story of an actual happening. Some ranch neighbors, who thought themselves to be sharp traders, were considering propositioning Ewing for a cattle deal. One said to the other, "Don't try to cheat old man Halsell. He has that little fat girl following him around, and she has that little black book, and she writes everything down. With the two of them, you can't win."[12]

Ewing enjoyed his friends who came and went. He entertained in the apartment or in the club downstairs. If there were only men, they talked, played poker, and had drinks. He still loved to mix the drinks for others but never for himself. If wives were also present, gin rummy usually took the place of poker.

The pastime Ewing enjoyed most was the hunting season in November and December at Farias. He, Mrs. Rider, and Helen spent hours planning each trip. Although Mrs. Rider was never strong enough to go, she helped with the plans.[13]

The last hunt took place in December 1965. Helen Campbell, an eyewitness to every detail, describes it far more vividly than could any secondhand account:

One of the happiest parties and one Mr. Halsell especially looked forward to was the Barnard-Lowrance party. This consisted of Mr. Horace Barnard and his son, Jim Bob, and Mr. Gus Lowrance and his son, Ed, plus many of Mr. Halsell's friends from San Antonio and

Eagle Pass. I remember one year, Mr. A. E. Bradshaw of Tulsa and Mr. Walter Jarboe of Parsons, Kansas, joined the party. Bob Cage, a ranch neighbor, was always an engaging guest. There was not a great deal of buck killing. The younger men each got his deer, but the old friends just loved to drive over the ranch, look at the cattle, play poker, talk, eat, and have an occasional drink.

On the last hunt, the crowd was going to the ranch on Wednesday, December 15, 1965. Mr. Halsell woke up that morning feeling bad. I suggested that I get a nurse to stay with him, and I would go to the ranch and get the party started, and then the guests could take care of themselves, and I would hurry back. He said that this would probably be Horace Barnard's last hunt, and he [Mr. Halsell] felt he had to be there.

We got him dressed, and with the help of the driver, downstairs to the car. I could tell the trip was most uncomfortable for him. Instead of his usual zest and interest in the country and cattle we passed along the road, he just lay back, propped up with pillows, was silent and nonobservant. When we arrived at the headquarters he went right to bed and never got out of it until we started home the next day. That night about 9:00 a pain hit him in the chest. He could trace it with his finger; it was a triangle shape. I gave him nitroglycerin tablets and administered oxygen. The tablets did not seem to help, but the oxygen did, and I kept it up all night.

I knew Dr. Minter was an early riser, and I called him at 6:00 in the morning. He was considerably alarmed at my report and said get him to the hospital in San Antonio as quickly as possible. I then called Captain Allee, who lived in Carrizo Springs, and asked if he could get an ambulance. He arrived in about an hour, followed by an ambulance. Mr. Halsell did not feel like moving until 2:30 in the afternoon. One of the cowboys helped me get Mr. Halsell dressed. He had a habit of always putting on his right shoe, or boot, first. The cowboy did not know about that and was trying desperately to put on his left shoe first. Mr. Halsell was kicking and protesting loudly, when I discovered what the problem was. I explained, and there was no more trouble.

The highway which ran through the ranch was being reworked, and the side road was very rough and gave Mr. Halsell a feeling he was going to roll off the stretcher. I rode on my knees beside him and held him on. After we were on good road, he asked, "Did you bring my nitroglycerin?" I said, "Yes." He asked, "Did you bring some Kleenex?" I answered, "Yes." Again he said, "I'll bet you forgot the stick candy." When I told him I had it, he chuckled, "Then I don't have a thing to worry about, except to think of something else you forgot."

Captain Allee drove in front of the ambulance at top speed with his lights flashing and his siren going. We made the trip in two hours, which usually took three. Two motorcycle traffic officers from San Antonio met us at Von Army. They got in front of Captain Allee with their sirens on. We sailed into town to the hospital at 80 miles an hour. I am naturally cautious and never dreamed I could do a thing like that. But we never know what we can do until it comes to an emergency for someone you love.

Dr. Minter was there, waiting, and although I did not then know it, he did not have much hope from the moment he saw Mr. Halsell. I am sure Mr. Halsell had no premonition of death. As soon as we got him in the hospital room and Dr. Minter had administered some strong tranquilizer, Mr. Halsell remembered that Red Murrell was to be in San Antonio that day. He told me to call the St. Anthony Hotel and reserve a room for him. I told him that we need not do that. Red could use his [Mr. Halsell's] room. He replied, "Go ahead and reserve a room, because I will be home tomorrow." Evidently I felt the same way because I ordered six bottles of oxygen sent to the apartment, to be delivered early next morning.

On such short notice, we had to take whatever nurse we could get. The one available was big, fat, and clumsy. Each time she went to the bed she bumped it, and Mr. Halsell's chest pains would start again. I finally told her to go out into the hall and sit in a chair and I would call her, if needed. When Mr. Halsell was quiet and apparently easy, I would doze off on a couch in the room. I slept so lightly that his slightest move would awaken me. About midnight I thought I heard him call. I went to the bed, and his eyes were open and bright. He asked what I was doing up, and I told him I thought I heard him call. He said, "No, I didn't call. Go back to bed. You did not get any rest at all last night." Those were his last words. As always he was thinking of the comfort of someone else. Apparently he was feeling no pain and went to sleep or into a coma. At 5:00 A.M. we realized he was dead.

In a daze I returned to the hotel and telephoned his sisters. Then I called Gilbert Denman, Jr. who came immediately and, seeing my foggy condition, took over. He was a tremendous source of strength, help, and comfort. Many other friends came and did what they could, but Gilbert was the one I relied on, as I have done so many times since.

We decided on two services, one on Sunday at 2:00 P.M. in Travis Park Methodist Church, San Antonio, where Dr. Browers officiated. The other was in Vinita in First Methodist Church at 2:00 P.M. Monday, December 20, 1965. So many people expressed a desire to go to Vinita that Gilbert suggested that we charter an airplane to take them and the family. Mr. Fred Shields of San Antonio was of valuable assistance in this chore and ended up with two planes. The body was taken overland to Vinita, and about 25 of his friends plus the family flew up. My brother, Carl Campbell, made arrangements for buses to meet the funeral party at the Tulsa Airport and take them to Vinita. Both services were wonderful, and I shall be eternally grateful to Dr. Browers for the tributes he paid him. It was a sad time, and I felt very lost and alone, but I am thankful he did not have to suffer.[14]

A Ranching Saga

Dr. Browers writes:

At the memorial service for Mr. Halsell . . . I looked out over a congregation of cowboys, ranchers, businessmen and women, rich and poor, educated and limited, and thought how appropriate it was to have these people at his last rites because this was his world. . . . No words were ever more fitting for a man than those of the text that I used for his memorial service, "Know ye not that there is a prince, and a great man fallen this day." (II Samuel 3:38).[15]

Representative Bill Clayton, Speaker of the House, Texas Legislature, was later to say of Ewing Halsell, "Looking back on this historical era, the name of Mr. Ewing Halsell comes to the forefront. He was a true pioneer—a man of his own making—a man who believed in the old fashioned way of working hard and getting ahead."[16]

Ewing Halsell was buried in the Vinita cemetery beside Lucile. A monument of handsome marble was erected for the two of them. It is similar in size and shape to the marble shaft which marks W. E. Halsell's grave a short distance away. These visible reminders testify to the achievements of two remarkable men, each responding to the challenges of his time in his own way.

Epilogue

Ewing Halsell's death does not end this saga. In his will he projected his own and his father's vision into the future. His great love of the lands entrusted to him appeared in the testament: he named off the properties given to him by his father and devised them to his sister's children; he named off other farms and pastures he had himself acquired and devised them to the old employees who had been his helpmates in his life's work; but he described the greatest of his landholdings and left them, along with all the rest and residue of his wealth, to a charitable trust dedicated to the broadest possible purposes for the public good.

A decade before his death, Ewing and Lucile decided that a charitable foundation was the vehicle which they desired to receive the bulk of their properties and use them for philanthropy. Ewing studied the legal instruments that the owners of great fortunes, such as Carnegie, Rockefeller, Mellon, and Ford, had adopted for such purposes, and also the documents that old friends in the Texas ranching industry, such as the Moody and Kleberg families, had utilized. By 1957, he had concluded the terms he wanted to guide his fortune and established a charitable trust for this purpose. Ewing wanted to call it The Ewing and Lucile Halsell Foundation, but Lucile quietly demanded that her first name be deleted. She said that her name had been Mrs. Ewing Halsell for almost sixty years, and that "The Ewing Halsell Foundation" described them both.

The Foundation was begun in a modest manner with the contribution of some shares of corporate stock. Its activities increased rapidly as it was funded with generous gifts from Ewing and Lucile. They were thrilled with the satisfaction they received from observing the results of the Foundation's early philanthropies. Lucile's sister, Grace Rider, shared their joy and became so convinced of its potential as an agency for private charity that she bequeathed her substantial estate to this same trust.

Thus, the Halsell fortunes, accumulated over a century of time, based on the love of the land and the understanding of mankind's simple and age-old dependence on the cow and the plow, came to be dedicated to some of our country's highest needs—to health, religion, education, the care of needy children and aged people, the arts, the pursuit of knowledge, social justice, and the conservation of the land and man's heritage.

Source References
Volume Two

CHAPTER 17

1. H. C. to E. H., 8-17-1938.
2. Map, Halsell Records, D-38, f-15.
3. Johnny Murrell to W. C. H., 2-25-1973.
4. Ibid.
5. Ibid.
6. Halsell Records, D-38, f-17, 9-28-1939.
7. George Kuykendall to W. C. H., 10-7-1974.
8. Ibid.
9. Halsell Records, separate books kept for the "Texas Ranch."
10. Johnny Murrell to W. C. H., 2-4-1973.
11. Halsell Records, D-11, f-9, 5-17-1937.
12. Ibid., D-31, f-14, 7-23-1942.
13. Newton Robison to W. C. H., 2-25-1974.
14. Ibid.
15. Ibid.
16. Ibid.
17. W. C. Holden, *Rollie Burns* (Dallas: Southwest Press, 1932), pp. 112-113.
18. Spur Records (Southwest Collection), X, 254.
19. Robison to W. C. H., 2-25-1974.
20. Halsell Records, D-28, f-9, 8-7-1933.
21. Ibid., D-30, f-28, 1-1-1933.
22. Ibid., D-30, f-28, 8-25-1925.
23. Ibid., D-30, f-30, 8-9-1932.
24. Ibid., D-30, f-30, 9-13-1933.
25. Ibid., D-30, f-28, 5-16-1932.
26. Ibid., D-30, f-28, 5-26-1932.
27. E. H. to W. J. Jarboe, 10-21-1938.
28. Mrs. Otis Langley to W. C. H., 2-24-1974.
29. Ibid.
30. Johnny Murrell to W. C. H., 2-4-1974.
31. N. B. H. to E. H., 5-19-1935.
32. H. C. to E. H., 8-9-1937.
33. John Mahoney to W. C. H., 8-24-1973.

CHAPTER 18

1. Halsell Records, D-15, f-5, 9-16-1939.
2. Halsell Records, D-15, f-1, 9-5-1939.
3. Ibid., D-30, f-2, 9-5-1939.
4. Ibid., D-30, f-2, 8-8-1939.
5. Ibid., D-30, f-2, 7-2-1941.
6. Ibid., D-30, f-2, 7-11-1941.
7. Ibid., D-30, f-2, 9-25-1939.
8. Ibid., D-30, f-2, 7-28-1941.
9. Halsell Records, D-10, f-2, 10-18-1938.
10. Ibid., D-30, f-2, 8-31-1939.
11. Ibid., D-30, f-2, 5-13-1941.
12. Ibid., D-16, f-1, 6-11-1941.
13. Ibid., D-16, f-1, 1-5-1942.
14. Ibid., D-30, f-2, 4-20-1940.
15. Ibid., D-15, f-1, 8-17-1942.
16. Halsell Records, D-30, f-5, 9-30-1942.
17. Ibid., D-16, f-1, 11-19-1942.
18. Ibid., D-15, f-21, 9-4-1942.
19. Ibid., D-15, f-21, 7-3-1942.
20. Ibid., D-15, f-21, 9-4-1942.
21. Halsell Records, D-15, f-1, 8-14-1937; also 8-11-1938; 7-28-1941.
22. Halsell Records, D-15, f-1, 9-28-1942.
23. Ibid., D-30, f-7, 4-29-1942.
24. Eva Halsell McCluskey to W. C. H., 2-15-1973.
25. Fred Davis to W. C. H., 7-28-1973.
26. Halsell Records, D-16, f-1, 12-30-1941.
27. Ibid., D-15, f-21, 10-28-1943; also, 3-13-1944.
28. Ibid., D-30, f-37, 7-17-1944.

CHAPTER 19

1. H. C. to W. C. H., 7-26-1973.
2. Ibid.
3. E. H. to W. C. Kitchen, 9-22-1942.
4. Halsell Records, D-30, f-7, 5-19-1938.
5. Oval Keen to E. H., 9-22-1942; also, E. H. to Oval Keen, 9-2-1942.
6. H. C. to W. C. H., 7-26-1973.
7. Ibid.

A Ranching Saga

8. W. H. George to W. C. H., 10-26-1973.
9. H. C. to W. C. H., 7-26-1973.
10. W. H. George to W. C. H., 10-26-1973.
11. H. C. to W. C. H., 8-15-1973.
12. Ibid.
13. W. H. George to W. C. H., 10-26-1973.
14. Halsell Records, D-30, f-13, 9-13-1944.
15. Ibid., D-30, f-13.
16. Halsell Records, Account Book, 1944.
17. Ibid.
18. Ibid.
19. Ibid.
20. Ibid.
21. Ibid.
22. W. H. George to W. C. H., 10-26-1973.
23. Les La Grange to E. H., 12-21-1945.
24. Halsell Records, Account Book, 1946.
25. H. C. to W. C. H., 11-9-1974.
26. Ibid.
27. Ibid.
28. Holman Cartwright to W. C. H., 11-12-1974.
29. Ibid.
30. H. C. to W. C. H., 11-9-1974.
31. Texas Almanac (*The Dallas News*, 1974–1975), pp. 558-561.
32. Red Caldwell to W. C. H., 10-26-1973.
33. Bob Cage to W. C. H., 10-26-1973.
34. W. H. George to W. C. H., 10-26-1973.
35. H. C. to W. C. H., 11-12-1974.
36. Gilbert M. Denman, Jr., to W. C. H., 11-13-1974.
37. H. C. to W. C. H., 10-28-1974.
38. Gilbert M. Denman, Jr. to W. C. H., 1974.
39. Allan Shephard to W. C. H., 1-10-1974.
40. H. C. to W. C. H., 7-24-1973.
41. Bob Cage to W. C. H., 10-26-1973.
42. Johnny Murrell to W. C. H., 2-25-1974.
43. Emerson Price to W. C. H., 10-24-1973.
44. Bob Cage to W. C. H., 10-20-1973.
45. J. Taylor (Carrizo Springs), to W. C. H., 10-24-1973.
46. Ibid.
47. Fred Shield to W. C. H., 1-10-1974.

CHAPTER 20

1. Halsell Records, D-30, f-30, 3-19-1938.
2. Ibid., D-30, f-29, 4-26-1938.
3. Ibid., D-30, f-30, no date.
4. H. C. to W. C. H., 1-10-1974.
5. Herb McSpadden to W. C. H., 8-23-1973.
6. Ibid.
7. E. H. to Horace Barnard, 8-28-1953.
8. Halsell Records, D-30, f-30, 9-9-1940.
9. Ibid., D-11, f-24, 9-13-1940.
10. Herb McSpadden to W. C. H., 8-23-1973.
11. H. C. to W. C. H., 8-15-1973.
12. Ibid.
13. Halsell Records, D-11, f-23, 8-19-1938.
14. H. C. to W. C. H., 7-2-1973.
15. Ibid.
16. Jack Barfield is a pseudonym.
17. Halsell Records, D-11, f-17, 7-30-1937.
18. Ibid., D-11, folders 22 and 24.
19. Ibid., D-11, f-23, 8-19-1938.
20. Ibid., D-11, f-24, 8-10-1940.
21. Ibid.
22. Ibid., D-11, f-23, 3-20-1945.
23. Ibid., D-11, f-23, 7-3-1945.
24. Holden, *Espuela Land and Cattle Company*, pp. 69-70.
25. Halsell Records, D-11, f-22, 8-18-1937.
26. Ibid., D-11, f-22, 9-15-1937.
27. Holden, *Espuela Land and Cattle Company*, pp. 148–149.
28. *Vinita Leader*, Vol. 7, 7-21-1904, p. 163.
29. Halsell Records, D-11, f-24, 3-30-1940.
30. Ibid., D-11, f-24, 9-13-1939.
31. Newt Robison to W. C. H., 2-25-1974.
32. Halsell Records, D-11, f-24, 9-18-1939.
33. Ibid., D-11, f-24, 9-26-1939.
34. H. C. to W. C. H., 10-26-1973.

CHAPTER 21

1. H. C. to W. C. H., 11-26-1973.

2. Mrs. Rex E. Dillard to H. C., 12-4-1952.

3. H. C. to W. C. H., 11-2-1973.

4. Halsell Records, D-58, f-Gaither, E. H. to L. D. Gaither, 7-25-1938; also see Ibid., D-58, f-Gaither, Gaither to E. H., 8-10-1938.

5. Bob Cage to W. C. H., 10-26-1973.

6. H. C. to W. C. H., 11-2-1973.

7. Ibid., 11-9-1974.

8. Johnny Murrell to W. C. H., 2-25-1974.

9. Bob Cage to W. C. H., 11-26-1973.

10. Johnny Murrell to W. C. H., 2-25-1974.

11. Ibid.

12. H. C. to W. C. H., 11-2-1973.

13. Halsell Records, D-58, f-Gaither, Gaither to E. H., 8-10-1938; also see Ibid., D-58, f-Gaither, E. H. to Gaither, 7-25-1938.

14. Ibid., D-58, f-Franklin, E. H. to George Franklin, 12-6-1940.

15. Ibid., D-15, f-5.

16. Ibid., D-58, f-Gaither, E. H. to Gaither, 9-2-1935.

17. Ibid.

18. Johnny Murrell to W. C. H., 2-25-1974.

19. Ibid.

20. Bob Cage to W. C. H., 10-26-1973.

21. Ibid.

22. Gus Parrish to W. C. H., 2-25-1974.

23. Johnny Murrell to W. C. H., 2-25-1974.

24. Bob Cage to W. C. H., 10-26-1973; also see Johnny Murrell to W. C. H., 2-25-1974.

25. H. C. to W. C. H., 11-2-1973.

26. Bob Cage to W. C. H., 10-26-1973.

27. Capt. Allee to W. C. H., 10-23-1973; also see H. C. to W. C. H., 11-2-1973; also see Bob Cage to W. C. H., 10-26-1973.

28. Johnny Murrell to W. C. H., 2-25-1974.

29. Capt. Allee to W. C. H., 10-23-1973.

30. Bob Cage to W. C. H., 10-26-1973.

31. Red Caldwell to W. C. H., 10-26-1973.

32. H. C. to W. C. H., 11-2-1973.

33. Johnny Murrell to W. C. H., 2-25-1974.

34. Bob Cage to W. C. H., 10-26-1973.

35. Ibid.

36. Ibid.

37. Ibid.

38. Halsell Records, D-58, f-Gaither, document of District Court of Lamb County, Texas 6-19-1953.

39. H. C. to W. C. H., 11-2-1973.

40. Halsell Records, D-58, f-Gaither, 8-15-1952.

41. Ibid., D-58, f-Gaither, Estate of Leslie D. Gaither, 1-12-1953.

42. H. C. to W. C. H., 11-2-1973.

43. Halsell Records, D-30, f-2, 11-?-1940; also see Johnny Murrell to W. C. H., 2-25-1974.

44. Johnny Murrell to W. C. H., 2-25-1974.

45. Ibid.

46. Halsell Records, D-30, f-15, 8-9-1929.

47. Johnny Murrell to W. C. H., 2-25-1974.

48. Ibid.

49. George Kuykendall to W. C. H., 11-7-1973.

50. Ibid.

51. Ibid.

52. George Kuykendall to W. C. H., 11-7-1973.

53. Ibid., 10-17-1973.

54. Ibid.; also see Johnny Murrell to W. C. H., 2-25-1974.

55. George Kuykendall to W. C. H., 10-17-1973.

56. Halsell Records, D-58, f-Huffman, 6-16-1943.

57. Ibid., D-30, f-2, 11-?-1940, November 1940, 11-25-1940, 7-26-1941.

58. Ibid., D-30, f-2, 7-26-1941

59. Ibid., D-16, f-1, 4-2-1942.

60. Johnny Murrell to W. C. H., 2-25-1974.

61. Ibid.

62. Ibid.

63. Ibid.

64. Ibid., also see Bob Cage to W. C. H., 10-26-1973.

65. Johnny Murrell to W. C. H., 2-25-1974.

66. Ibid.

67. Halsell Records, D-16, f-1, 4-2-1942.

CHAPTER 22

1. H. C. to W. C. H., 8-19-1974.

2. Halsell Records, D-58, f-John K. Skinner, *The Bomb Cite*, Milan Arsenal, Milan, Tennessee, 10-1-1950.

3. Paul Howe to W. C. H., 8-26-1973.

4. Ibid.

5. Halsell Records, D-58, f-John K. Skinner, *The Bomb Cite*, Milan Arsenal, Milan, Tennessee, 10-1-1950.

6. Paul Howe to W. C. H., 8-26-1973.

7. Halsell Records, D-58, f-John K. Skinner, 8-7-1942; also see H. C. to W. C. H., 8-19-1974.

8. H. C. to W. C. H., 8-19-1974; also see Halsell Records, D-58, f-John K. Skinner, *The Bomb Cite*, Milan Arsenal, Milan, Tennessee, 10-1-1950.

9. H. C. to W. C. H., 8-19-1974.

10. Halsell Records, D-58, f-John K. Skinner, 7-13-1946, also see Paul Howe to W. C. H., 8-26-1973.

11. Halsell Records, D-58, f-John K. Skinner, 8-7-1942.

12. Paul Howe to W. C. H., 8-26-1973.

13. Bill Eden to W. C. H., 8-23-1973.

14. H. C. to W. C. H., 8-19-1974.

15. Halsell Records, D-58, f-John K. Skinner, 4-?-1946.

16. Ibid., D-58, f-John K. Skinner, 3-20-1946.

17. Ibid., D-58, f-John K. Skinner, 4-?-1946.

18. Paul Howe to W. C. H., 8-26-1973; also see H. C. to W. C. H., 8-26-1973.

19. Halsell Records, D-58, f-John K. Skinner, 4-?-1946.

20. Ibid., D-58, f-John K. Skinner, 12-23-1945.

CHAPTER 23

1. Capt. Allee to W. C. H., 10-23-1973.

2. Halsell Records, D-12, f-24, 8-12-1939.

3. Ibid., D-15, f-4, pk. 3, 5-28-1936; D-15, f-5, pk. 2, 5-18-1938; D-15, f-5, pk. 2, 5-21-1938; D-58, f-Hands, 9-18-1939; D-11, f-24, 9-15-1939.

4. Ibid., D-58, f-Hands, 9-28-1943.

5. Ibid., D-58, f-Hands, 10-18-1943.

6. Ibid., D-58, f-Hands, 3-12-1943.

7. Ibid., D-58, f-Hands, 3-20-1943.

8. Bill Eden to W. C. H., 8-23-1973.

9. Halsell Records, D-58, f-Hands, 6-25-1945, 9-?-1945, 9-19-1945, undated letter from Tom Hannon to E. H.

10. Ibid., D-58, f-Hands, 9-19-1939.

11. Ibid., D-58, f-Hands, 9-21-1939.

12. Ibid., D-58, f-Hands, 9-2-1937, 10-26-1937, 2-9-1938; also see H. C. to W. C. H., 8-23-1973.

13. Ibid., D-58, f-Hands, 8-22-1945.

14. Ibid., D-58, f-Hands, 12-13-1937.

15. Ibid., D-58, f-Hands, 8-27-1937, 8-22-1938, 9-28-1939, 9-11-1937, 9-6-1938.
16. Ibid., D-24, f-7, 12-18-1945, 12-21-1945.
17. Ibid., D-58, f-Hands, 8-28-1939, 8-29-1939, 9-9-1940.
18. Ibid., D-58, f-Hands, 12-24-1940.
19. Ibid., D-58, f-Hands, 7-26-1939.
20. Johnny Murrell to W. C. H., 2-4-1974.
21. Halsell Records, D-30, f-27, 7-26-1943.
22. Halsell Cattle Company Record Books, 1930–1950.
23. Halsell Records, D-30, f-27, 8-25-1942.
24. Ibid., D-58, f-Hands, Saturday 23.
25. Ibid., D-58, f-Hands, Monday Sept. 7.
26. Ibid., D-58, f-Hands, Friday.
27. Ibid., D-58, f-Hands, 8-1-1938.
28. Doc Vann to W. C. H., 8-26-1973.
29. H. C. to W. C. H., 8-26-1973.
30. Eva Halsell McCluskey, 7-14-1973.
31. Ibid.
32. Ibid., also see Cleve Hamilton to W. C. H., 11-23-1973.
33. H. C. to W. C. H., 11-2-1973.
34. George Kuykendall to W. C. H., 10-17-1973; also see Billy McCluskey to W. C. H., 11-15-1973.
35. H. C. to W. C. H., 11-2-1973.
36. Halsell Records, D-58, f-Hands, 7-?-1940.
37. Ibid., D-58, f-Hands, 9-6-1940.
38. Ibid., D-58, f-Hands, 7-18-1941, 7-22-1941, 8-1-1941, 9-11-1941.
39. H. C. to W. C. H., 6-2-1973.
40. Lupe Garza to W. C. H., 10-26-1973.
41. H. C. to W. C. H., 11-8-1974.
42. Lupe Garza to W. C. H., 10-26-1973.
43. Ibid.
44. Ibid.
45. H. C. to W. C. H., 10-26-1973.

CHAPTER 24

1. Billy McCluskey to W. C. H., 11-15-1973.
2. Vinita Tatum to W. C. H., 12-10-1973.
3. John Mahoney to W. C. H., 8-24-1973.
4. H. C. to W. C. H., 11-8-1974.
5. Billy McCluskey to W. C. H., 11-15-1973.

6. Ibid., also see John Mahoney to W. C. H., 8-24-1973.

7. Ibid.

8. Ibid.

9. Clyte Harlan to W. C. H., 8-24-1973.

10. Ibid., also see Bob Cotton to W. C. H., 8-27-1973.

11. *Chieftain*, vol. 6, 5-16-1901, p. 141a.

12. Cleve Hamilton to W. C. H., 11-23-1973.

13. *Chieftain*, vol. 5, 9-25-1890, p. 31a, 10-23-1890, p. 42.

14. Ibid., vol. 2, 9-21-1899, p. 61; also see *Chieftain Weekly*, vol. 6, 10-19-1899, pp. 66-69, 72, 73-76.

15. Cleve Hamilton to W. C. H., 11-23-1973; also see H. C. to W. C. H., 8-28-1973.

16. George Kuykendall to W. C. H., 11-7-1973.

17. Cleve Hamilton to W. C. H., 11-23-1973.

18. Halsell Records, D-58, f-Law and Order, *The Tulia Herald*, 6-6-1919.

19. George Kuykendall to W. C. H., 11-7-1973; also see Cleve Hamilton to W. C. H., 11-23-1973.

20. Halsell Records, D-58, f-Halsell Family, Record of Birth and Death of Family of Electious and Elizabeth Jane Halsell.

21. Ibid., D-58, f-Ann Waggoner Will, Correspondence and documents dated June and July 1928.

22. Ibid., D-58, f-Ann Waggoner Will, Auditor's Report, Estate Syclly Ann Waggoner, Fort Worth, Texas, 6-24-1929; also see Ibid., D-58, f-Law and Order, Will of Syclly Ann Waggoner, 1926.

23. Ibid., D-58, f-Halsell Family, Waggoner Family genealogy.

24. Ibid., D-58, f-Ann Waggoner Will, Bruce Young to E. H., 6-21-1928.

25. Ibid., D-58, f-Ann Waggoner Will, Bill of Sale, 6-8-1928.

26. Ibid., D-58, f-Ann Waggoner Will, Bruce Young to E. H., 6-20-1928.

27. Ibid., D-58, f-Ann Waggoner Will, E. H., to Ella Waggoner, 6-27-1928.

28. Ibid., D-58, f-Ann Waggoner Will.

29. Ibid., D-58, f-Ann Waggoner Will, telegram, 6-9-1928.

30. Ibid., D-58, f-Ann Waggoner Will, telegram, 6-9-1928.

31. Ibid., D-58, f-Ann Waggoner Will.

32. Ibid., D-58, f-Ann Waggoner Will, Furd Halsell to E. H., 6-23-1928.

33. Ibid., D-58, f-Ann Waggoner Will, Bruce Young to E. H., 7-17-1928.

34. Ibid., D-58, f-Ann Waggoner Will.

35. Ibid., D-58, f-Ann Waggoner Will, undated letter to Oscar Halsell.

36. Ibid., D-58, f-Ann Waggoner Will, 7-14-1928.

37. Ibid., D-58, f-Ranch Maps.

38. Ibid., D-30, f-2, 8-16-1939, 8-23-1939.

39. Ibid., D-30, f-2, 11-25-1939.

40. Ibid., D-30, f-2, 8-23-1939, 11-19-1941.
41. Ibid., D-30, f-2, 9-17-1941.
42. Ibid., D-30, f-2, 5-26-1941.
43. Ibid., D-30, f-2, 7-13-1940.
44. Ibid., D-30, f-2, 9-17-1941.
45. Ibid., D-30, f-2, 9-19-1941.
46. Ibid., D-24, f-7, 10-20-1946, 1-23-1946.
47. Ibid., D-6, f-Halsell vs. Santa Fe.
48. H. C. to W. C. H., 7-26-1973.
49. Ibid.
50. Ibid.

CHAPTER 25

1. Eva Halsell McCluskey to W. C. H., 8-16-1973.
2. *Chieftain*, vol. 1, 10-18-1888, p. 281.
3. Ibid., vol. 5, 9-2-1898, p. 316.
4. *Leader*, vol. 8, 5-24-1906, p. 44.
5. *Chieftain Daily*, vol. 4, 5-18-1907, p. 324.
6. *Chieftain*, vol. 1, 3-31-1887, p. 222.
7. Ibid., vol. 5, 9-28-1893, p. 180.
8. Ibid., vol. 5, 5-28-1896, p. 240.
9. Ibid., vol. 5, 9-30-1897, p. 278.
10. Ibid., vol. 6, 1-25-1900, p. 88.
11. *Chieftain Daily*, vol. 3, 6-20-1902, p. 242.
12. *Chieftain*, vol. 2, 10-12-1891, p. 236.
13. Newt Robison to W. C. H., 2-16-1974.
14. Eva Halsell McCluskey to W. C. H., 8-16-1973.
15. Dr. Merton Minter to W. C. H., 10-11-73.
16. Ibid.
17. Halsell Records, D-11, f-24, 12-3-1940.
18. Ibid., D-11, f-23, 8-17-1945.
19. H. C. to W. C. H., 6-2-1973.
20. Halsell Records, D-58, f-Horses, 11-11-1950.
21. Clyte Harlan to W. C. H., 8-24-1973.
22. Ibid.
23. Ibid.
24. Ibid.
25. H. C. to W. C. H., 8-24-1973.
26. Clyte Harlan to W. C. H., 8-24-1973.

27. Doc Vann to W. C. H., 8-26-1973.

28. Paul Howe to W. C. H., 8-26-1973.

29. Ibid.

30. Ibid.

31. Ibid.

32. H. C. to W. C. H., 8-26-1973.

33. Paul Howe to W. C. H., 8-26-1973.

34. Halsell Records, D-11, f-24, 12-27-1940; D-11, f-23, 2-19-1942, 4-27-1942, 8-14-1944, 8-16-1945; D-30, f-37, 9-5-45.

35. Jean Holmes McDonald to W. C. H., 11-17-1973.

36. Newt Robison to W. C. H., 2-16-1974.

37. H. C. to W. C. H., 8-26-1973; also see Johnny Murrell to W. C. H., 2-25-1974.

38. Johnny Murrell to W. C. H., 2-25-1974.

CHAPTER 26

1. Tom Burckhalter to W. C. H., 8-24-1973.

2. Halsell Records, D-58, f-Benevolences, 8-30-1935.

3. Bob Love to W. C. H., 8-24-1973.

4. Halsell Records, D-16, f-1, 6-4-1937.

5. Bob Love to W. C. H., 8-24-1973.

6. Ibid.

7. Ibid.

8. Halsell Records, D-58, f-Benevolences.

9. Bob Love to W. C. H., 8-24-1973.

10. Ibid.

11. H. C. to W. C. H., 11-8-1974.

12. Bob Love to W. C. H., 8-24-1973.

13. Ibid.

14. Ibid.

15. Ibid., also see Halsell Records, D-30, f-37, 5-26-1944.

16. Bob Love to W. C. H., 8-24-1973.

17. H. C. to W. C. H., 11-8-1974.

18. H. C. to W. C. H., 9-10-1973.

19. Bob Love to W. C. H., 8-24-1973.

20. H. C. to W. C. H., 9-10-1973.

21. Ibid.

22. Ibid.

23. Ibid.

24. Halsell Records, D-58, f-Contributions, 1959, 1960, 1961.

25. H. C. to W. C. H., 11-11-1973, 8-23-1973.
26. Ibid., 11-11-1973.
27. Ibid.
28. J. W. B. to W. C. H., 1975.
29. H. C. to W. C. H., 11-11-1973, 8-23-1973.
30. J. W. B. to W. C. H., 1975.
31. J. and A. Rodriguez to W. C. H., 10-27-1973.
32. Dr. Merton Minter to W. C. H., 10-11-1973.
33. Ibid.
34. Halsell Records, D-58, f-Benevolences, 4-13-1961.
35. H. C. to W. C. H., 11-8-1974.
36. Ibid.
37. Halsell Records, D-30, f-2, 12-21-1933.
38. H. C. to W. C. H., 11-11-1973.
39. Emerson Price to W. C. H., 10-24-1973.

CHAPTER 27

1. H. C. to W. C. H., 8-6-1973.
2. Halsell Records, D-58, f-Last Hunt, Lucile 1960–1963.
3. H. C. to W. C. H., 8-6-1973.
4. Halsell Records, D-58, f-Last Hunt.
5. H. C. to W. C. H., 8-6-1973.
6. Ibid.
7. Ibid.
8. Halsell Records, D-58, f-Last Hunt, Laura Wood to E. H., 9-10-1963.
9. Ibid., D-58, f-Last Hunt, 1962–1963.
10. H. C. to W. C. H., 10-24-1973.
11. Ibid., 8-6-1973.
12. Ibid.
13. Ibid.
14. Ibid.
15. J. W. B. to W. C. H., 1975.
16. B. C. to W. C. H., 12-22-74.

Our gratitude goes to all who contributed useful information. They are listed in alphabetical order as follows: Captain Alfred Y. Allee; Kling L. Anderson; Ida McMurtry Barnett; Tom Bell; Mrs. Ina Boggs; A. E. Bradshaw; Paul Brady; J. Walter Browers; Elgie Brown; Tom Burckhalter; D. Burns; Bob Cage; Red Caldwell; Helen Campbell; O. B. Campbell; Holman Cartwright; Judge Glenn Chappell; Glenn Christian; Wayne Christian; Price Clark; Bill Clayton; Maurice Cohen; Bob Cotton; Herb Couch; Gail and Denny Cresap; Charley Dailey; Duval Davidson; Fred Davis; Gilbert Denman, Jr.; Christine De Vitt; "Chuck" Drummond; Fred Drummond; R. C. Drummond; Don D. Dwyer; Bill Eden; Odie B. Faulk; Joe Finley, Jr.; Joe Finley, Sr.; Lucile Wood Francis; Simon Freese; H. M. Galloway; Lupe Garza; Bill George; Sothoron George; Irene Gibson; Eva Gillett; Russell Gillett; James E. Graves; Fenton Gray; Walter Gray; Max H. Grossenbacher; Jim Hacker; Franklin Halsell; Mrs. Furd Halsell; George Halsell; Glenn Halsell; Mrs. H. H. Halsell; Cleve Hamilton; Clyte Harlan; Jack R. Harlan; Kelly Hartley; Robert Hartley; H. O. Hodson; Clare Halsell Holmes; Wallace Hough; Paul Howe; Maita Hughes; Amos Jackson; Helen De Vitt Jones; Joe Jarboe; Clarence Stafford Kornegay; George Kuykendall; Mrs. Lester La Grange; Mrs. Otis Langley; Tom Lasater; Bob Love; Ed Lowrance; Russ and Marg Magee; John Mahoney; Hugh McClure; Billy McCluskey; Eva Halsell McCluskey; Bill McDaniel; Jean Holmes McDonald; Judge Lacey McKenzie; W. E. McMurphy; Herb McSpadden; Robert McSpadden; Dr. Merton Minter; Jess Moore; Ronnie Moore; R. D. Morrison; Ruth Morrison; H. O. Murrell; Johnny Murrell; Larry Murrell; Mary Murrell; Oma Pearl Murrell; Phelps Murrell; T. V. (Red) Murrell; A. B. Nelson; Gus Parrish; V. M. Peterman; Guy Pickard; Jim Pond; Emerson Price; Jane Price; John Rice; John Robertson; Albert Rodriguez; Joe Rodriguez; Frank Rogers; Mrs. Frank Rogers; L. M. Rommann; Bean Salinas; Ken Sawyer; Arch Sequichie; Allan Shephard; Fred Shield; Tom Simmons; Mrs. L. E. Slate; Mike and Jane Snedden; Anne Snyder; Etta Lee Stevens; Vinita Tatum; Jay Taylor (Amarillo); J. Taylor (Carrizo Springs); Gene Templeton; Jim Templeton; Leonard Traylor; Doc Vann; Edna Waldrop; George R. Waller; Mrs. Roger Willet; Emil Weilbacher; Grady and Katheryn York; Terry Thrift.

INDEX

health of, 203, 315; and Helen Campbell, 294, *passim*; helping Harlans, 334–35; helping George Snedden, 331–34; helping Medical Center, 523–25; helping Southwest Texas Methodist Hospital, 584; hired John K. Skinner, 414; as a host, 355–56; interest in Billy McCluskey, 389, 392, 435–36; interest in hands, 435; interest in Johnny Murrell, 409–11; joined church, 522; Keller murder, 465–67; law and order man, 460; lawsuit against W. E. by Claud, 467–77; lawsuit, truck accident, 479–80; learning cattle business as child, 142; love of fishing, 477; love of growing things, 311; manager, Halsell Cattle Company, 292; manager, Spring Lake Ranch, 215–17; method of "pear burning," 348–50; move to San Antonio, 340; negotiations to purchase Farias, 337–38; Osage lease, 217–18; philosophy about giving, 424–25; philosophy about women on ranches, 311; plans to move from VVN, 340–41; as a poker player, 358–59; powers of attorney, 239; preparations for World War II, 321–30; president of baseball club, 178; purchase of Farias, 337–39; ranch operation, 291, 369–70; relationship with C. K. Warren, 306–308; relationship with cooks, 444–45; relationship with Edward Warren, 308–309; relationship with Huffman, 296, 404–405; relationship with W. E., 142, 198; rodeos, 488; roping, 200–202; school in Decatur, 143–44, 200; schooling, 200–206; self-sustaining ranches, 311, 328; showing Farias, 361; spayed heifer experiment, 364–65; Syclly Ann's will, 466–77; teetotaler, 206; thoroughness of, 310; traits of, 197, 200–206, 214, 226; use of mechanization, 324; wedding of, 210; Will Rogers Memorial and Tomb, 506–17; in Willie Halsell College, 200, 203; in Worcester Academy, 200

Halsell Farms Company: Amherst office, 237; formation of, 237; land office manager, 240; operation of, 237, 240; publicity for land sales, 237–38; 240; sale lands surveyed, 237; sales method, 237, 240; townsite located, 238, 240

Halsell, Ferdinand. *See* Halsell, Furd

Halsell, Furd, 108, 143–44, 150, 475, 477

Halsell, George, 7, 11, 15; birth of, 4; characteristics of, 32; death and burial of, 66–69; learns cattle business, 53; loses toe, 53, 54; school, 13; trail drive, 55; works for Dan Waggoner, 37, 38, 39, 40, 62, 63

Halsell, Glenn "Honey" (Mrs. Tom Yarbrough), 108

Halsell, Harry Hurrinden, 66, 69, 108, 110

Halsell home, Vinita, 216–17; to public schools, 517

Halsell, Ida (Mrs. J. M. Embry), 4, 6, 31, 37, 40, 46, 69, 74, 76, 77, 78, 102

Halsell, James Thompson (Thomas), 7, 9, 53, 66, 69, 72, 73, 74, 77, 78; birth of, 4; in Civil War, 36; marriage of, 6; name change, 36; rescues Electious from mob, 46–47

Halsell, John Glenn, 7, 11, 15, 32, 51, 76, 77, 97,

passim; birth of, 4; children of, 77, 108; death of, 146; establishes facilities at Triangle D Ranch, 63; freighting trips, 32, 33, 34, 58; health of, 110; house in Decatur, 108; knowledge of cattle business, 101, 102; marriage of, 50; more land in Archer County, 110; other partnerships of, 74; partnership with W. E., 34, 62, 64, 74, 75, 98, 99, 100; partnership dissolved with W. E., 109, 121; rears Ida and Keach, 74; resigns as Waggoner foreman, 75; school, 13; works for Dan Waggoner, 37, 38, 39, 40, 55, 74, *passim*

Halsell, Mrs. John H. (Josephine Halsell), 108

Halsell, Julia Earhart (Mrs. John Glenn Halsell), 4, 50, 74, 97

Halsell, Josie Crutchfield (Mrs. W. E. Halsell): after W. E.'s death, 262–71; art collection of, 270; death of, 269; description of, 171, 183; financial problems, 269; house in California, 268; letter to Mrs. Lutie Perry, 265; life in Vinita, 172–79; life with W. E., 258–61; marriage to W. E., 170–72, 180–82; niece of Mary Alice, 152; receives Fairlawn, 221; relationship with Halsell family, 268; Reversionary trust, 264; sale of collection, 270; W. E.'s will, 262–63; will of, 270; *passim*

Halsell, Lucile Fortner (Mrs. Ewing Halsell): background, 207–208; courtship of, 208; illness and death of, 531–33; description of, 208; funeral of, 533; schooling, 208; at Spring Lake Ranch, 215–16; teacher, 208; wedding, 210; *passim*

Halsell, Mary Alice Crutchfield (Mrs. W. E. Halsell): birth, 79; birth of Clarence, 149; birth of Eva, 145–46; birth of Ewing, 107; birth of Mary, 151; birth of Willie, 102; at Bridgeport stage stand, 83, 134; in carriage accident, 152; death of, 152–53; decline in health, 123, 124, 128; description of, 77; effects of Willie's death on, 140–44, 152; marriage of, 81; meets W. E., 77, 79; move to Henrietta, 108; one-quarter Cherokee, 79; parents of, 78–79; religion of, 97; *passim*

Halsell, Mary (Mary Halsell Wood Vilan), 230; birth of, 151; as a girl, 210

Halsell, Maud, 77

Halsell, Oscar, 250, 475, 477

Halsell Ranch records: day book, 432–34; after Ewing takes over, 434

Halsell, Roswell Keach, 11, 37, 40, 53, 69, 74, 77, 86, 468

Halsell Switch. *See* Railroads

Halsell, Syclly Ann. *See* Syclly Ann Halsell Waggoner

Halsell Tavern: building of, 19; Colonel Hunt moves in, 37; description of, 23; Halsells leave, 37; operation of, 25, 31; rented by Jack Moore, 46; used as courthouse, 23

Halsell Theater. *See* Theaters

Halsell Valley, 11, 12, 18, 78

Halsell, W. E. (William Electious): adopted citizen,

560   *Index*

Newspapers: *Amherst Advocate*, 246; *Cherokee Advocate*, 192; *Denver Post*, 179; *Littlefield Leader*, 246; *Kansas City Star*, 256; *Vinita Indian Chieftain*, 135, 136, 138, 144, 147, 149, 166, 172–78, 189, 460; *Vinita Leader*, 215
New York, 35, 75
North Carolina, 4, 35, 56, 78
"Northerners," 40–41
Nowata County. *See* Counties, Oklahoma
Nurse. *See* Lizzie

Oak trees. *See* Trees
Oates, W. S., 17
Oklahoma: Catoosa, 128; Claremore, 92, 119, 127, 159, 160; Guthrie, 87, 107, 108; Hominy, 218; Inola, 123; Mingo, 128; Pawhuska, 120, 218; Tulsa, 85, 116, 119, 120, 177–78; Wagoner, 116, 127. *See also* Counties, Oklahoma; Vinita
Oklahoma Territory, 85, 195
Old Chili. *See* Horses
Old Ginger. *See* Horses
Oliver's Creek, 78
Olton. *See* Texas
O'Neal, S., 247
Osage Indians, 217
Osage lease: breeding, 218; Ewing cattle business, 217–18; gave up lease, 219; size of, 217–18; stocking, 218; use of cotton seed for supplement, 218
Ouachita Mountains. *See* Mountains
Ozark Mountains. *See* Mountains

Palmer, Mrs. Robert, 444–47
Palo Pinto County. *See* Counties, Texas
Panic of 1873, 103
Parker County. *See* Counties, Texas
Parrish, Gus, 398
Partnership of Glenn and W. E. Halsell: Archer county ranch, 104; brand of, 34; dissolved partnership, 109; duration of Creek lease, 107; established separate herd, 75; formation of, 34; lawsuit against, 110; leased Creek lands, 107; length of stay in Cimarron, 108–109; location of Creek lease, 107; move to Cimarron, 108; operation of, 102; plans for, 103–104; preparations to move to Cimarron, 107; rearrangement of, 74; sell herd and range rights, 110; size of herd, 109; terms of Creek lease, 107; trail drive to Abilene, 64; trail drive to Vinita, 105
Pasture burning, 385
Pauley family, 13
Pawhuska. *See* Oklahoma
Payne, Lee, 248, 254
Peace Party, 41, 45
Pear burning, 348–50
Pease, E. M., 36
Pecan Bayou, 6
Pecan trees. *See* Trees

Penn, Mrs. Mary A., 50
Pennsylvania, 35
Perry, Mrs. Lutie, 265
Pets, 187–88
Pierce, Shanghai, 124–25
Pierce. *See* Texas
Pigeon. *See* Horses
Politics: Cattlemen-Cherokee confrontation, 135–36; Cherokee Nation, 135–36; Cherokee Outlet scandal, 135; Immigrant claim, 163–64
Ponderosa pasture. *See* Big Creek Ranch
Post, Wiley, 390, 392
Potts-Turnbull, 240
Prairie fires. *See* Fires
Prairie Point. *See* Texas
Price, Emerson, 356–58
Price, L. S., 441
Price, Mrs. L. S., 441, 444
Principal Chief. *See* Bushyhead, Dennis Wolf; Downing, Lewis
Proctor, Mr. and Mrs. Joe, 18
Proctor Hill, 18
Public domain, 14, 16
Public library, Vinita, 169
Punch and Judy. *See* Mules
Puncheon floor, 7

Railroads: Atlantic and Pacific, 85; Buffalo Bayou, 16; Brazos Valley and Colorado Railroad, 16; early Texas law, 16; excessive rates of, 80; Frisco, 85, 116, 119, 123, 125, 127, 131, 133, 150; Gulf, Colorado and Santa Fe, 236; Halsell Switch, 236; importance of, 126; lands of, 16; from Memphis, 56; Missouri, Kansas and Texas, 81, 85, 95, 116, 123, 125, 130; railheads, 63; rate war, 75; Santa Fe, 84, 236; shipping rates to eastern markets, 75, 80
Ranch records: of free range era, 432; of enclosed ranch span, 432; of corporate ranches, 432
Ranch work, 298, 369–70
Ranches: Archer County, 75, 76, 97, 102, 103, 107, 108; Camp Supply, 193–94; canning on, 311; Clay County, 73; Chittum, 340; Dan Waggoner's, 38, *passim*; Dunn league, 292; Fall River, 225, 291, 338; Mallet, 292; meat on, 311–12; menu on, 311–15; Muleshoe, 291; Running Water, 236; as self-sustaining units, 311, 328; Surratt, 219, 389; "Texas" Ranch, 291–92, 338; Three D, 76, 106; Triangle D, 59; Trinity Pasture, 86, 102; Trinity River, 49, 63; Triple D, 86, 103; Wallen, 331, 338; Warren lease, 291, 292, 297, 306; West Trinity River, 34, 53, 73, 81; XIT, 214–15, 227, 236; Yellow House, 236. *See also* Big Creek Ranch; Bird Creek Ranch, Cimarron Ranch, Farias Ranch; King Ranch; Osage lease; Spring Lake Ranch; VVN Ranch; Women on ranches
Range conditions of 1884, 136
Ratcliff, Fred, 231–32

About the author

William Curry Holden, a teacher, historian, archaeologist, author. In 1929 Dr. Holden went to Texas Technological College in Lubbock as Professor of History and Director of The Museum and has taught there continuously, interspersed with visiting professorships in history at the University of Texas. He served as head of the Department of History, Sociology and Anthropology, Dean of Archaeological and Social Science Research, and Dean of the Graduate School. He retired as Director of The Museum in 1965.

Dr. Holden has published a remarkable number of articles and books, including *Alkali Trails*; *Rollie Burns*; *The Spur Ranch*; *Studies of the Yaqui Indians of Sonora, Mexico*; *Hill of the Rooster*; *The Espuela Land and Cattle Company* (which won the Amon G. Carter Award for best book on Southwest history for 1970 from the Texas Institute of Letters and the Award of Merit from the American Association for State and Social History), *The Flamboyant Judge*, co-authored with J. Evetts Haley, and *Alton Hutson: Reminiscences of a South Plains Youth*.

His distinguished career has been honored with awards and recognition. In 1972 Holden Hall was dedicated at Texas Tech and the William Curry Holden and Frances M. Holden Fund was established. Dr. Holden is listed in Who's Who in America, American Men of Science, Who's Who in the South and Southwest, The Authors and Writers Who's Who, Dictionary of International Biography, and the International Directory of Anthropologists.

About the artist

José Cisneros was born in the Mexican state of Durango, was raised in Juarez, and, in 1934, moved to El Paso where he has since lived. He became a U. S. citizen in 1948. His knowledge of art and history is evident in his beautiful drawings. In addition to illustrating magazines, Cisneros has had his work published in more than forty books, most of which deal with the Southwest. In 1969 Cisneros was the recipient of a residence fellowship given by The University of Texas and spent six months at J. Frank Dobie's Paisano Ranch, where he completed the drawings for *Riders of the Border: A Selection of Thirty Drawings* by José Cisneros, with text by the artist (El Paso: Texas Western Press, 1971). Other books in which his illustrations appear include *Journey of Fray Marcos de Niza* by Cleve Hallenback, *The Spanish Heritage of the Southwest* by Francis Fugate, *Morelos of Mexico* by William Timmons, and *Spanish and Mexican Land Grants* by J. J. Bowden.